CLARK GABLE AND JEAN HARLOW IN *RED DUST*, 1932

GINGER ROGERS AND FRED ASTAIRE IN *FLYING DOWN TO RIO*, 1933

INTRODUCTION BY ROBERT OSBORNE

TEXT BY FRANK MILLER

LEADING**COUPLES**

THE MOST UNFORGETTABLE SCREEN ROMANCES OF THE STUDIO ERA

CHRONICLE BOOKS

SAN FRANCISCO

All of the films in this book, along with countless other classics, can be seen every day, completely commercial-free, on Turner Classic Movies.

A concerted effort has been made to trace the ownership of all material included in this book. Any errors that may have occurred are inadvertent and will be corrected in subsequent editions, provided sufficient notification is sent to the publisher in a timely manner.

Library of Congress Cataloging-in-Publication Data:
    Miller, Frank, 1954–
    Leading couples : the most unforgettable screen romances of the studio era / introduction by Robert Osborne ; text by Frank Miller.
        p. cm.
    ISBN 978-0-8118-6301-8
    1. Motion picture actors and actresses—United States—Biography.
    2. Love in motion pictures. I. Title.

    PN1998.2.M498 2008
    791.4302'80922—dc22
    [B]

                        2008009917

Manufactured in China

Designed by Affiche Design

10 9 8 7 6 5 4 3 2 1

Chronicle Books LLC
85 Second Street
San Francisco, California 94105
www.chroniclebooks.com

ACKNOWLEDGMENTS

Like all great film productions, this book reflects the collaborative efforts of many: from the Academy of Motion Picture Arts and Sciences & Margaret Herrick Library, Faye Thompson; from the Everett Collection, Glenn Bradie and Ron Harvey; from the Getty Collection, Ann Marshall; from Corbis, Meghan Wright; from MPTV, Beth Jacques; from Photofest, Howard Mandelbaum; from the Warner Bros. Corporate Image Archive, Steve Bingen, Jeff Briggs and Geoff Murillo; from Turner Broadcasting System, Inc. Image Management, David Diodate, Christopher Grakal, Brandy Ivins Wright, Melissa Jacobson, Cynthia Martinez, Christian Pierce, Matthew Rond, Kim Vardeman, and Jason Williams.

TCM contributors to project development and management and to editorial and research include: Carrie Beers, Charlie Coates, Tanya Coventry-Strader, Alexa Foreman, Randy Gragg, Les Howell, Scott McGee, Genevieve McGillicuddy, Dennis Millay, Claire Monson, Robert Osborne, Pamela Reisel, Mary Rindlesbach, John Renaud, Jeff Stafford, Richard Steiner, Charles Tabesh, and Lee Tsiantis.

Thanks to our friends and colleagues for their relentless enthusiasm and commitment to TCM: Britt Else, Signal, Inc., Debra Lemonds, Frank Miller, and Michon Wise.

INTRODUCTION **ROBERT OSBORNE**

Variety, it's said, is the spice of life. But not always . . .

Certainly one of the great pleasures of moviegoing during the so-called "studio era" of filmmaking was seeing a favorite star working with a wide mix of different costars— Audrey Hepburn, for instance, delighting us in a film with Gregory Peck, then showing up teamed with Humphrey Bogart and William Holden, followed by Henry Fonda, Fred Astaire, Gary Cooper, and later Burt Lancaster, Rex Harrison, Peter O'Toole, Albert Finney, and so on.

But in my opinion, even more of a pleasure through the years have been those filmgoing times when the two people up on that magical movie screen seemed to fit together so well, so seamlessly, you couldn't wait to see them teamed again. And again. And again. They became like old friends to us, dependable chums, or even like family.

The tough guy Bogart with the barbed babe Bacall? Nothing better. The sexy-adorable Betty Grable and affable dancing man Dan Dailey? A match made in movie heaven. Moody Alan Ladd and even moodier Veronica Lake? Nothing steamier. And while Fred Astaire partnered beautifully and successfully with many different light-footed ladies—from Rita Hayworth, Cyd Charisse, and Vera-Ellen to Audrey Hepburn, Leslie Caron, and two Powells (Eleanor and Jane)—he never seemed quite as comfortable, or more perfectly matched (at least in the minds of most moviegoers), than when he was dancing cheek-to-cheek with Ginger Rogers.

That's what this book is all about. We're toasting more than three dozen great movie teams, twenty-five comprising duos who teased, flirted, fought, loved, suffered, laughed, sometimes sang, and often danced together in not one but several films, along with twelve who worked together but once. All of the pairings made an impact that captivated audiences during the Hollywood era from the late 1920s into the early 1960s, when a few major studios ruled the film industry, each with a list of contract players at its bidding. And our fascination with the couples' on- and sometimes offscreen chemistry hasn't dimmed to this day.

Each of the great teams celebrated in this book was unique. Janet Gaynor and Charles Farrell, who made twelve films together at Fox between 1927 and 1934, were sweet, noble, and unsophisticated babes in the woods. Greta Garbo and John Gilbert, teammates four times at MGM from 1927 to 1933, were stormy, sensual, and complex (and often doomed). Gene Tierney and Tyrone Power were, singularly and together, almost illegally attractive, the epitome of movie stars obviously made for each other. Marie Dressler and Wallace Beery were the antithesis of Power and Tierney—both looking shopworn and bulky, but inherently decent. Doris Day and Rock Hudson were playful and fun. Jane Russell and Robert Mitchum—worldly and cynical. But all these combos had one thing strikingly in common: a double-edged bond with moviegoers that earned their support and enthusiasm, whether the film the couple was in was a joy or a dud.

What's amazing is that some of these million-dollar teamings happened strictly by accident. Robert Donat, for instance, was supposed to star in Warner Bros.' 1935 adventure tale *Captain Blood* but was forced to relinquish the title role because of illness. Warners, in a quandary with its expensive film ready to roll, tried to borrow Clark Gable from MGM and Gary Cooper from Paramount to no avail, so it started testing newcomers for the juicy part. The result: The unknown Errol Flynn got the break of a lifetime, and not only was a new star born, but with Olivia de Havilland as his costar, a magnificent new movie team was launched as well. It's unlikely that audiences would still connect the names of Flynn and de Havilland seventy-plus years later if Mr. Donat had possessed a healthier constitution.

When director Howard Hawks cast nineteen-year-old *Harper's Bazaar* cover girl Lauren Bacall opposite forty-five-year-old superstar Humphrey Bogart in the 1944 movie *To Have and Have Not*, no one had a clue that the teaming would turn out to be the stuff of which legends are made, in addition to adding mountains of moola to the coffers at Warner Bros. Not only was an indelible screen partnership created on that Burbank soundstage, but an offscreen romance as well, which would endure until Bogart's death thirteen years later.

When Myrna Loy and William Powell made their first film together, a 1934 Hollywood melodrama called *Manhattan Melodrama*, they were just two contract stars doing what contract stars did in those days—working on what was his fifty-ninth movie and her eightieth. No crystal ball foretold that they would eventually make fourteen films together and become so strongly identified as a couple that when both later went to do some location filming in San Francisco, the management of the St. Francis Hotel automatically booked "Mr. and Mrs. Powell" into the same suite. (Bill and Myrna quickly rebooked themselves into separate quarters.)

And so it was with the other couples we've profiled in this book, whether they starred together in numerous films or just once, still managing to create enough electrifying sparks that they're together forever after in our collective minds. Who knows exactly why these particular combos clicked so mightily? As Rodgers and Hammerstein once told us in a song, "Fools give you reasons. Wise men never try."

An inevitable question is: How did we pick the combinations that did end up on our list? Not in any scientific way, certainly, but it was accomplished with surprising ease. A panel of ten did the choosing; no fistfights transpired, but a few spirited arguments ensued. The amazing thing is how this list of great screen couples basically compiled itself. Rogers and Astaire—a given. Jeanette MacDonald and Nelson Eddy—absolutely.

And no way could you not include Judy Garland and Mickey Rooney, Greer Garson and Walter Pidgeon, Katharine Hepburn and Spencer Tracy, and most of the others.

Since we set our sights on Hollywood's studio era, we didn't want to ignore couples from the silent era, such as Garbo and Gilbert, or Gaynor and Farrell, nor could we omit others who worked their magic when the studio system was beginning to fade out in the late 1950s and early 1960s, such as Doris Day and Rock Hudson, and Elizabeth Taylor and Richard Burton. Only a few of the slots gave us pause. That's where the arguments started, and a few coins were ultimately tossed.

We also followed one rule: No actor or actress could appear in the top twenty-five multiple-movie pairs more than once (although they were allowed a chance to fill out the twelve single-movie slots with another partner), which is why you'll find several teams missing that you might otherwise have expected: Katharine Hepburn and Cary Grant, for instance. They certainly qualify—but Kate had already made the list with Spencer Tracy and, in our unscientific opinion, the nine on-camera alliances of Hepburn and Tracy outranked the four of Hepburn and Grant.

Cary Grant, in fact, is the one among all others who ended up getting somewhat short shrift from that only-one-teaming-per-person rule: You won't find Cary anywhere among the top twenty-five leading couples, but for several reasons. Certainly, Cary and Deborah Kerr qualify as one of the great screen couples, but so do Cary and Irene Dunne, Cary and Myrna Loy, Cary and Ingrid Bergman, and Cary and Katharine Hepburn. All were incredible screen partnerships, and it seemed unfair to him, and to the ladies, to choose one of those duos above all the others. You will, however, find Cary definitely represented in the company of our twelve one-shot champs. And, yes, that list is totally subjective as well.

As with any compiled list, you'll find many reasons to argue, but those who made the selections for this book had reasons for each and every decision. If we'd gone for totals, Dale Evans and Roy Rogers would have made the list. (They made twenty-eight features together.) But we were looking for combinations that created sparks, excitement, and more than the usual interest. Take Tyrone Power. He had three successful teamings with Alice Faye, four with Linda Darnell, and five with Loretta Young, but we felt none of those matches made quite the impact of Power with Gene Tierney in the trio of films they did together. Clark Gable could have been in these pages with any number of ladies—Joan Crawford, Myrna Loy, Lana Turner, and Ava Gardner, all of whom made an enormous impact with The King. None of those duos, however, seemed stronger than his pairing with Jean Harlow—no doubt helped by the fact that when the Gable-Harlow movies were made, both were young and in their primes.

We couldn't resist having some fun as well, which is why we included Margaret Dumont and Groucho Marx as one of the great screen teams. However, when you think about it, who deserves a spot on such a list more? Their scenes together practically define the word *teamwork*. The same goes for Maureen O'Sullivan and Johnny Weissmuller, who went barefoot, skinny-dipped (until the Hollywood Production Code ruled otherwise), and swung from vines through six Tarzan movies, making an unforgettable pair. John Wayne worked with almost every important leading lady in films, from Dietrich to Crawford to Bacall to Hepburn, but did anyone ever suit him better than Maureen O'Hara? Again, subjective, but Maureen O. got our vote.

A number of popular couples did not make the list, including Vilma Banky and Ronald Colman, Bette Davis and George Brent, Claudette Colbert and Fred MacMurray, Kay Francis and Ian Hunter, Maria Montez and Jon Hall, June Allyson and Van Johnson, Janet Leigh and Tony Curtis, Joanne Woodward and Paul Newman, and so many others who struck sparks in the numerous films they made together. And the self-imposed rule of only one-time-per-list kept us from including such popular twosomes as June Allyson and Jimmy Stewart, Judy Garland and Gene Kelly, Elizabeth Taylor and Montgomery Clift, Gene Tierney and Dana Andrews, and others.

We also kept that one-time rule for our list of the dozen teams who worked together but once—which is why, for one example, you won't find Bogart and Katharine Hepburn in *The African Queen* (1951) on the list, because Bogie's already there with Ingrid Bergman in *Casablanca* (1942). For another example, Douglas Fairbanks and Mary Pickford are also missing, because it was their real-life marriage that made them such a famous movie twosome, not their one screen appearance together in *The Taming of the Shrew* (1929).

Like our earlier companion book, *Leading Ladies: The 50 Most Unforgettable Actresses of the Studio Era*, and its follow-up, *Leading Men*, this tome also comes crammed with some nifty extras. Besides statistics on each of the stars involved (who knew that Bacall at 5'8" was a half-inch taller than Bogie, or that Ingrid Bergman stood an inch and a half taller than her *Casablanca* costar?), there are also great photographs from the Turner archives that have never been published before, samples of movie posters in rich color, and a wealth of fascinating information. I hadn't realized until reading these pages that Ginger Rogers was married to actor Lew Ayres, the movies' famous Dr. Kildare, for the entire time she was making those musicals with Fred Astaire at RKO. Nor had I known that two decades after Jeanette and Nelson had made their final film together—1942's *I Married an Angel*—producer Ross Hunter tried to get them to play the older couple in the Doris Day–James Garner comedy *The Thrill of It All* (1963). They declined.

Enjoy the view and the read. Besides the facts, the fun, and the photographs, you'll also learn about the offscreen relationships of these onscreen titans. Which reminds me of something Ginger Rogers told me in an interview when I asked her if it was true, as some had said, that she and Fred Astaire were never very friendly. "That's pure bunk," she said. "I adored Fred. We were good friends." Then she said, somewhat ruefully, "Our only problem is that we never aspired to be any kind of a team. We didn't want to be Abbott and Costello. We thought of ourselves as individuals. We didn't intend to be another Frick and Frack." Then she said, after a pause and with a smile, "But it happened anyway, didn't it? And I'll be forever grateful it did."

We're grateful, too, for the movies' most famous dance team, which was often referred to by a single word: *Fred'n'Ginger*. And we're also grateful for each and every one of the other magical film couples in the spotlight in this book.

With a spin, a lift, and a burst of taps, they became the greatest dancing team in film, making ballroom dancing sexy, sophisticated, silly, and just downright fun.

FRED ASTAIRE
GINGER ROGERS

Film critic Pauline Kael once called their teamwork a "great American courtship told in dance." Critic Arlene Croce called them the only screen musical team to transform dance into "a vehicle of serious emotion between a man and a woman." Fred Astaire and Ginger Rogers were the screen's first great dancing team and are still the sexiest, classiest duo ever to cut an onscreen rug. In nine films over the course of five years at RKO, followed by a curtain call at MGM a decade later, they were the epitome of grace, style, and fun. Maybe it was the intriguing mix of opposites: the sophisticate in top hat, white tie, and tails and the plucky little girl from America's heartland. Or maybe it was the simple fact that they didn't stop acting when the dancing began—each number was an extension of the characters and their relationships. Either way, no dance team before or since has risen to such heights. Even seven decades after their reign as stars, the names "Fred and Ginger" are still the ultimate compliment for any dance team. The Astaire–Rogers partnership was never supposed to be. When David O. Selznick first signed Astaire to an RKO contract, he was slated to dance "The Carioca" in *Flying Down to Rio* (1933) with Dorothy Jordan. But Jordan had fallen in love with producer Merian C. Cooper when she read for *King Kong* (1933), and their honeymoon coincided with *Rio*'s production dates. Instead, the studio rushed in recent contractee Rogers. She was billed fourth and he fifth, but their brief turn on the dance floor stole the picture, and the studio's exhibitors demanded that Fred and Ginger have a film of their own. Astaire wanted nothing to do with it at first. Having risen to stardom in a vaudeville act with his sister, Adele, he was afraid of becoming half of another twosome. He only agreed to costar with Rogers after producer Pandro S. Berman offered him 10 percent of the film's profits. Thanks largely to their pictures, in 1935 RKO posted its first profit in five years; *Top Hat* was one of only two pictures that year (the other was MGM's *Mutiny on the Bounty*) to gross over $3 million. RKO knew better than to meddle with success like that. Most of the Astaire–Rogers musicals recycled the same plot: Cocky young man falls for independent woman, but just as she sees the charm beneath the brash façade, some misunderstanding sends her packing until they dance off into the sunset together. The studio also kept many of the same production personnel on the films. Choreographer Hermes Pan worked on every one of Astaire's RKO films and later followed him to other studios. Sets were always overseen by art-department head Van Nest Polglase, whose art-deco designs became a trademark of the series. Also helping give the series an identity was a recurring supporting cast, including Helen Broderick and Erik Rhodes (two films each), Edward Everett Horton (three), and Eric Blore (four). But even at the height of their success together, Astaire and Rogers had other plans. As early as

1936, he was clamoring for an end to the partnership, while she dreamed of establishing herself as a dramatic actress. When the box office for their films began to decline, RKO finally realized it might be time to put an end to their lavish productions. In *The Story of Vernon and Irene Castle* (1939), the team played the famous ballroom dancers of days gone by, their first biographical roles and the first time they were cast as husband and wife. Reviews were ecstatic, but box-office returns weren't as strong as they'd once been. Astaire moved to other studios and other dance partners—including Rita Hayworth and Judy Garland—and Rogers scored an Oscar for Best Actress in the dramatic *Kitty Foyle* (1940). Neither expected a permanent end to the partnership, but it would be a decade before they reunited—and once again, it was by accident. When Garland's health problems forced her to withdraw from *The Barkleys of Broadway* (1949), producer Arthur Freed thought it would provide the perfect vehicle for an Astaire–Rogers reunion. As in their previous pairing, they played a happily married dancing team, with the crisis, fittingly enough, growing from her desire to branch out as a dramatic actress. The results turned a solid profit for MGM, but the decline in musical production meant that this would be their last picture. It wasn't their last dance, however. In 1967, they were reunited as Oscar presenters. On the way to the podium, Astaire spun Rogers into an impromptu routine that brought the house down, a testament to their enduring popularity as the screen's greatest dancing team.

FOLLOW THE FLEET, 1936

WITH COMPOSER IRVING BERLIN, 1938

BEHINDTHESCENES

KATHARINE HEPBURN ON FRED ASTAIRE AND GINGER ROGERS: "SHE GIVES HIM SEX; HE GIVES HER CLASS."

THE ASTAIRE–ROGERS MUSICALS GARNERED SEVEN OSCAR NOMINATIONS FOR BEST SONG (INCLUDING GEORGE GERSHWIN'S ONLY NOMINATION, FOR "THEY CAN'T TAKE THAT AWAY FROM ME" IN 1937'S *SHALL WE DANCE*). THE FILMS WON TWICE, WITH *THE GAY DIVORCEE* (1934) TAKING THE FIRST BEST SONG OSCAR FOR "THE CONTINENTAL," AND *SWING TIME* WINNING TWO YEARS LATER FOR "THE WAY YOU LOOK TONIGHT."

GINGER ROGERS HAD ONLY TWO DANCE SOLOS IN THE TEN FILMS SHE MADE WITH FRED: "LET YOURSELF GO" IN *FOLLOW THE FLEET* (1936), AND "THE YAMA YAMA MAN" IN *THE STORY OF VERNON AND IRENE CASTLE* (1939). MOST OF HER VOCAL SOLOS WERE DELIVERED BEFORE THEIR DANCE NUMBERS, AND SOME, LIKE "THE PICCOLINO" IN *TOP HAT* (1935) AND "THE YAM" IN *CAREFREE* (1938), WERE GIVEN TO HER ONLY BECAUSE FRED ASTAIRE DIDN'T WANT TO SING THEM.

THE FIRST FRED ASTAIRE–GINGER ROGERS DANCE DUET, "THE CARIOCA" IN *FLYING DOWN TO RIO* (1933), LASTED A MERE TWO MINUTES.

ALTHOUGH FRED ASTAIRE FAVORED DOING MUSICAL NUMBERS IN ONE LONG TAKE, THE "NEVER GONNA DANCE" NUMBER FROM *SWING TIME* (1936) WAS SO COMPLICATED IT REQUIRED MULTIPLE SETUPS. IT TOOK FORTY-SEVEN TAKES TO GET GINGER ROGERS' PIROUETTE DOWN A FLIGHT OF STAIRS; THEN THEY HAD TO STOP SHOOTING BECAUSE HER FEET WERE BLEEDING.

MANY, INCLUDING TEXAS POLITICIAN ANN RICHARDS AND GINGER ROGERS HERSELF, HAVE BEEN CREDITED WITH SAYING, "SURE, HE WAS GREAT, BUT DON'T FORGET THAT GINGER ROGERS DID EVERYTHING HE DID, BACKWARD . . . AND IN HIGH HEELS!" BUT THE LINE ACTUALLY ORIGINATED IN A 1982 EDITION OF THE COMIC STRIP *FRANK AND ERNEST* BY BOB THAVES.

OFFSCREEN **RELATIONSHIP**

Fred Astaire on his partnership with Ginger Rogers: "Of course, Ginger was able to accomplish sex through dance. We told more through our movements instead of the big clinch. We did it all in the dance."

Ginger Rogers on her partnership with Fred Astaire: "We had fun, and it shows. True, we were never bosom buddies off the screen; we were different people with different interests. We were only a couple on film."

Although they were simply "no more than" acquaintances while making their films together, Fred Astaire and Ginger Rogers had dated briefly during their New York theater days. He was called in to help restage her dance to "Embraceable You" in *Girl Crazy* in 1930, then asked her out dancing. They loved hitting the dance floor together, particularly at the Casino in Central Park, but never dreamed that they would become stars dancing together.

Although Ginger Rogers worked tirelessly mastering her dance steps, the studio kept her so busy on other pictures that she rarely got involved in the actual choreography. Fred Astaire worked out their dances, with choreographer Hermes Pan standing in for Ginger. Pan would then take Fred's role to teach his leading lady her part.

On *Follow the Fleet*, Ginger Rogers surprised Fred Astaire with a heavy beaded gown for "Let's Face the Music and Dance." During the first take, one of the sleeves hit him in the face after a turn, almost knocking him out. He finished the dance in a daze. They tried the number twenty-three times in all but could never get it right again, and director Mark Sandrich ended up using that first take.

SWING TIME, 1936

Hers

BORN
Virginia Katherine McMath
July 16, 1911
Independence, Missouri

DIED
April 25, 1995
Rancho Mirage, California,
of congestive heart failure

STAR SIGN
Cancer

HEIGHT
5′4½″

HUSBANDS
Singer Jack Culpepper
(1929–1931, divorced)

Actor Lew Ayres
(1934–1941, divorced)

Marine Jack Briggs
(1943–1949, divorced)

Actor Jacques Bergerac
(1953–1957, divorced)

Actor William Marshall
(1961–1969, divorced)

ESSENTIAL**TEAM-UPS**

THE GAY DIVORCEE (1934, RKO)
Their first costarring vehicle set up the standard Astaire–Rogers plot, with Fred
as a dancing star whose courtship of Ginger is hindered when she thinks he's the
married gigolo hired to get her out of a loveless marriage.

TOP HAT (1935, RKO)
At the height of their popularity, Fred and Ginger dance, fight, and cross wires
(this time she thinks he's her best friend's husband) through Hollywood versions
of London and Venice.

SWING TIME (1936, RKO)
As dancers whose partnership and romance is threatened by the small-minded
small-town girl he left behind, they perform to one of their best scores (including
the Oscar-winning "The Way You Look Tonight") in a film often hailed as their best.

THE STORY OF IRENE AND VERNON CASTLE (1939, RKO)
A series of firsts—their first historical film, their first real-life characters, their first
film playing a married couple, and Fred's first death scene—help make their last
RKO picture, a musical biography of the famed ballroom dancers, a memorable
experience.

THE BARKLEYS OF BROADWAY (1949, MGM)
Their reunion, after ten years apart, gave the duo the MGM touch for this tale of
married hoofers who separate when the missus decides to tackle heavy drama,
leading to some superb musical numbers and a supremely silly performance of
Rogers' big dramatic hit.

The gruff cynic and the tough glamour girl were united by their freewheeling battle against anything that smacked of phoniness.

HUMPHREY **BOGART**
LAUREN **BACALL**

They were cool before anybody had picked up the word. Humphrey Bogart and Lauren Bacall were united by their deep love and respect for each other and their disdain for anybody who didn't get it. When they insulted each other, it was loving banter between two people who were happiest when dishing it out to somebody who could take it. When they turned a withering gaze on anyone else, it was trouble— trouble for crooks, trouble for killers, trouble for anyone. They made insolence sexy. And though their love scenes were more about taking a slap than locking lips, audiences kept coming back for more. With the role of Marie in her first film, *To Have and Have Not* (1944), Bacall became one of the first women in screen history who could hold her own against even the toughest man. For Bogie, the film was the first in which his character actually seemed to take pleasure in romance, a quality that cemented his surprising move to romantic lead following the success of *Casablanca* (1942). Reviewing *To Have and Have Not* in the *New York Herald Tribune*, critic Otis L. Guernsey said, "They take their romance without frills—as straight as a shot of whiskey." Through four films and a twelve-year offscreen relationship, they reigned as one of Hollywood's hottest couples. Their teamwork could brighten even the most formulaic script. Hollywood's hostesses competed to get them on their guest lists; any party they attended was a guaranteed success. There was no great chemistry between the two when they first met on the set of Bogie's 1943 war film *Passage to Marseilles*. Bacall had come to Hollywood after producer–director Howard Hawks' second wife, Nancy "Slim" Gross, saw her modeling in the pages of *Harper's Bazaar*. Although she was up for a role opposite Bogart in *To Have and Have Not*, she told Hawks she'd rather work with Cary Grant. But when the costars shot their first scene, sparks flew. By that point, Hawks had coached her extensively in the role. Bacall was still nervous, but Bogart kidded her through her first days on the set. Kidding led to friendship, which soon blossomed into love. The actors' blossoming love affair gave their onscreen relationship a sexual charge that dominated the film. Hawks even had Bacall's role expanded, at the expense of the more conventional character set up as her romantic rival. The studio wanted more of that charge in their next film together, the Raymond Chandler film noir *The Big Sleep* (1946). When Hawks and studio head Jack Warner didn't see enough of it onscreen, they held the film back from release to build up Bacall's role, most notably in the classic scene during which their discussion of horse racing masks some blatant sexual teasing. By the time that scene was shot, Bogart had freed himself of his third wife, actress Mayo Methot, and wed Bacall. In *Dark Passage* (1947), their first film as husband and wife, their onscreen relationship matured. For once, they started out on the same side, united in their rebellion against a justice system gone wrong. The kidding banter was still there, but the warmth between the characters and the stars was beginning to eclipse the more blatant sexuality of their earlier films. In their final collaboration, *Key Largo* (1948), their rebel characters were more muted. But their continuing love for each other helped make their more conventional romance emotionally satisfying for fans. Bacall was never afraid to put her career on the back burner to support Bogart, first accompanying him during location work on *The Treasure of the Sierra Madre* (1948) and *The African Queen* (1951), and later taking time off for two pregnancies, giving Bogie his only children. They were planning a fifth film when Bogart was diagnosed with cancer. For over a year, she nursed him through what would turn out to be a terminal illness. They faced the inevitable together with the same toughness that made their onscreen image as a couple immortal. Despite another marriage (to actor Jason Robards Jr.) and other notable romances, Bacall herself would say that she never met a man—or an acting partner—to match her first love.

DARK PASSAGE, 1947

CIRCA 1945

BEHINDTHESCENES

PRODUCER–DIRECTOR HOWARD HAWKS' INITIAL ATTRACTION TO LAUREN BACALL WAS DUE TO HER RESEMBLANCE TO HIS WIFE, SLIM. THE TWO WOMEN BECAME FRIENDS, AND BACALL EVEN STARTED TO DRESS AND TALK LIKE HER. FOR HIS PART, HAWKS HAD HUMPHREY BOGART'S AND BACALL'S CHARACTERS IN *TO HAVE AND HAVE NOT* (1944) CALL EACH OTHER STEVE AND SLIM, HIS AND HIS WIFE'S OWN NICKNAMES FOR EACH OTHER. SLIM WOULD LATER CLAIM THAT MANY OF BACALL'S LINES IN THE FILM WERE EITHER HER SUGGESTIONS OR COPIED BY HAWKS FROM HER CONVERSATION.

THE CHEMISTRY BETWEEN HUMPHREY BOGART AND LAUREN BACALL IN THEIR FIRST TEAM–UP WAS CAREFULLY PLANNED BY PRODUCER–DIRECTOR HOWARD HAWKS. NOTING THAT BOGIE WAS EASILY THE MOST INSOLENT ACTOR ONSCREEN, HE ASKED WRITER JULES FURTHMAN, "DO YOU SUPPOSE WE COULD MAKE A GIRL WHO IS INSOLENT, WHO INSULTS PEOPLE, WHO GRINS WHEN SHE DOES IT, AND PEOPLE LIKE IT?"

HUMPHREY BOGART HAD OPTIONED THE RIGHTS TO J. P. MARQUAND'S 1951 NOVEL *MELVILLE GOODWIN, U.S.A.* AS A VEHICLE FOR HIMSELF AND LAUREN BACALL. THEY HAD SHOT COSTUME TESTS WHEN BOGART WAS DIAGNOSED WITH ESOPHAGEAL CANCER. HE HAD TO DROP OUT OF THE FILM TO DEAL WITH THE ILLNESS THAT WOULD EVENTUALLY TAKE HIS LIFE.

His

BORN
Humphrey DeForest Bogart
December 25, 1899
New York, New York

DIED
January 14, 1957
Holmby Hills, California,
of throat cancer

STAR SIGN
Capricorn

HEIGHT
5'8"

WIVES AND CHILDREN
Actress Helen Menken
(1926–1927, divorced)

Actress Mary Phillips
(1928–1937, divorced)

Actress Mayo Methot
(1938–1945, divorced)

Actress Lauren Bacall
(1945–1957, his death)
son, Stephen Humphrey
daughter, Leslie Howard

KEY QUOTE

**From *The Big Sleep*
(1946)**

Bacall
You've forgotten one
thing—me.

Bogart
What's wrong with you?

Bacall
Nothing you can't fix.

OFFSCREEN**RELATIONSHIP**

Humphrey Bogart on acting with Lauren Bacall: "She gives you back what you send. It's like a fast game of tennis. If you put over a good ball and somebody muffs it, you can't have a good game. But if somebody drives it back hard, you drive back hard, and pretty soon you have a good game."

Lauren Bacall on her relationship with Humphrey Bogart: "For myself, I can only say that he changed me. He was my teacher, my husband, my friend. In his life and his work, Bogie was integrity, truth, and courage. He taught me how to live. That it was okay to trust. He taught me to keep going on, no matter what. He did. And he is."

Humphrey Bogart and Lauren Bacall were married May 21, 1945, just eleven days after his divorce from Mayo Methot. The wedding took place on his friend Louis Bromfield's farm in Ohio; they then had to take the train back to Los Angeles, as both were due to report to work less than a week later.

When Lauren Bacall was pregnant for the first time, President Harry Truman bet Humphrey Bogart $20 the child would be a boy. After Stephen Bogart's birth, Bogie sent the president a check and asked him to cash it, so the child would have his autograph. Instead, Truman endorsed the check to the child and told Bogie to buy a savings bond for the boy's college education.

Humphrey Bogart was cremated and his ashes were interred at Forest Lawn in Los Angeles. In the urn, Lauren Bacall put a gold whistle he had given her on the closing day of *To Have and Have Not*. The inscription read, "If you need anything, just whistle."

DARK PASSAGE, 1947

Hers

BORN
Betty Joan Perske
September 16, 1924
Bronx, New York

STAR SIGN
Virgo

HEIGHT
5'8½"

HUSBANDS AND CHILDREN
Actor Humphrey Bogart
(1945–1957, his death)
son, Stephen Humphrey
daughter, Leslie Howard

Actor Jason Robards Jr.
(1961–1969, divorced)
son, Sam

ESSENTIAL TEAM-UPS

TO HAVE AND HAVE NOT (1944, Warner Bros.)
Ship's captain Humphrey Bogart locks horns with Nazi agents and a sexy pickpocket (Lauren Bacall), who would soon become his leading lady offscreen.

THE BIG SLEEP (1946, Warner Bros.)
As a private eye and the society dame whose sister he's been hired to look out for, Bogie and Bacall strike more sparks off each other in a mystery so convoluted that even the original author, Raymond Chandler, couldn't say conclusively who committed one of the murders.

DARK PASSAGE (1947, Warner Bros.)
Bogie and Baby take on the establishment as an escaped man wrongly convicted of his wife's murder and an heiress whose father was executed on circumstantial evidence.

KEY LARGO (1948, Warner Bros.)
The sexuality is subtler as Bogart stars as a disenchanted war veteran bringing widow Bacall her late husband's war medal on a Florida island that's under assault by a hurricane and a brutal gangster.

The cynic and his long-lost flame became a pair of lovers that would always have Paris in the screen's greatest romantic thriller.

HUMPHREY **BOGART**
INGRID **BERGMAN**

IN *Casablanca*

Boy meets girl. Boy loses girl. Boy gets girl. Boy gives up girl in the name of a larger cause. It was the stuff of tragedy and romance, rarely played as effectively as the final reel of *Casablanca* (1942). Filmed as the United States was entering World War II, it has become one of Hollywood's most iconic love stories. Nobody could have envisioned its position as a classic at the time producer Hal Wallis, director Michael Curtiz, and a raft of writers were scrambling to get the film together. As cowriter Howard Koch described it, *Casablanca* was "conceived in sin and born in travail." It all started with what one studio insider dubbed "the worst play ever written," *Everybody Comes to Rick's*. Inspired by the topical story with an exotic setting reminiscent of Algiers, Warner Bros. picked up the rights for $20,000. Although a famous press release touted Ronald Reagan and Ann Sheridan for the leads, Wallis envisioned the film as the next step in his drive to make Bogart a major star. Sheridan actually was considered for the female lead, because the character in the play is an American woman involved with resistance leader Victor Laszlo. Writer Casey Robinson suggested that making the leading lady European would strengthen the film's conflict, which opened the door for Bergman. Ultimate credit for the film's lasting impact must go to the inspired, one-time-only pairing of Bogart and Bergman. Only Bogie could have shown the vulnerability beneath the tough-guy persona he had honed in his earlier gangster films. Only Bergman could have maintained the purity of a woman in love with one man while married to another. Although they had no chemistry offscreen, all they had to do was look at each other in the film to bring the characters' passions to life. Bergman took on the role with trepidation over the unfinished screenplay. For the first weeks of filming, she didn't know whether her character would end up with her lover or her husband. Curtiz told her to "play it . . . in between," which raised the romantic tension. *Casablanca* turned Bergman and Bogart into superstars. Nonetheless, Bergman never really appreciated the picture. She saw it only once during its initial release, and was unreceptive to Warner Bros.' discussions of a possible sequel. Even as the film continued to grow in popularity in later years, its charms continued to elude her, until she was invited to speak on the picture at the British Film Institute in the 1970s. Seeing the film for the first time in three decades, she finally understood its appeal. When the lights came up, all she could say was, "What a good movie that was!" Audiences have shared her feelings for more than half a century.

BORN
Humphrey DeForest Bogart
December 25, 1899
New York, New York

DIED
January 14, 1957
Holmby Hills, California,
of throat cancer

STAR SIGN
Capricorn

HEIGHT
5'8"

WIVES AND CHILDREN
Actress Helen Menken
(1926–1927, divorced)

Actress Mary Phillips
(1928–1937, divorced)

Actress Mayo Methot
(1938–1945, divorced)

Actress Lauren Bacall
(1945–1957, his death)
son, Stephen Humphrey
daughter, Leslie Howard

KEY QUOTE

Bergman
With the whole world
crumbling, we pick this
time to fall in love.

Bogart
Yeah, it's pretty bad
timing. Where were you,
say, ten years ago?

OFFSCREEN**RELATIONSHIP**

Humphrey Bogart on his performance in *Casablanca*: "I didn't do anything I've never done before, but when the camera moves in on that Bergman face, and she's saying she loves you, it would make anybody feel romantic."

Because Ingrid Bergman was actually an inch and a half taller than Humphrey Bogart, director Michael Curtiz used various tricks to make his leading man seem taller. Bogie stood on boxes or wore five-inch platform shoes in some scenes, and sat on pillows on the sofa with Bergman, who had to slouch. Throughout the film, however, the height difference between the two changes noticeably.

Humphrey Bogart had little to say to Ingrid Bergman between scenes while shooting *Casablanca*. She finally got to know him, or at least his acting style and screen image, by watching *The Maltese Falcon* repeatedly. She would later say, "I kissed him, but I never knew him."

Lack of certainty over the script caused numerous production delays, with actors barely able to remember lines they were getting the night before or even the morning of shooting. Humphrey Bogart added to the delays the day they shot his parting scene with Ingrid Bergman by getting into a big disagreement with director Michael Curtiz. The issue was whether or not Rick should kiss Ilsa before sending her off with Victor. Curtiz wanted the kiss; Bogart thought it was out of character. Finally producer Hal Wallis had to be called in to settle the matter, which he did by siding with Bogart. The publicity department made light of it by issuing a press release questioning how any man could turn down the chance to kiss Ingrid Bergman.

ON SET, 1942

Hers

BORN
Ingrid Bergman
August 29, 1915
Stockholm, Sweden

DIED
August 29, 1982
London, England,
of lymphoma complications
following a breast cancer
operation

STAR SIGN
Virgo

HEIGHT
5'9½"

HUSBANDS AND CHILDREN
Dr. Aron Petter Lindstrom
(1937–1950, divorced)
daughter, Pia

Director Roberto Rossellini
(1950–1957, divorced)
son, Roberto Ingmar
daughters, Isabella and
Isotta

Swedish stage producer
Lars Schmidt
(1958–1975, divorced)

BEHINDTHESCENES

CONTRARY TO LEGEND, GEORGE RAFT NEVER HAD THE OPPORTUNITY TO
TURN DOWN *CASABLANCA*. IN FACT, HE CAMPAIGNED FOR THE ROLE, ONLY TO
HAVE PRODUCER HAL WALLIS TURN HIM DOWN. THE LEGEND MAY HAVE ITS
SOURCE IN RAFT'S REJECTION OF TWO OTHER FILMS—*THE MALTESE FALCON*
AND *HIGH SIERRA* (BOTH 1941)—THAT HELPED PROPEL HUMPHREY BOGART
TO STARDOM.

ALTHOUGH INGRID BERGMAN ALWAYS CLAIMED SHE DIDN'T KNOW
CASABLANCA'S ENDING UNTIL THE LAST DAY OF FILMING, PRODUCTION
REPORTS REVEAL THAT THE FINAL SCENE AT THE AIRPORT WAS ACTUALLY
SHOT MUCH EARLIER IN THE SCHEDULE. SHE FILMED MANY OF HER KEY
SCENES AFTER LEARNING THAT ILSA LEFT WITH HER HUSBAND.

WHEN MAX STEINER STARTED WORKING ON THE SCORE FOR *CASABLANCA*,
HE CONVINCED PRODUCER HAL WALLIS TO LET HIM WRITE A NEW SONG TO
REPLACE "AS TIME GOES BY," EVEN THOUGH IT WOULD REQUIRE RETAKES.
BY THAT TIME, HOWEVER, INGRID BERGMAN HAD CUT HER HAIR FOR A ROLE
IN *FOR WHOM THE BELL TOLLS* (1943), MAKING RETAKES IMPOSSIBLE, SO THE
SONG STAYED IN.

THE ALLIED LANDING IN CASABLANCA INSPIRED EXECUTIVES IN WARNER
BROS.' NEW YORK SALES OFFICES TO DEMAND A NEW FINAL SCENE FOR
CASABLANCA, SHOWING HUMPHREY BOGART AND CLAUDE RAINS ON
SHIPBOARD LISTENING TO PRESIDENT ROOSEVELT'S ADDRESS TO THE MILITARY
PRIOR TO THE LANDING. FORTUNATELY, PRODUCER DAVID O. SELZNICK, WHO
HELD INGRID BERGMAN'S CONTRACT, SAW A PREVIEW AND TOLD STUDIO HEAD
JACK WARNER THAT CHANGING THE ENDING WOULD BE A HUGE MISTAKE.

They were a vision of doomed, exotic romance so vivid that their one film together would haunt these two onscreen lovers for the rest of their lives.

CHARLES **BOYER**
HEDY **LAMARR**

IN *Algiers*

The romance between a thief on the run and a kept woman with a romantic heart was a chestnut that predated the movies, even if *Algiers* (1938) was based on a 1937 French novel. But with Charles Boyer at his dramatic best and Hedy Lamarr at her most beautiful, few fans had time to remember any other variations on the theme. Even critics who had seen the story's first film version, director Julien Duvivier's *Pépé le Moko* (1937), had to admit that the Hollywood rendition was every bit as romantic. And like many of the screen's most potent romantic pairings, it's all the more powerful because it marked the only time the great lover and the exotic beauty worked together. There are no other onscreen memories to dim the film's luster. Less romantic was the reason for *Algiers*'s production—economic necessity. Boyer had a contract with independent producer Walter Wanger, who needed a surefire hit to offset some recent box-office duds. The star actually turned down *Algiers* at first. The last thing Boyer wanted was to court comparison with Jean Gabin, who had starred in the original. But when he turned down all of Wanger's other picture ideas, he had to give in. Wanger had wanted to cast Sylvia Sidney as Gaby, the woman whose love lures Pépé out of the Casbah to his death, but her recent films had tanked, and he began looking for a more bankable choice. There are conflicting stories about Hedy Lamarr's casting in her first U.S. film. In her memoirs, she claims that a chance meeting with Boyer and Wanger at a party brought her the role. Other sources suggest that although he had signed her to an MGM contract, studio head Louis B. Mayer didn't want to take a chance on the untried actress himself and had been shopping around Hollywood for the right loan-out. Boyer was pleased when Wanger hired "actor's director" John Cromwell to helm the film, but not so pleased when Wanger ordered Cromwell to remake the French original frame for frame. The actor felt trapped into mimicking Gabin's performance, though Cromwell would later state that the actor, perhaps unconsciously, found subtle shadings that made the role his own. Boyer also helped mold Lamarr by manipulating her with praise or indifference as the scene required. As a result, *Algiers* made Lamarr a star. But it also typed Boyer as a lover, just as he had won respect for his acting in films like *Mayerling* (1936) and *Conquest* (1937). For all the problems the film ultimately caused him, however, *Algiers* also gave him the chance to play one of film's greatest doomed romantics, opposite one of the most beautiful faces ever to grace a movie screen.

His

BORN
Charles Boyer
August 28, 1899
Figeac, Lot, Midi–Pyrénées,
France

DIED
August 26, 1978
Phoenix, Arizona,
of suicide, by pill overdose

STAR SIGN
Virgo

HEIGHT
5'7"

WIFE AND CHILD
British actress Pat Paterson
(1934–1978, her death)
son, Michael

KEY QUOTE

Boyer
For two years I've been
lost, like walking in
my sleep, suddenly I
wake up, that's you.
I don't know what I've
been doing all that
time waiting for you
without knowing it.
Do you know what you
are to me? Paris, that's
you, Paris. With you
I escape, follow me? The
whole town, the
spring morning in Paris.
You're lovely, you're
marvelous. Do you know
what you remind
me of? The subway.
Close your eyes, listen,
can you hear it?

Lamarr
That's my heart beating.

Boyer
Does it go like a
subway train?

Lamarr
Faster.

OFFSCREEN**RELATIONSHIP**

According to Hedy Lamarr's memoirs, she first met Charles Boyer at a party she attended on the spur of the moment. Able to see only her back, he commented, "I have not seen your face, but from the back, your hair and your figure assure me you are a beautiful woman." When she mentioned she was under contract at MGM but had only appeared in "a few minor films in Vienna," he instantly realized she was Hedy Lamarr.

Director John Cromwell on Charles Boyer's working relationship with Hedy Lamarr: "He pulled Hedy through so delicately. . . He acted with sincerity and with integrity, and she responded to it. Any actor, good or bad, responds to another actor's level. . . In *Algiers* Hedy plays off Boyer, and he's incredible. The love scenes are so strong that you don't see it's all *him*."

When independent producer Walter Wanger bought the rights to *Pépé le Moko*, he also bought all prints of the film so it could not be shown in the United States and compared to *Algiers*. In addition to remaking the original virtually frame-for-frame, he had large portions of the score used in his own version.

ALGIERS, 1938

Hers

BORN
Hedwig Eva Maria Kiesler
November 9, 1913
Vienna, Austria

DIED
January 19, 2000
Orlando, Florida,
of natural causes

STAR SIGN
Scorpio

HEIGHT
5′7″

HUSBANDS AND CHILDREN
Multimillionaire
manufacturer Fritz Mandl
(1933–1937, divorced)

Screenwriter Gene Markey
(1939–1940, divorced)
adopted son, James

Actor John Loder
(1943–1947, divorced)
daughter, Denise Hedy
son, Anthony

Restaurateur Ted Stauffer
(1951–1952, divorced)

Oil millionaire W. Howard Lee
(1953–1960, divorced)

Attorney Lewis Boies
(1963–1965, divorced)

BEHIND THE SCENES

THE PRODUCTION CODE ADMINISTRATION ORDERED CHANGES IN JOHN HOWARD LAWSON'S SCRIPT TO REMOVE ANY SUGGESTION THAT THE CHARACTERS PLAYED BY HEDY LAMARR AND SIGRID GURIE WERE KEPT WOMEN. THEY ALSO DEMANDED THAT THE ENDING BE REWRITTEN TO MAKE IT CLEAR THAT CHARLES BOYER'S CHARACTER DID NOT COMMIT SUICIDE TO ESCAPE ARREST.

CHARLES BOYER'S PERFORMANCE IN *ALGIERS* WAS BREAD AND BUTTER TO IMPRESSIONISTS, WHO COULD ALWAYS GET A LAUGH WITH THE LINE "COME WIZ ME TO ZE CASBAH." THIS LINE, HOWEVER, WAS NOT DELIVERED IN THE FILM.

ALTHOUGH THEY NEVER WORKED TOGETHER AGAIN, CHARLES BOYER AND HEDY LAMARR CAME CLOSE WHEN SHE WAS OFFERED THE LEADING ROLE IN *GASLIGHT* (1944), IN WHICH BOYER PLAYED THE DEVIOUS HUSBAND OUT TO DRIVE HIS WIFE MAD. IN ONE OF THE BIGGEST CAREER BLUNDERS IN HOLLYWOOD HISTORY, LAMARR TURNED DOWN THE ROLE, WHICH BROUGHT AN OSCAR TO INGRID BERGMAN.

They were the anti-stars, a pair of authentic mugs who brought to life a gallery of outrageously funny, irresistibly touching characters with so much heart that glamour was unnecessary.

MARIE **DRESSLER**
WALLACE **BEERY**

Battered by life, weathered by experience, Marie Dressler and Wallace Beery reveled in their wrinkles and jowls. Although they made only three films together, and only two in which they actually costarred, they left an indelible impression. In a Hollywood dominated by glamour girls and debonair gentlemen, their pairing was risky. But MGM production head Irving G. Thalberg had the foresight to see that Depression-era audiences were ripe for a change of pace. While most films of the day created dreams of luxury, audiences were drawn to the very ordinariness of Dressler and Beery. The two looked like any other married couple dealing with the same problems—paying bills, raising children, dealing with life's little temptations—the audience faced every day. And no matter how hard things got for them, they always came out on top. Even when they cleaned up for the society comedy *Dinner at Eight* (1933), audiences saw it as an inverted form of slumming. Dressler and Beery swanned through the elite dinner party in the finest eveningwear as if they knew they were only a few steps removed from the gutter. Beyond their maturity, the characterizations came naturally to them simply because they had been down so many times themselves. During a long stage career, Dressler lost everything twice and was even blacklisted for her early support of Actor's Equity, the stage-actors' union. It had taken Beery years to establish himself as a film actor, and the 1929 stock-market crash had pretty much wiped out his savings. The team was born because of a good deed Dressler had done in earlier days, granting an interview to a struggling female writer. Years later that woman, Frances Marion, was one of the top screenwriters at MGM. Hearing that Dressler had fallen on hard times, she urged Thalberg to cast her in *The Callahans and the Murphys* (1927), passing her off as a major stage star. She kept creating roles for Dressler, building up a one-scene bit in *Anna Christie* (1930) into a scene-stealing showcase. With fan mail pouring in, Marion had little trouble convincing executives to buy the rights to Lorna Moon's novel *Dark Star*, about a beaten-up bar owner raising another woman's child as her own. Beery had just scored a hit as the childlike killer in *The Big House* (1930), which made him the obvious choice to play Dressler's hard-drinking, sometimes abusive boyfriend, even though he was actually seventeen years her junior. Marion even named the film after their characters, *Min and Bill* (1930). The result was MGM's highest-grossing film of the year and made Dressler, at the tender age of sixty-two, the year's top box-office star, with Beery ranked seventh. Among the glamorous figures she beat out were Norma Shearer, Joan Crawford, and Greta Garbo. *Min and Bill* also brought Dressler the Oscar for Best Actress, industry recognition of her new status as the world's most popular actress. MGM was quick to develop other properties for her, even though her health had begun to fail. She would make three films in one six-month period, with her workdays often cut back to three hours to conserve her energies. That wasn't hard to do with *Dinner at Eight*, an ensemble film featuring Dressler in just three scenes, two of them with Beery. But it was a much bigger challenge on *Tugboat Annie* (1933). In transferring the Tugboat Annie stories to the screen, MGM's writers changed her husband from fond memory to living partner (and sometime pain in the neck) so they could reteam the unlikely stars. But even with the use of a double in long shots and rehearsals, Dressler had to survive a storm at sea—created in the studio water tanks, of course—that the real sailors working on the film said was rougher than anything they'd ever experienced in the real world. The result, once again, was the studio's top-grossing film. Dressler and Beery might have continued their winning streak—the studio was working on a *Tugboat Annie* sequel—had she not passed away in 1934, leaving a nation in mourning. Although her reign as a star and her partnership with Beery were short, they were unique. No other character actress has ever risen to the same heights. And though MGM paired Beery with Marjorie Rambeau and Marjorie Main in later years, no screen team could match the original for authenticity, earthiness, and sheer heart.

MIN AND BILL, 1930

WITH DIRECTOR MERVYN LEROY ON THE SET OF *TUGBOAT ANNIE*, 1933

BEHINDTHESCENES

MGM SHOT *MIN AND BILL* ALMOST ENTIRELY ON LOCATION—A RARITY AT THE TIME—AT FISH HARBOR, THE LOW-RENT FISHING DISTRICT IN LOS ANGELES. THE SMELL OF FISH FROM THE NEARBY CANNERIES MADE EVERYONE SICK. AT ONE POINT PRODUCTION ACTUALLY HAD TO BE SHUT DOWN FOR A WEEK AND A HALF BECAUSE BOTH STARS WERE ILL.

ON JANUARY 31, 1931, MARIE DRESSLER AND WALLACE BEERY LEFT THEIR FOOTPRINTS IN CEMENT IN FRONT OF GRAUMAN'S CHINESE THEATER. SID GRAUMAN WROTE IN THE CEMENT, "AMERICA'S NEW SWEETHEARTS, MIN AND BILL."

IN ADDITION TO THEIR THREE FILMS TOGETHER, MARIE DRESSLER AND WALLACE BEERY APPEARED IN A PUBLIC-SERVICE ANNOUNCEMENT CAMPAIGNING AGAINST THE CREATION OF DAYLIGHT SAVINGS TIME. IT ENDED WITH HER SAYING, "THEY *PAY* MEN TO THINK UP THINGS LIKE THAT?"

WITH THE SUCCESS OF *MIN AND BILL*, OTHER STUDIOS TRIED TO CREATE THEIR OWN VERSIONS OF MARIE DRESSLER AND WALLACE BEERY. RKO TEAMED CHARACTER COMICS EDNA MAY OLIVER AND HUGH HERBERT IN *LAUGH AND GET RICH* (1931), WHILE PARAMOUNT HAD MORE SUCCESS PAIRING W. C. FIELDS AND ALISON SKIPWORTH IN A SERIES OF FILMS, INCLUDING *IF I HAD A MILLION* (1932).

His

BORN
Wallace Fitzgerald Beery
April 1, 1885
Kansas City, Missouri

DIED
April 15, 1949
Beverly Hills, California,
of a heart attack

STAR SIGN
Aries

HEIGHT
6'1"

WIVES AND CHILD
Actress Gloria Swanson
(1916–1919, divorced)

Actress Rita Gilman
(1924–1939, divorced)
daughter, Carol Ann

KEY QUOTE

From *Tugboat Annie* (1933)

Beery
Ah! This is a great day for the Brennans.

Dressler
Oh, go on away, you big ape, you kiss like a wet paintbrush.

OFFSCREEN**RELATIONSHIP**

Wallace Beery on working with Marie Dressler: "I've seen her work and smile when she was in actual pain. They don't come any better than Marie."

Marie Dressler's official line on Wallace Beery: "Wally is that rare creature, a perfectly natural human. If he likes you, he shows it; if he doesn't like you, he shows it. No matter whether he is talking to Mr. Louis B. Mayer himself or the humblest prop boy on the lot, he is exactly the same."

Director George Hill (*Min and Bill*) on working with Marie Dressler and Wallace Beery: "When they gave me two such unconscious scene-stealers as Marie and Wally to work with, I had visions of having to tear them apart when they were before the camera. It worked just the other way around. I had to fight them separately, to keep their faces in front of the camera. Each wanted the other to have all the business. It must be love!"

With the success of *Min and Bill*, MGM's publicity department fanned rumors that Marie Dressler and Wallace Beery had fallen in love.

Despite a reputation for crude and inconsiderate behavior, Wallace Beery not only opened Marie Dressler's limousine door for her at the Los Angeles premiere of *Min and Bill* but also bowed as she got out. He then led her to the dais to be interviewed for the radio and kissed her.

MARIE DRESSLER WALLACE BEERY

A GEORGE HILL PRODUCTION

SUGGESTED FROM THE BOOK "DARK STAR" BY LORNA MOON · SCENARIO AND DIALOGUE BY FRANCES MARION AND MARION JACKSON · DIRECTED BY GEORGE HILL

A METRO·GOLDWYN·MAYER PICTURE

MIN AND BILL

MIN AND BILL, 1930

Hers

BORN
Leila Marie Koerber
November 9, 1868
Cobourg, Ontario, Canada

DIED
July 28, 1934
Santa Barbara, California,
of cancer

STAR SIGN
Scorpio

HEIGHT
5'7"

HUSBAND
George Hoppert
(1899–1906, divorced)

ESSENTIAL**TEAM-UPS**

MIN AND BILL (1930, MGM)
In the title roles, Marie Dressler and Wallace Beery have a relationship that is sometimes contentious, but more often comforting, as Dressler tries to protect her adopted daughter in a seedy waterfront bar.

TUGBOAT ANNIE (1933, MGM)
Dressler risked her health to play a tugboat captain trying to deal with a drunken Beery and a son (Robert Young) who's just been promoted to captain a cruise ship.

DINNER AT EIGHT (1933, MGM)
Dressler, as aging actress Carlotta Vance, and Beery, as nouveau-riche tycoon Dan Packard, barely share any screen time but steal the film in this comedy of bad manners about a disastrous society dinner party.

There never was a high concept more stratospheric than the teaming of the screen's most bombastic con artist with the woman who cornered the market on sex appeal.

W. C. FIELDS
MAE WEST
in *My Little Chickadee*

W. C. Fields and Mae West were an almost irresistible pairing. The potential for subtle barbs about his drinking and her allure would have delighted any writer. Surprisingly, though, that's not what happened when they finally got together onscreen for *My Little Chickadee* (1940). For one thing, the two shared relatively little screen time together. The plot—in which West engineers a sham marriage to Fields in order to keep up her romance with a masked bandit—permitted the stars to go their own ways for much of the running time. And when they did get together, their scenes were surprisingly sweet, with Fields fussing over West's "symmetrical digits," and West ultimately standing up for him when he's mistaken for the outlaw. That may have been a wise choice, since West's polished double entendres and Fields' whimsical, off-the-cuff ad-libs weren't the most compatible of comic styles. Yet the mere thought of their working together was so powerful that *My Little Chickadee* has continued to be a fan favorite and one of the best remembered in both stars' canons. Fields' first film since he'd left Paramount for Universal, *You Can't Cheat an Honest Man* (1939), was doing such good business that the studio asked him to make another. He wanted to star in an adaptation of Charles Dickens' *The Pickwick Papers*, but Universal decided to go with something more commercial. Although he and West had both worked at Paramount at the same time in the 1930s, they had never appeared together, partly because of West's low tolerance for heavy drinkers. When Universal approached her about the teaming, she insisted on a contract clause that would allow her to have him removed from the set should he ever turn up inebriated. Finding a script was a major battle. The studio wanted a run-of-the-mill Western into which the stars were expected to insert their specialties. After numerous arguments with Universal's executives, Fields finally appealed to West for help and even offered to support one of her story ideas. When he finally got a look at her script, he was amazed at how well she had captured his particular brand of humor. Ultimately Fields would write his own scenes, while West handled the rest of the picture, including their scenes together. Of course, Fields' penchant for ad-libbing guaranteed that he would hold his own with her. The two got along well during filming, each respecting the other's professionalism. In later years, West, bitter over having to share her writing credit with Fields, would disparage the film and her costar's contribution to it. Nothing she could say, however, could keep audiences from making *My Little Chickadee* the most popular of either star's films, a movie people would come up and see not just sometime, but time and time again.

His

BORN
William Claude Dukenfield
January 29, 1880
Darby, Pennsylvania

DIED
December 25, 1946
Pasadena, California,
of a stomach hemorrhage

STAR SIGN
Aquarius

HEIGHT
5'8"

WIFE AND CHILDREN
Harriet Hughes
(1900–1946, his death)
son, William Jr.

son, William Rexford
Fields Morris, born to
girlfriend Bessie Poole
out of wedlock

OFFSCREEN**RELATIONSHIP**

Although Paramount publicists had reported that W. C. Fields had considered Mae West his favorite movie actress back when they worked at the studio, in private he was somewhat more judgmental. He once described her as "a plumber's idea of Cleopatra."

W. C. Fields on writing the script with Mae West: "During my entire experience in the entertainment world, I have never had anyone catch my character as Miss West has. In fact, she is the only author that has ever known what I was trying to do."

Despite the success of *My Little Chickadee*, Mae West tended to disparage it in later years. Still bitter over having made a third of W. C. Fields' salary on the film, she said, "I sorta stepped off my pedestal when I made that movie." She also quipped, "Some people have gotten the quaint idea that I made more than one film with W. C. Fields. No way, baby. Once was enough."

Mae West, on keeping W. C. Fields in line: "There were a few times when Bill wouldn't play a scene the way I thought it should be played. But I would never stop him. I'd just blow a line myself, or forget one. Then we would give each other a look, have a laugh, and do the scene right."

MY LITTLE CHICKADEE, 1940

Hers

BORN
Mary Jane West
August 17, 1893
Brooklyn, New York

DIED
November 22, 1980
Hollywood, California,
of heart failure following
multiple strokes

STAR SIGN
Leo

HEIGHT
5'1"

HUSBAND
Vaudeville partner
Frank Wallace
(1911–1942, divorced)

BEHIND THE SCENES

ALTHOUGH HE WAS THE HIGHER-PAID OF THE TWO STARS, W. C. FIELDS GAVE MAE WEST TOP BILLING IN RETURN FOR SCRIPT APPROVAL. THAT TURNED OUT TO BE A WISE MOVE WHEN HE DIDN'T LIKE ANY OF THE SCRIPTS UNIVERSAL'S WRITERS CAME UP WITH.

DESPITE MAE WEST'S MISGIVINGS AND HIS JOKES ABOUT HEAVY DRINKING, THERE HAS NEVER BEEN A SINGLE STORY FROM ANYONE WHO EVER SAW W. C. FIELDS INEBRIATED.

ONE BATTLE THE INDUSTRY'S CENSORS LOST WAS OVER THE WEDDING-NIGHT SCENE, IN WHICH MAE WEST SLIPS A GOAT INTO THE BED SHE'S SUPPOSED TO BE SHARING WITH W. C. FIELDS. ALTHOUGH HIS LINE, "DARLING, HAVE YOU CHANGED YOUR PERFUME?" WAS CUT, THE SCENE STAYED. THE ENTIRE SCENE WAS CUT BY CENSORS IN AUSTRALIA AND BRITISH COLUMBIA.

THERE WAS A GREAT DEAL OF DEBATE OVER HOW TO END THE FILM, EVEN AFTER IT WAS FINISHED. W. C. FIELDS DIDN'T WANT A FUNNY FINAL SCENE WITH MAE WEST. INSTEAD, HE ASKED TO PLAY UP THE CHARACTERS' GROWING REGARD FOR EACH OTHER BY HAVING THEM SWITCH CATCHPHRASES, WITH WEST CALLING HIM "MY LITTLE CHICKADEE" AND FIELDS TELLING HER TO "COME UP AND SEE ME SOMETIME." WHEN THE STUDIO DECIDED NOT TO PAY FOR RETAKES, THE SCENE STAYED IN.

TAG LINE FOR *MY LITTLE CHICKADEE*: "IT'S THE LAFFTIME OF A LIFETIME! . . . AS 'WILD BILL' FIELDS TRIES TO TAME THE WEST!"

KEY QUOTE

Fields
May I present
my card?

West
"Novelties and
Notions." What kind
of notions you got?

Fields
You'd be surprised.
Some are old,
some are new.

They were the definitive swashbuckling couple, a striking combination of masculine swagger and feminist pluck.

ERROL **FLYNN**
OLIVIA **DE HAVILLAND**

Errol Flynn and Olivia de Havilland set the bar—and set it very high—for the swashbuckler genre. His combination of a devil-may-care attitude and earnest devotion to whatever cause was at hand had critics hailing him as a worthy successor to Douglas Fairbanks Sr. Where other leading ladies in the genre were merely decorative window dressing, de Havilland brought a touch of rebellion to her roles opposite Flynn. Perhaps it was a reflection of her own rebelliousness under the studio contract system, but she always found a way to give her leading ladies a bit more backbone than audiences expected. And that was the ideal counterpoint to Flynn's braggadocio. They weren't the perfect match just because the script said so, or because they were the prettiest people onscreen. Rather, she was the ultimate challenge: a feisty, independent female whose tongue was sharper than any sword Flynn could ever beat down. Later screen teams might try to imitate their verbal sparring but could never match their electricity for one simple reason—as each would admit later, Flynn and de Havilland had a very real attraction to each other. That connection made their love scenes thrillingly sexy. It also made it possible for them to make films in which they didn't always live happily ever after at the final fade-out. Not even death could diminish the electrical charge between them. They first met when Warner Bros. remade the silent action classic *Captain Blood* (1923), spurred by the success of *The Count of Monte Cristo* and *Treasure Island* (both 1934). Studio head Jack Warner decided to risk the expensive production on a newcomer and ordered director Michael Curtiz to test Errol Flynn. The actor had only recently arrived at the studio, where he had thus far played two small roles. When he tested opposite de Havilland, all thought of other actors vanished. Their romantic byplay, along with dazzling action and some footage borrowed from the earlier film, made *Captain Blood* (1935) a hit and turned both actors into stars. It also set the form for their future adventures. When a scheduling conflict forced Anita Louise out of Flynn's *The Charge of the Light Brigade* (1936), Warner heeded the fans' demands for another pairing and put de Havilland into the role. Eventually they would team for eight films. Working mostly with Curtiz, they scored hit after hit, though Flynn was increasingly unhappy working with the autocratic director and de Havilland increasingly distressed over the lack of solid dramatic roles for her at Warner Bros. In retrospect, however, it's clear that as she grew as an actress, her roles opposite Flynn got stronger. Not only did she clash onscreen with her costar in films like *The Adventures of Robin Hood* (1938), *Dodge City* (1939), and *Santa Fe Trail* (1940), but she also stood by his side against corruption, be it in medieval England, a town in the Wild West, or even the U.S. government. The films also grew increasingly elaborate; *The Adventures of Robin Hood*, *Dodge City*, and *The Private Lives of Elizabeth and Essex* (1939) were all shot in Technicolor. However, de Havilland's restlessness at Warner Bros. would eventually put an end to their partnership. When Flynn started work on *They Died with Their Boots On* (1941), the studio's fanciful biography of General George Armstrong Custer, he requested de Havilland as his leading lady, knowing full well that it would probably be their last film together. For the only time, they played a happily married couple onscreen. And as had happened in several other of their best films, they were ultimately torn apart by destiny, sharing a heartbreaking scene in which de Havilland sends Flynn off to certain death at the Battle of Little Big Horn. Ironically, it was the last scene they ever shot together, made all the more poignant by Flynn's realization that it was, indeed, his final chance to work with her. But though they went their separate ways, they left a significant legacy on film. As de Havilland once said, "Of course we did have a life together as Peter Blood and Arabella Bishop, as Maid Marian and Robin Hood, as George Custer and his Libby. And those were happy lives, and perhaps that was enough."

FOUR'S A CROWD, 1938

THEY DIED WITH THEIR BOOTS ON, 1941

BEHINDTHESCENES

OLIVIA DE HAVILLAND BEAT OUT JEAN MUIR AND BETTE DAVIS FOR THE FEMALE LEAD IN *CAPTAIN BLOOD* (1935).

HISTORICAL ACCURACY WAS HARDLY AN ISSUE IN THE FLYNN–DE HAVILLAND FILMS. *THE CHARGE OF THE LIGHT BRIGADE* (1936) TURNED THE FAMED CHARGE FROM MILITARY MISTAKE TO NOBLE ACT OF SELF-SACRIFICE. *SANTA FE TRAIL* (1940), SET NOWHERE NEAR NEW MEXICO, MADE COLLEGE CHUMS OF FUTURE GENERALS JEB STUART (ERROL FLYNN) AND GEORGE ARMSTRONG CUSTER (RONALD REAGAN), EVEN THOUGH THE LATTER WAS ONLY A CHILD WHEN THE FORMER GRADUATED FROM WEST POINT. MOST EGREGIOUS OF ALL WAS THE REWRITING OF HISTORY IN *THEY DIED WITH THEIR BOOTS ON* (1941), WHICH PAINTED GEORGE ARMSTRONG CUSTER AS A FORWARD-THINKING NATIVE-RIGHTS ACTIVIST, WHEN IN TRUTH HE WAS UNDER INVESTIGATION FOR STEALING NATIVE LANDS AND ONLY MADE HIS FAMOUS LAST STAND IN A BID TO IMPROVE HIS REPUTATION.

OLIVIA DE HAVILLAND FILMED HER ROLE IN *THE PRIVATE LIVES OF ELIZABETH AND ESSEX* (1939) AFTER COMPLETING PRINCIPAL PHOTOGRAPHY ON *GONE WITH THE WIND* (1939). NOT ONLY WAS HER THIRD-BILLED ROLE IN THE FLYNN FILM A LETDOWN, BUT HER PREOCCUPATION WITH SHOOTING RETAKES ON THE CIVIL WAR EPIC ALSO MADE THE SHOOT ESPECIALLY CHALLENGING.

His

BORN
Errol Leslie Thomson Flynn
June 20, 1909
Hobart, Tasmania, Australia

DIED
October 14, 1959
Vancouver, British Columbia,
Canada, of a heart attack

STAR SIGN
Gemini

HEIGHT
6'2½"

WIVES AND CHILDREN
Actress Lili Damita
(1935–1942, divorced)
son, Sean

Actress Nora Eddington
(1943–1948, divorced)
daughters, Deirdre and Rory

Actress Patrice Wymore
(1950–1959, his death)
daughter, Arnella Roma

OFFSCREEN**RELATIONSHIP**

Olivia de Havilland on testing for *Captain Blood* with Errol Flynn: "I reported to the set and saw this tall young man in costume ready to make this test. We were very formal with each other, but I thought, 'Oh . . . oh . . . he is the handsomest, most charming, most magnetic, most virile young man in the entire world.'"

While filming *The Adventures of Robin Hood*, Errol Flynn told Olivia de Havilland that his marriage to Lili Damita was over, which would leave him free to marry her. She advised him to wait until he had straightened things out with his wife. When Damita showed up on the set, it was clear the marriage was far from over. De Havilland would later describe how she got back at him: "I thought, 'Oh, well, I'm going to torture Errol Flynn, that's what I'm going to do.' And so we had one kissing scene, which I looked forward to with great delight. I remember I'd ruin every take—at least six in a row, maybe seven, maybe eight—and we had to kiss all over again. And Errol Flynn got really rather uncomfortable and he had, if I may say so, a little trouble with his tights."

As an outlet for his unrequited affection for Olivia de Havilland, Errol Flynn tormented her with practical jokes throughout the making of *The Charge of the Light Brigade*, most famously putting a dead snake in her underwear drawer.

After years of denigrating her films with Errol Flynn, Olivia de Havilland saw *The Adventures of Robin Hood* in Paris in 1959 and remarked, "Seeing *Robin Hood* after all these years made me realize how good all our adventure films were." De Havilland was so moved by the screening that she started writing Flynn a letter, but then she tore it up, afraid he might find her too sentimental. Flynn died a couple of weeks later, and de Havilland later stated that she regretted not having sent the letter.

CAPTAIN BLOOD, 1935

Hers

BORN
Olivia Mary de Havilland
July 1, 1916
Tokyo, Japan

STAR SIGN
Cancer

HEIGHT
5'3½"

HUSBANDS AND CHILDREN
Writer Marcus Goodrich
(1946–1953, divorced)
son, Benjamin

Paris Match editor
Pierre Galante
(1955–1979, divorced)
daughter, Gisele

ESSENTIAL**TEAM-UPS**

CAPTAIN BLOOD (1935, Warner Bros.)
Escaped slave Errol Flynn and colonial governor's daughter Olivia de Havilland spar in their first swashbuckling epic.

THE CHARGE OF THE LIGHT BRIGADE (1936, Warner Bros.)
Before Flynn takes off on his famous charge, he rescues de Havilland from a rebel attack in this sumptuous spectacle.

THE ADVENTURES OF ROBIN HOOD (1938, Warner Bros.)
In their greatest film together, Flynn and de Havilland enjoy romance when they're not busy trying to keep King John (Claude Rains) and Sir Guy of Gisbourne (Basil Rathbone) from stealing the British throne.

SANTA FE TRAIL (1940, Warner Bros.)
De Havilland had one of her best roles in the series as the strong-willed frontierswoman who realizes that Flynn's defeat of John Brown (Raymond Massey) will do little to ease hostilities between North and South.

THEY DIED WITH THEIR BOOTS ON (1941, Warner Bros.)
In their last film together, Flynn and de Havilland costar as the Custers, whose mature and multilayered relationship provides a contrast to the general's involvement in the Civil War and Native uprisings.

KEY QUOTE

**From *The Adventures of Robin Hood*
(1938)**

De Havilland
What's your reward
for all this?

Flynn
My reward? You
just don't understand,
do you?

De Havilland
I'm sorry.
Yes, I do begin
to see . . . a
little . . . now.

Flynn
If that's true . . .
then I want
no greater reward.

They were the hottest screen team of the 1930s, exhibiting a raw, unembarrassed sexuality that belied their inherent vulnerabilities.

CLARK **GABLE**
JEAN **HARLOW**

Jean Harlow's hard-boiled, peroxided exterior masked a street-smart but sensitive girl looking for love. Clark Gable's all-American image combined a passionate soul with a tender heart. He was more than just her most frequent costar. As Harlow was rising to stardom, he was the actor who brought more out of her—more fight and more passion—than had any other costar up untill then. Each had such a strong personality, their scenes were like contests. Even the simplest exchange could be overwhelmingly sexy. When they played it platonic, as boss and assistant in *Wife vs. Secretary* (1936), audiences still observed the attraction between them, even though the closest they got to romance was a scene in which Harlow removed her sleeping boss's shoes. The stars' offscreen relationship played out much the same. Although Gable had a reputation for romancing his leading ladies, and gossip hinted at an affair, they were really more like siblings. While everyone else at MGM called Harlow "Baby," to Gable she was just "Sis." Like an affectionate brother and sister, the two were constantly wrestling with or poking each other, which made it easy for them to "heat up the negative," as studio photographer Clarence Bull Sinclair used to describe it. It was sheer horseplay, but it made their love scenes even more searing. Harlow had been hard and sexy in pictures like *Hell's Angels* (1930) and *Red-Headed Woman* (1932), and she didn't leave those qualities behind when working with Gable. He had become a sex symbol by manhandling leading ladies like Norma Shearer in *A Free Soul* (1931). But when they got together, their obvious affection brought a new depth to their screen work. Their films trace both performers' growing maturity as stars and, more important, as artists. Interestingly, their first pairing was unofficial. Jean Harlow's leading men in *The Secret Six* (1931) were Wallace Beery and Johnny Mack Brown. During filming, however, MGM production head Irving G. Thalberg had Gable's role in the film expanded. It was in their second film, *Red Dust* (1932), that the team took off. As a plantation manager and a streetwalker, they literally steamed up the film's Southeast Asia setting. Harlow also showed an unexpected flair for self-deprecating humor, while Gable proved his ruggedness could appeal to both men and women. Their open sexuality raised problems with the Production Code. Studio head Louis B. Mayer wanted to exploit their chemistry in another film, but asked writer Anita Loos to come up with something more appealing to potential censors. The result was *Hold Your Man* (1933), an amiable tale of romantic con artists. To appease the moralists, Loos sent the characters to prison at the end, in a series of dramatic scenes that reviewers hated. But audiences were so eager to see the stars together that they gave the pair another hit. Commitments to other films meant that it would take two years to get them back together, for the rousing adventure film

China Seas (1935). With their next-to-last film, *Wife vs. Secretary*, the two softened their images, a bow to changing tastes. Fans complained about the film's lack of comedy, but they still bought tickets, many hoping Gable would dump highbrow wife Myrna Loy for adoring secretary Harlow (she landed the young James Stewart at the end instead). The racetrack comedy *Saratoga* (1937) marked their sixth teaming, and there might have been many more had Harlow not died of kidney failure during production. MGM finished *Saratoga* with a double filling in for her in long shots. After years of offscreen friendship, supporting Harlow through husband Paul Bern's suicide and her on-again, off-again relationship with actor William Powell, Gable was devastated. He stated that finishing the film without her was like being in the arms of a ghost. But the notoriety surrounding her death made *Saratoga* the highest-grossing picture of 1937. The studio and Hollywood moved on. But though Gable would team with two other generations' blonde bombshells—Lana Turner, in four pictures, and Marilyn Monroe, in his final film, *The Misfits* (1961)—he rarely found a costar who could release his combination of sensitivity and intense masculinity as entertainingly as had Harlow.

WIFE VS. SECRETARY, 1936

RED DUST, 1932

BEHINDTHESCENES

AFTER SEEING ONE OF CLARK GABLE'S EARLY FILMS, *RED DUST* SCREEN-WRITER JOHN LEE MAHIN TOLD PRODUCER HUNT STROMBERG, "THERE'S THIS GUY, MY GOD, HE'S GOT THE EYES OF A WOMAN AND THE BUILD OF A BULL. HE IS REALLY GOING TO BE SOMETHING. . . . HE AND HARLOW WILL BE A NATURAL."

FILMING *RED DUST* WAS A PHYSICALLY UNPLEASANT EXPERIENCE. TO RE-CREATE AN INDOCHINESE JUNGLE ON THE SOUNDSTAGE REQUIRED A COMBINATION OF DIRT AND VEGETATION THAT OFTEN STANK, PARTICULARLY WHEN IT RAINED—THE WATER WOULD LEAK INTO THE SOUNDSTAGE, TURNING THE EARTH INTO MUD. THE PROP DEPARTMENT HAD TO HEAT THE WATER SPRAYED ON THE ACTORS FOR A RAINSTORM SCENE SO IT WOULDN'T STEAM UNDER THE HOT LIGHTS.

CHINA SEAS (1935) WAS PLANNED AS A CLARK GABLE–JEAN HARLOW VEHICLE AS EARLY AS 1932. EVEN HARLOW'S SECOND HUSBAND, MGM EXECUTIVE PAUL BERN, CONTRIBUTED TO THE SCRIPT. IT TOOK THREE YEARS TO COME UP WITH A SCREENPLAY THAT COULD PASS THE PRODUCTION CODE ADMINISTRATION. THE CHIEF PROBLEMS WERE CAUSED BY THE SEA CAPTAIN GABLE'S AFFAIR WITH AN ASIAN WOMAN, WHICH PRODUCED AN ILLEGITIMATE CHILD, AND REFERENCES TO OPIUM USE. NONE OF THOSE PLOT ELEMENTS REMAINED IN THE FILM.

WHEN JEAN HARLOW PASSED AWAY WITH 90 PERCENT OF *SARATOGA* (1937) COMPLETED, MGM CONSIDERED RESHOOTING THE ENTIRE PICTURE WITH EITHER VIRGINIA BRUCE, JEAN ARTHUR, OR CAROLE LOMBARD. BUT WITH FAN MAIL BEGGING THEM TO RELEASE THE FILM WITH HARLOW, IT PREVIEWED A PARTIAL PRINT TO GREAT SUCCESS. AS A RESULT, THE FILM WAS FINISHED WITH A DOUBLE OF THE LATE STAR SHOT FROM AFAR, FROM BEHIND, OR MASKED BY BINOCULARS OR LARGE HATS, AND A RADIO ACTRESS WAS BROUGHT IN TO LOOP ADDITIONAL DIALOGUE.

WHEN MGM REMADE *RED DUST* IN 1953 AS *MOGAMBO*, CLARK GABLE REPRISED HIS ORIGINAL PART. AVA GARDNER WON AN OSCAR NOMINATION FOR HER PERFORMANCE IN THE JEAN HARLOW ROLE.

BORN
William Clark Gable
February 1, 1901
Cadiz, Ohio

DIED
November 16, 1960
Los Angeles, California,
of a heart attack

STAR SIGN
Aquarius

HEIGHT
6'1"

WIVES AND CHILDREN
Drama teacher
Josephine Dillon
(1924–1930, divorced)

Houston socialite
Maria (Ria) Franklin
Prentiss Lucas Langham
(1931–1939, divorced)

daughter, Judy Lewis,
born to actress Loretta
Young out of wedlock in 1935

Actress Carole Lombard
(1939–1942, her death)

Lady Sylvia Ashley
(1949–1952, divorced)

Kay Williams Spreckles
(1955–1960, his death)
son, John Clark

KEY QUOTE
From *Red Dust* (1932)

Harlow
You can check your
wings and
halo at the desk.

Gable
I'll be right up.

OFFSCREEN**RELATIONSHIP**

Clark Gable on acting with Jean Harlow: "She sets a pace for me that keeps me on my toes every minute. . . . She anticipates every move and meets you more than halfway. When it comes to weighing dramatic values, Jean's scales need no adjusting."

Jean Harlow was one of the few people who could get Clark Gable to submit gladly to production photos, which were usually scheduled during the actors' free time. She would put on her favorite jazz recordings and tell the photographer to work fast as she and Gable clowned around. The pair also enjoyed kidding each other between shots. She jokingly called him a "big Ohio hillbilly," while he dubbed her "the chromium blonde."

When Jean Harlow and boyfriend William Powell quarreled during production of *Saratoga*, he made up with her by ordering a third-birthday cake in honor of the third anniversary of their dating. Not to be outdone, Clark Gable announced on the set that this was the sixth anniversary of his working with Harlow. Although the scene they were filming called for only a discreet peck, he pulled her into a passionate embrace as the crew cheered and whistled.

Clark Gable got word of Jean Harlow's passing while he was on the set of *Saratoga*. He was so upset that he raced home, refusing to speak to reporters who wanted his reaction. Gable served as a pallbearer and an usher at her funeral.

CHINA SEAS, 1935

Hers

BORN
Harlean Harlow Carpenter
March 3, 1911
Kansas City, Missouri

DIED
June 7, 1937
Los Angeles, California,
of uremic poisoning

STAR SIGN
Pisces

HEIGHT
5'2"

HUSBANDS
Chicago socialite
Charles McGrew III
(1927–1929, divorced)

MGM executive Paul Bern
(1932–1932, his death)

Cameraman Harold Rosson
(1933–1935, divorced)

ESSENTIAL TEAM-UPS

RED DUST (1932, MGM)
Clark Gable stars as a rubber-plantation manager whose station is invaded by
two ladies who tempt his heart—fallen woman Jean Harlow and the patrician
Mary Astor.

HOLD YOUR MAN (1933, MGM)
Harlow marries con artist Gable and even does jail time for him in the most
proletarian of their films together.

CHINA SEAS (1935, MGM)
MGM recycled key plot elements from *Red Dust*, laundered for the Production
Code era, with Gable as a ship's captain fighting off pirates while torn between
upper-class Rosalind Russell and ex-love Harlow.

WIFE VS. SECRETARY (1936, MGM)
Gable stars as a publishing magnate caught between legal wife Myrna Loy and
office wife Harlow.

SARATOGA (1937, MGM)
In her final film, Harlow is the daughter of a horse breeder who's forced to
romance gambler Gable to save the family farm.

Theirs was the ultimate battle of masculine vs. feminine in an epic tale of love, war, and home that captivated fans from the moment the film was announced.

CLARK GABLE
VIVIEN LEIGH
in *Gone with The Wind*

Clark Gable and Vivien Leigh shared the definitive one-time pairing in *Gone with The Wind* (1939). Not only were they letter-perfect in their performances, but the fact that this was their only film together makes their teamwork even more treasured. No other film could have possibly followed the Civil War epic, so it may have been fortunate that Leigh's career path—she made relatively few American films—kept the two from working together again. Although it might have seemed to many that Rhett and Scarlett were fated to create a dynamic screen team, the actors did more than their fair share to make the characters work. Scarlett O'Hara was one of the most selfish, destructive leading ladies in film history. That she generated enough sympathy to carry audiences through nearly four hours of screen time can be credited to the collaboration of independent producer David O. Selznick and actors Gable and Leigh. Selznick had the intelligence to build the film around her love of Tara, a commitment to home that struck a powerful chord with audiences as America was coming out of the Depression and watching the world explode in the early days of World War II. Finding the right Rhett and Scarlett was a battle as furious as any military maneuver, involving the most elaborate, hotly debated casting process in film history. Although most readers associated Gable with the role of Rhett Butler, Selznick also considered the likes of Ronald Colman, Gary Cooper, and Errol Flynn before agreeing to a distribution deal with MGM, the studio holding Gable's contract. The star had his misgivings about taking the role. He didn't think he could live up to audience expectations, and he was terrified of the scene in which Rhett cries over the death of his daughter. But he also was desperate to divorce his second wife, Ria Langham, and marry longtime love Carole Lombard, and when MGM offered to pay Langham off, he had to accept the role. The real furor, though, attended the search for Scarlett O'Hara. Selznick tested thirty-five actresses and sent talent scouts roaming the nation, at a cost of about $100,000, and supposedly didn't make his final decision until he had already started filming. According to legend, his brother, agent Myron Selznick, introduced him to Leigh the night they filmed the burning of Atlanta. Other records suggest that he had seen her work earlier in *Fire over England* (1937) and *A Yank at Oxford* (1938). Although there is one memo from 1937 saying that Leigh was out of the running, historians have suggested that Selznick wanted to cast her all along and simply used the talent search for publicity. Either way, he created a one-time pairing whose appeal has reached across generations and cultures to capture the imaginations of fans from post-World War II France to contemporary Japan.

His

BORN
William Clark Gable
February 1, 1901
Cadiz, Ohio

DIED
November 16, 1960
Los Angeles, California,
of a heart attack

STAR SIGN
Aquarius

HEIGHT
6'1"

WIVES AND CHILDREN
Drama teacher
Josephine Dillon
(1924–1930, divorced)

Houston socialite
Maria (Ria) Franklin Prentiss
Lucas Langham
(1931–1939, divorced)

daughter, Judy Lewis,
born to actress Loretta
Young out of wedlock in 1935

Actress Carole Lombard
(1939–1942, her death)

Lady Sylvia Ashley
(1949–1952, divorced)

Kay Williams Spreckles
(1955–1960, his death),
son, John Clark

KEY QUOTE

Leigh
Sir, you are no
gentleman.

Gable
And you, Miss,
are no lady.

OFFSCREEN **RELATIONSHIP**

Clark Gable and Vivien Leigh met for the first time at a publicity shoot for *Gone with The Wind*. When Leigh was over an hour late, Gable complained, "I couldn't make love to that dame now if she were the most beautiful woman in the world!" Leigh showed up just in time to hear him. She touched his shoulder and said, "I quite agree, Mr. Gable. If I were a man, I'd tell that Vivien Leigh to go right back to merry old England. . . ."

Clark Gable greatly resented the rapport that developed between director George Cukor and Vivien Leigh. With Cukor's reputation as a women's director, Gable was justly afraid that the film would favor his leading lady. When Cukor was fired, Leigh was crushed. When he was replaced by Gable's favorite director, Victor Fleming, she couldn't help but resent her costar, particularly since Fleming rarely gave her any helpful notes. She continued seeing Cukor on the sly for coaching in the role.

One thing Vivien Leigh hated about Clark Gable was the smell of his dentures. The notoriously thrifty star had not bought himself the best possible pair, which made kissing him an ordeal.

Despite their difficulties at the start, Clark Gable taught Vivien Leigh how to play backgammon to pass the time as the lengthy shoot wore on. She returned the favor by teaching him to play battleship. From then on, they spent their time between setups together.

ON SET, 1939

Hers

BORN
Vivian Mary Hartley
November 5, 1913
Darjeeling, West Bengal,
British India (now India)

DIED
July 7, 1967
London, England,
of chronic tuberculosis

STAR SIGN
Scorpio

HEIGHT
5'3"

HUSBANDS AND CHILD
Attorney Herbert Leigh
Holman (1932–1940,
divorced)
daughter, Suzanne

Actor Laurence Olivier
(1940–1960, divorced)

BEHIND THE SCENES

CLARK GABLE'S MOST FAMOUS LINE IN *GONE WITH THE WIND* WAS SLIGHTLY DIFFERENT FROM WHAT MARGARET MITCHELL HAD WRITTEN. IN THE NOVEL, RHETT SIMPLY SAYS, "MY DEAR, I DON'T GIVE A DAMN." IN HIS FIRST DRAFT OF THE SCREENPLAY, PLAYWRIGHT SIDNEY HOWARD ADDED THE WORD "FRANKLY" AT THE BEGINNING OF THE SENTENCE, CREATING THE PERFECT RHYTHM TO HELP THE LINE GO DOWN IN FILM HISTORY.

CLARK GABLE WAS MAKING $4,500 A WEEK WHILE SHOOTING *GONE WITH THE WIND*. THE LENGTHY PRODUCTION EARNED HIM $120,000. VIVIEN LEIGH MADE THE FILM FOR JUST $25,000.

LONELY BECAUSE OF TIME SPENT AWAY FROM HER THEN-LOVER, LAURENCE OLIVIER, VIVIEN LEIGH BEGAN TO RESENT *GONE WITH THE WIND*. AFTER HAVING WORKED SO HARD TO WIN THE ROLE, SHE WROTE A FRIEND, "IT IS REALLY VERY MISERABLE AND GOING VERY SLOWLY. I WAS A FOOL TO HAVE DONE IT."

ONE CONCERN CLARK GABLE HAD ABOUT PLAYING RHETT BUTLER WAS SIMPLY THE LENGTH OF THE ROLE. IT IS ACTUALLY THE SHORTEST OF THE FOUR PRINCIPAL ROLES IN THE FILM. HE FELT THAT, AS RHETT WAS WRITTEN, HE HAD TO JUMP IN AND GRAB THE AUDIENCE'S ATTENTION WITHOUT THE CAREFUL BUILDUP GIVEN SCARLETT, MELANIE, AND ASHLEY.

They were the silent cinema's sexiest couple, drawing on their mutual offscreen passion to create some of the movies' greatest love scenes.

GRETA **GARBO**
JOHN **GILBERT**

A romantic view of Greta Garbo's life would suggest that she was never happier in the United States than when she was involved with John Gilbert. He was the only actor who could persuade her to attend a film premiere and smile for the camera. He taught her how to maneuver in the choppy seas of studio politics. And he came closer to getting the reclusive Swede to the altar than anybody else. Even after their affair was over, Garbo tried to help his failing career by demanding that he be cast as her leading man in *Queen Christina* (1933). The gesture seemed appropriate, as, ironically, Gilbert's love for her helped lead to his own fall from stardom. Their tragic romance—doomed by Gilbert's brash devotion and Garbo's driving need for independence—permeates every inch of celluloid they shared. Their first love scenes in *Flesh and the Devil* (1926) mirror the offscreen affair that started soon after they began work on the film. During production, director Clarence Brown and his crew often tiptoed off the set after shooting a scene, because the two refused to let their love scenes end. The passion that Garbo displayed was rooted in her initial experience in Hollywood films. The actress brought surprising dimension to the hackneyed vamp roles MGM stuck her with. For most actresses, playing vamp scenes was a one-sided affair, in which they reduced their romantic partners to quivering children. But when Garbo vamped Gilbert, her aggressive romancing actually made him look sexier. With Gilbert, she carried the innovation further. She was such a force of nature that her desire and his willing surrender made him seem like any woman's ideal. The Gilbert-Garbo team was born out of a time-honored Hollywood tradition: pairing an established star with a newcomer to boost the latter's career. Rarely has it worked so brilliantly. With Rudolph Valentino's death, Gilbert had become Hollywood's top male star. Garbo was still a relative newcomer, imported from Sweden as an afterthought when studio head Louis B. Mayer signed her mentor, director Mauritz Stiller. She almost turned down *Flesh and the Devil*, afraid of being typecast forever as a vamp, but her teaming with Gilbert turned a routine tale of forbidden love into a romantic tragedy. Capitalizing on the affair, the MGM publicity department issued progress reports on the stars' romance, priming audiences to expect some of the most passionate love scenes in film history. They weren't disappointed. Offscreen, their connection developed quickly and went far beyond sex. Gilbert helped her with her English, taught her to play tennis, and even turned her into a Hollywood hostess, a role she would give up when they eventually parted. Following his urging, Garbo went on strike for a better contract. Mayer was well aware of Gilbert's influence on Garbo, and it added to his enmity toward an actor he already considered a troublemaker. But he couldn't deny their power as a screen team. When he gave in to Garbo's pleas to film *Anna Karenina*, retitled *Love* (1927), Gilbert was the ideal choice to play her illicit lover. Garbo then turned flapper for *A Woman of Affairs* (1928), in which her bohemian lifestyle alienates Gilbert's patrician family. By this point, their on-again, off-again romance had become a Hollywood legend, with ever more fanciful stories of her leaving him at the altar. After she refused Gilbert's marriage proposals for the last time, both started exploring other relationships. Shortly after that, the coming of sound made Garbo bigger than ever but ended Gilbert's days as a star (many have suggested that Mayer sabotaged his career). There was to be one final reunion, however. When the young Laurence Olivier was cast as her leading man in *Queen Christina* (1933), she insisted the role be given to Gilbert. Although they had not seen each other in three years, they fell into their old working relationship quickly, although she remained aloof when the cameras weren't running. The film came too late to end Gilbert's downward spiral, the product of too many bad scripts and too much liquor, but it provided fans with their last golden moments onscreen together. Three years later, Gilbert died of a heart attack at the relatively young age of thirty-eight. According to friends, shortly before his death he admitted, "There's never been a day since [Garbo] and I parted that I haven't been lonely for her."

BARDELYS THE MAGNIFICENT PREMIERE, 1926

CIRCA 1926

BEHINDTHESCENES

BEFORE PRODUCTION ON *FLESH AND THE DEVIL* (1926), MGM PRODUCTION HEAD IRVING G. THALBERG ASKED JOHN GILBERT IF HE WOULD BE WILLING TO SHARE COSTARRING BILLING WITH GRETA GARBO, EVEN THOUGH HIS CONTRACT GUARANTEED HIM SOLE BILLING ABOVE THE TITLE. HE WAS ONLY TOO HAPPY TO GIVE THE RELATIVE NEWCOMER A CAREER BOOST.

LOVE (1927) WAS ORIGINALLY TO BE CALLED *HEAT* UNTIL SOMEBODY AT MGM REALIZED THAT MARQUEES READING "JOHN GILBERT AND GRETA GARBO IN *HEAT*" MIGHT BE EMBARRASSING. BUT "JOHN GILBERT AND GRETA GARBO IN *LOVE*" WOULD PROVIDE THE PERFECT OPPORTUNITY TO CAPITALIZE ON THE PAIR'S HIGHLY PUBLICIZED AFFAIR.

STUDIO EXECUTIVES COULDN'T AGREE ON WHETHER TO KEEP THE ORIGINAL DOWNBEAT ENDING OF *LOVE* OR TO CREATE A HAPPY ENDING REUNITING JOHN GILBERT AND GRETA GARBO. ON PRODUCTION CHIEF IRVING G. THALBERG'S ORDERS, THE STUDIO SHOT TWO DIFFERENT ENDINGS AND ALLOWED EXHIBITORS TO CHOOSE THE ONE THEY WANTED. MOST EAST COAST AND WEST COAST THEATERS SHOWED THE FAITHFUL ENDING, IN WHICH GARBO THROWS HERSELF IN FRONT OF A TRAIN. IN THE FLYOVER STATES, HOWEVER, THE STARS HAD A HAPPY ENDING. RECENT HOME VIDEO RELEASES HAVE INCLUDED BOTH VERSIONS.

His

BORN
John Cecil Pringle
July 10, 1897
Logan, Utah

DIED
January 9, 1936
Los Angeles, California,
of heart failure

STAR SIGN
Cancer

HEIGHT
5'11"

WIVES AND CHILDREN
Olivia Burwell
(1918–1921, divorced)

Actress Leatrice Joy
(1921–1925, divorced)
daughter, Leatrice
Gilbert Fountain

Actress Ina Claire
(1929–1931, divorced)

Actress Virginia Bruce
(1932–1934, divorced)
daughter, Susan Ann

OFFSCREEN **RELATIONSHIP**

Greta Garbo on John Gilbert: "I am very happy when I am told that I am to do a picture with Mr. Gilbert. He is a great artist. He lifts me up and carries me along with him. It is not scenes I am doing. I am living."

John Gilbert built a small cabin for Greta Garbo on his estate and had it surrounded with pine trees to remind her of her native Sweden.

During their affair, the solitary Swede was much more sociable than she would be in later years. She and Gilbert hosted several parties at his estate and frequently attended gatherings thrown by his friends. She even allowed herself to be photographed at the premiere of his film *Bardelys the Magnificent* (1926). It was the only time she ever posed for a photograph at a movie premiere.

Greta Garbo resisted all of John Gilbert's efforts to marry her. He even tried proposing in front of other people, hoping that this would embarrass her into saying yes. At one point he was so frustrated with her behavior that he sent her a note suggesting she start paying rent for living with him.

Six years before Greta Garbo starred in the comedy *Ninotchka* (1939), she had to laugh onscreen, in the scene in which she first meets John Gilbert in *Queen Christina*. Studio insiders had warned director Rouben Mamoulian that she could not laugh, even though he had seen her laugh in private moments. To help her, he asked Gilbert to make funny faces at her from offscreen when she sees him trapped in the snow. He then warned her to keep going in the scene no matter what happened. The trick worked perfectly.

Greta Garbo learned of John Gilbert's death while in Stockholm. When a rumor spread that she had commented on his passing, "What is that to me?" she was so upset that she held a rare press conference to dispute it.

QUEEN CHRISTINA, 1933

Hers

BORN
Greta Lovisa Gustafson
September 18, 1905
Stockholm, Sweden

DIED
April 15, 1990
New York, New York,
of pneumonia

STAR SIGN
Virgo

HEIGHT
5'7½"

ESSENTIAL**TEAM-UPS**

FLESH AND THE DEVIL (1926, MGM)
In their first pairing, Garbo plays a doomed temptress with the bad luck of always
being married to other men whenever Gilbert is available.

LOVE (1927, MGM)
This adaptation of Tolstoy's *Anna Karenina* casts Garbo and Gilbert as illicit lovers
torn apart by her devotion to her son and his commitment to his military career.

A WOMAN OF AFFAIRS (1928, MGM)
Adapted from Michael Arlen's scandalous *The Green Hat*, the film casts Garbo as a
playgirl whose scarlet reputation masks a purity of heart that only true love
Gilbert can see.

QUEEN CHRISTINA (1933, MGM)
In a liberal retelling of history, Garbo plays the famed Swedish monarch who,
at least according to Hollywood, gave up her throne for the love of Spanish
nobleman Gilbert.

KEY QUOTE

**From *Queen Christina*
(1933)**

Gilbert
There's a mystery
in you.

Garbo
Is there not in every
human being?

Through sheer physical presence, they turned a tale of doomed love into one of the screen's greatest romances.

GRETA **GARBO**
ROBERT **TAYLOR**
IN *Camille*

Camille, the story of a young innocent whose love transforms a kept woman, was almost a century old when MGM released it in 1937, but the once-in-a-lifetime casting of Greta Garbo and Robert Taylor made it seem new. Their romantic scenes marked the definitive meeting of female experience and male naïveté, both on- and offscreen. Taylor was terrified to be working with Garbo, which played well into his character. In addition, the athletic young actor from Nebraska was ill-prepared for her approach to onscreen lovemaking. As she had done with frequent costar and offscreen lover John Gilbert, Garbo played the aggressor's role. In one scene, without laying a hand on Taylor, she leaned in and covered his face with short kisses. He was afraid the scene would reinforce his "pretty boy" image, but female fans adored it. The film may have been Garbo's acting triumph, but for Taylor it was a very important step up the ladder to stardom. Inexperienced as he was, he turned out to be Garbo's most effective costar since Gilbert, justifying MGM production head Irving G. Thalberg's faith in him. Thalberg had begun working on an adaptation of *Camille* in 1933. The novel had been a favorite of his mother's, and he was convinced Garbo was the only film actress who could follow in the footsteps of such stage legends as Sarah Bernhardt and Eleonora Duse in the tragic role. With her busy schedule and problems coming up with a suitable screenplay, it took three years to finally get the picture in front of the cameras. Thalberg knew that one problem with most productions of *Camille* was the casting of her young lover, Armand. Actors in the role were usually overaged or overly priggish, making them far from believable or sympathetic. Most of Thalberg's fellow executives thought Taylor, who had only gotten into movies two years earlier, wouldn't be able to hold his own against Garbo. But the producer was convinced the actor's youthful innocence and sheer beauty made him a good match for the role—and for Garbo. With the help of director George Cukor and Garbo's imaginative playing, Taylor came off better than anybody had expected. Nor did it hurt that the costars looked terrific together. Their scenes captured a sense of romantic longing that still resonates today. Taylor's move into tougher roles and Garbo's limited production schedule made future teamings unlikely, which only makes their single encounter in *Camille* more special. In years to come, Taylor would speak affectionately of his surprisingly warm encounters with Garbo, the Swedish Sphinx. And Garbo would consistently call the film her favorite, a sentiment echoed by generations of critics and fans.

His

BORN
Spangler Arlington Brugh
August 5, 1911
Filley, Nebraska

DIED
June 8, 1969
Santa Monica, California,
of lung cancer

STAR SIGN
Leo

HEIGHT
5'11½"

WIVES AND CHILDREN
Actress Barbara Stanwyck
(1939–1951, divorced)

Actress Ursula Thiess
(1954–1969, his death)
son, Terrence
daughter, Theresa

KEY QUOTE

Garbo

I must give you up.
I've told you before
that you should
forget me. So
you go on your trip
around the world
and put me
out of your mind.

Taylor

I thought I meant
something to you.

Garbo

You mean too
much already.

OFFSCREEN **RELATIONSHIP**

When director George Cukor introduced Greta Garbo to Robert Taylor for the first time, the young actor froze. He couldn't even speak when she said, "How do you do?" and, after what seemed an endless silence, he left the room in a sweat.

While filming their first love scene, Greta Garbo and Robert Taylor slipped off the divan and fell to the floor. Taylor was terrified until she started laughing.

Greta Garbo on her costar: "Robert Taylor was actually a kind and well-bred man. I really appreciated what he did when he visited Stockholm for the premiere of *Camille*, which was to send flowers to my mother, twelve gorgeous orchids."

Robert Taylor on working with Greta Garbo: "I don't know why I was so frightened of her, because her acting was as natural as her breathing. She thought with her eyes—they expressed exactly what was needed. I considered working with her my greatest acting lesson, but I confess it didn't teach me anything because what she had was inborn—not method."

Robert Taylor actually had one date with Greta Garbo while making *Camille*. When he arrived at her house to pick her up, she was seated on the floor, meditating, with a long, flowing dress arranged carefully around her. She barely acknowledged his entrance. He never told anybody what happened next.

In the mid-1950s, Taylor was lunching in the MGM commissary when he spotted Garbo at another table. He didn't dare approach her, not wanting to invade her privacy and half afraid she wouldn't remember him.

CAMILLE, 1937

Hers

BORN
Greta Lovisa Gustafson
September 18, 1905
Stockholm, Sweden

DIED
April 15, 1990
New York, New York,
of pneumonia

STAR SIGN
Virgo

HEIGHT
5'7½"

BEHIND THE SCENES

MGM'S *CAMILLE* WAS AT LEAST THE FIFTEENTH FILM VERSION OF THE STORY. PROMINENT EARLIER VERSIONS INCLUDED A SHORT WITH SARAH BERNHARDT FROM 1911, THEDA BARA'S 1917 RENDITION, A 1920 POLA NEGRI FILM, ALLA NAZIMOVA'S 1921 MODERN-DRESS ADAPTATION WITH RUDOLPH VALENTINO, AND A 1926 FILM WITH NORMA TALMADGE AND GILBERT ROLAND.

AFRAID THAT THE PRODUCTION CODE ADMINISTRATION WOULD CUT THE TEETH OUT OF HIS SCRIPT, MGM PRODUCTION HEAD IRVING G. THALBERG GOT GRETA GARBO TO AGREE TO MAKE A SCREEN VERSION OF *CARMEN* IF THEY COULDN'T WORK OUT A SUITABLE COMPROMISE OVER *CAMILLE*'S DEPICTION OF PROSTITUTION.

PLAYING THE DYING MARGUERITE EXHAUSTED GRETA GARBO. ON SOME NIGHTS, SHE WOULD COME HOME FROM THE SET BARELY ABLE TO CLIMB THE STAIRS TO HER BEDROOM. YEARS LATER SHE WOULD TELL AN INTERVIEWER, "IF YOU'RE GOING TO DIE ONSCREEN, YOU'VE GOT TO BE STRONG AND IN GOOD HEALTH."

WHEN ROBERT TAYLOR FINALLY RETURNED TO RECONCILE WITH GRETA GARBO AT THE END OF *CAMILLE*, AUDIENCES IN SOME THEATERS OPENLY CHEERED.

CAMILLE INSPIRED THE SONG "I'LL LOVE LIKE ROBERT TAYLOR, BE MY GRETA GARBO" BY MILTON BENJAMIN.

They created an indelible image of self-sacrifice that struck a powerful chord with audiences eager for hope in the midst of war.

GREER **GARSON**
WALTER **PIDGEON**

Greer Garson and Walter Pidgeon were the epitome of grace under fire. They embodied a dream of dignity and good manners that complemented MGM's brand of class and elegance. In each of their eight films together, they played married couples, almost always working for some good cause. One of studio head Louis B. Mayer's favorite actresses, Garson was usually cast as the sentimental but resilient wife opposite tall, deep-voiced Pidgeon as her supportive husband. History has not been kind to the team. Changing tastes have led many to overlook the solid quality of their acting, as they brought a subtle humanity and warmth to their do-gooder roles. Their honesty and restraint helped keep their films from sinking into bathos, making them among the top-grossing and most honored pictures of the 1940s. Garson was Mayer's personal discovery, though he initially could find little to do with her after bringing her to the studio from the London stage. Pidgeon, himself recently signed to an MGM contract, first worked with her on one of her early screen tests. He dubbed her "Duchess" for her impeccable manners and insisted that they would work together someday. His prediction came true when they were cast in *Blossoms in the Dust* (1941), a biography of children's-rights crusader Edna Gladney. Having scored with *Boys Town* (1938) and *Men of Boys Town* (1941), two films focusing on child welfare, MGM decided to showcase Garson in a similar role following her triumphant appearance as Robert Donat's wife in *Goodbye, Mr. Chips* (1939). At the same time, Pidgeon was promoted to top projects after a successful loan-out to 20th Century Fox for *How Green Was My Valley* (1941). *Blossoms in the Dust* set the tone for their most popular vehicles—hushed, respectful, and relentlessly gallant. Pidgeon provided manly solace, while Garson did most of the suffering. Their greatest success came with their second teaming, in *Mrs. Miniver* (1942). MGM bought the rights to Jan Struther's Mrs. Miniver stories as a vehicle for Garson, but she initially turned it down because she didn't want to play a woman with a grown son. It took a major appeal from Mayer to convince her to accept what would become her most famous role. The part of an average British homemaker braving the Blitz would bring her an Oscar for Best Actress. The film also clearly established Garson and Pidgeon as one of Hollywood's most potent box-office teams. That was a lucky choice for Garson, as Pidgeon's solid underplaying provided the perfect foundation for her more emotional scenes. The indelible images of the pair watching over their terrified children in a bomb shelter, Garson knitting to maintain a calm facade while Pidgeon reads aloud from *Alice's Adventures in Wonderland*, helped fuel support for the war. By 1943, they were the only natural choice for *Madame Curie*, a laudatory biography of the famous physicist and her husband. By their next picture,

Mrs. Parkington (1944), the magic seemed to be fading. The film dealt with a nouveau-riche couple's rise to high society. Critics complained that with no cause to which to dedicate themselves, the stars were cut adrift, and the story seemed little more than soap opera. With the end of World War II, audiences were tired of sacrifice, no matter how noble or well played. Moreover, the new MGM management under Dore Schary appeared to have little understanding of what had made the Garson-Pidgeon team tick. An attempt to alter their image with the comedy *Julia Misbehaves* (1948) fell flat, partly because audiences couldn't accept Garson as an actress who deserts her husband and infant daughter for the stage. *The Miniver Story* (1950), a postwar sequel to *Mrs. Miniver*, was inferior to the original; thanks to a lackluster script that had Garson's character solving the problems of the world while secretly dying of cancer, critics openly derided the nobility that had made the pair stars. After the pallid *Scandal at Scourie* (1953)—ironically, a film about orphans, the topic of their first film— Garson left MGM. The two remained friends, but they never made another film together. Greer Garson and Walter Pidgeon were a pair that best flourished in the Hollywood that had generated *Mrs. Miniver*, a more genteel place where movie stars could play out dreams of heroism and self-sacrifice.

MADAME CURIE, 1943

ON THE SET OF *THE MINIVER STORY*, 1950

BEHINDTHESCENES

ALTHOUGH *BLOSSOMS IN THE DUST* (1941) STARTED HER RISE TO STARDOM, GREER GARSON DIDN'T REALLY LIKE THE FILM. A 1942 *NEW YORK TIMES* ARTICLE QUOTED HER AS SAYING, "THE SCREEN IS NEITHER A PLATFORM OR A PULPIT."

A GALLUP POLL CONDUCTED IN SEPTEMBER 1942 INDICATED THAT AUDIENCES WHO HAD SEEN *MRS. MINIVER* AND TWO OTHER PRO-BRITISH FILMS OF THAT YEAR (*THIS ABOVE ALL* AND *EAGLE SQUADRON*) WERE 17 PERCENT MORE FAVORABLE TOWARD THE BRITISH THAN THOSE WHO HAD NOT. ACCORDING TO BRITISH PRIME MINISTER WINSTON CHURCHILL, *MRS. MINIVER* DID MORE FOR THE WAR EFFORT THAN SIX MILITARY DIVISIONS COULD HAVE.

IN ADDITION TO GREER GARSON AND WALTER PIDGEON, SEVERAL OTHERS INVOLVED WITH *MRS. MINIVER* (1942) ALSO REUNITED FOR *MADAME CURIE* (1943): ACTORS DAME MAY WHITTY AND HENRY TRAVERS, PRODUCER SIDNEY FRANKLIN, AND CAMERAMAN JOSEPH RUTTENBERG.

MADAME CURIE WAS WALTER PIDGEON'S FAVORITE OF HIS EIGHT FILMS WITH GREER GARSON AND, WITH *COMMAND DECISION* (1949), THE PERFORMANCE HE CONSIDERED HIS BEST.

GREER GARSON USUALLY WORE PERFUMES CHOSEN TO PUT HER IN THE MOOD FOR DIFFERENT TYPES OF SCENES. AS HE BECAME ACCUSTOMED TO THE SMELLS, PIDGEON GAVE THEM HIS OWN PET NAMES, INCLUDING "GIVE HIM A CHANCE" AND "SHOW HIM NO MERCY."

TAG LINE FOR *MADAME CURIE*: "MR. AND MRS. MINIVER TOGETHER AGAIN."

His

BORN
Walter Davis Pidgeon
September 23, 1897
Saint John, New Brunswick,
Canada

DIED
September 25, 1984
Santa Monica, California,
of a stroke

STAR SIGN
Libra

HEIGHT
6′2½″

WIVES AND CHILD
Muriel Pickles
(1922–1926, her death)
daughter, Edna Verne

Secretary Ruth Walker
(1931–1984, his death)

KEY QUOTE

**From *Mrs. Miniver*
(1942)**

Pidgeon
What's all that about a
German pilot?

Garson
Oh, nothing, dear.
Nothing at all.

Pidgeon
What do you mean,
nothing at all?

Garson
Well, darling, we just
had a German pilot
in for ham and eggs this
morning, that's all.

OFFSCREEN**RELATIONSHIP**

After acting with Greer Garson for the first time, in a screen test, Walter Pidgeon quipped, "I'll bet we're starring together before you know it and running this studio!"

Greer Garson on teaming with Walter Pidgeon: "I couldn't have had any leading man I would have liked better. He represented the kind of strong yet gentle, warm, kind man that every woman thinks will make a wonderful husband."

Walter Pidgeon on his professional relationship with Greer Garson: "Greer and I have worked well from the first. She's a fine, professional actress—and a hell of a woman. I've done eight pictures with that gal, and we never had a bad word between us. I went with her through her romances and her marriages. A great lady, I think."

Although Greer Garson played Walter Pidgeon's wife onscreen in seven films, they were never romantically involved. In fact, she married their son from *Mrs. Miniver*, Richard Ney, and later met her third husband, Texas businessman E. E. Fogelson, on the set of their *Julia Misbehaves*.

Greer Garson on Walter Pidgeon's death: "My heart turned over when I heard from Mrs. Pidgeon on the phone today. I've lost a dear friend and a wonderful partner. He was a solid-gold gentleman. Even on the difficult days on the set, I looked forward to working, because he was such a delightful man and a splendid actor. This is a sad, sad day."

MRS. MINIVER, 1942

Hers

BORN
Eileen Evelyn Greer Garson
September 29, 1904
London, England

DIED
April 6, 1996
Dallas, Texas,
of heart failure

STAR SIGN
Virgo

HEIGHT
5'6"

HUSBANDS
Civil servant
Edwin A. Snelson
(1933–1937, divorced)

Actor Richard Ney
(1943–1947, divorced)

Texas businessman
E. E. Fogelson
(1949–1987, his death)

ESSENTIAL**TEAM-UPS**

BLOSSOMS IN THE DUST (1941, MGM)
In their first film together, Greer Garson clearly dominates as Walter Pidgeon's loving wife, who devotes her life to helping orphans find good homes and social acceptance.

MRS. MINIVER (1942, MGM)
As a proper British couple, Pidgeon and Garson face the early days of World War II together in a film that played a major role in winning U.S. support for the British cause.

MADAME CURIE (1943, MGM)
Garson and Pidgeon bring their usual nobility to the careers of the crusading physicists who pioneered the study of radioactivity.

MRS. PARKINGTON (1944, MGM)
After three years of nobility, Garson and Pidgeon cut loose and have some fun as a western hotel maid and the philandering oilman who turns her into a society matron.

THAT FORSYTE WOMAN (1949, MGM)
Garson bounced back from a career slump with this truncated adaptation of John Galsworthy's tale of twisted passions in a Victorian business dynasty, with her character trapped in a loveless marriage and Pidgeon as the family pariah who comes to her rescue.

They represented the triumph of purity and innocence, becoming, in the words of studio publicists, "America's favorite lovebirds."

JANET **GAYNOR**
CHARLES **FARRELL**

Janet Gaynor and Charles Farrell were just the right screen team to carry Hollywood into the dawn of the talking era in films. The silent era's more exotic figures—Latin lovers and kohl-eyed vamps—were out. Instead, audiences wanted simple working-class characters. Gaynor and Farrell provided a more wholesome alternative to silent greats like John Gilbert and Greta Garbo, and were the reigning screen team when they starred in *Seventh Heaven* (1927). Gaynor usually played the type of girl whose options were marriage, hard work, or a life on the streets. Farrell strayed into upper-crust roles in their talking films, but functioned most effectively as a working stiff who finds his purpose in life when he meets his leading lady. Like some of Hollywood's greatest twosomes, their mystique was shaped through work with a single, visionary director. Humphrey Bogart and Lauren Bacall had Howard Hawks. John Wayne and Maureen O'Hara had John Ford. And Farrell and Gaynor had Frank Borzage, a lyrical romantic who invested them with his love of ordinary people possessed of extraordinary emotions. The opening title of their second film with him, *Street Angel* (1928), was a perfect expression of the team at their best: "Everywhere . . . in every town, in every street . . . we pass, unknowing, human souls made great by love and adversity." Audiences warmed to the genuine innocence that they portrayed onscreen. In their first two films, they played couples who lived together platonically—nobody questioned the nature of their relationship. Gaynor was already being touted as the next Mary Pickford or Lillian Gish when Borzage cast her as Diane in *Seventh Heaven*. Farrell had been working his way up the Hollywood ladder for years when he won the role of Chico. These were characters who couldn't hide their feelings, and the stars' naked emotions made tired plots about the redemptive powers of love seem fresh. *Seventh Heaven* was a box-office smash hailed by many critics as one of the greatest movies ever made. Fox reunited the actors and the director twice more, first for the Italy-set *Street Angel*, then for their first American drama, *Lucky Star* (1929). The latter included a few sound scenes that proved both stars had what it took for talking pictures. Fox went whole hog with their first full-fledged talkie, *Sunny Side Up* (1929), putting them into a musical that showed off both to good effect. With sound, the team moved into more contemporary films and American characters that matched their talents well. Over time, sound films worked better for Gaynor's career than for Farrell's. The emotional openness of her silent-screen acting made it easier for her to adapt to spoken dialogue, giving her a simple, natural delivery. Away from Farrell, astute choices like *Daddy Long Legs* (1931) and *State Fair* (1933) improved her box-office standing. Farrell, however, ran into problems. He played the title role in *Liliom* (1930), revealed his limits as an actor, and failed at the box office. Moreover, some of their pairings, like *High Society Blues* (1930), as seen on p. 74, and *The Man Who Came Back* (1931), weren't very good films. They returned to favor with the gentle comedy of *The First Year* (1932), but with Farrell's declining popularity, Fox kept them apart for two years afterward. When they reunited in 1934, it was for an ensemble comedy, *Change of Heart*, but the meatie r roles were given to costars James Dunn and Ginger Rogers. And though their few romantic scenes in the film prompted happy memories of *Seventh Heaven*, the team's time had passed. With the rise of more sophisticated teams like William Powell and Myrna Loy and harder–edged couples like Clark Gable and Jean Harlow, Farrell and Gaynor's winsome ways seemed out-of-date. *Change of Heart* would mark the end of Farrell's Fox contract. When Fox merged with Darryl F. Zanuck's 20th Century Pictures, Gaynor found herself out of favor with her new boss. She left the studio in 1936 and, despite hits in *A Star Is Born* (1936) and *The Young in Heart* (1938), retired from acting to raise her son with her second husband, costume designer Gilbert Adrian. The team's swan song was a 1951 radio version of *Seventh Heaven*, presented to celebrate the film's twenty–fifth anniversary. Younger stars like June Allyson and Van Johnson had long since replaced the pair as the screen's prime purveyors of youthful innocence. By 1951, Gaynor and Farrell were in middle age. But on radio, the audience's imaginations could return them to the days when a nation opened its heart to a pair of youngsters in search of heaven on earth.

LUCKY STAR, 1929

AT THE *SEVENTH HEAVEN* RADIO SHOW BROADCAST, 1951

BEHINDTHESCENES

FANS WERE SO INVESTED IN CHARLES FARRELL AND JANET GAYNOR AS A ROMANTIC TEAM THAT THE STUDIO KEPT NEWS OF GAYNOR'S MARRIAGE TO PUBLICIST LYDELL PECK OUT OF THE PRESS. THEY COULDN'T KEEP IT QUIET, HOWEVER, WHEN FARRELL MARRIED ACTRESS VIRGINIA VALLI, AND THE NEWS HURT THEIR FILMS AT THE BOX OFFICE.

WHEN FILMS LIKE *HIGH SOCIETY BLUES* AND *THE MAN WHO CAME BACK* FARED POORLY WITH THE CRITICS AND SUFFERED AT THE BOX OFFICE, FOX DECIDED TO GIVE *DELICIOUS* (1932) A WIDER-THAN-USUAL RELEASE TO GET IT TO LARGER AUDIENCES, PARTICULARLY IN RURAL AREAS, BEFORE THE CRITICS COULD DO ANY DAMAGE. IT MUST HAVE WORKED, AS THE BOX-OFFICE TOP TEN FOR 1932 PLACED JANET GAYNOR SECOND (BEHIND MARIE DRESSLER) AND CHARLES FARRELL FOURTH.

THERE ARE NO SURVIVING PRINTS OR NEGATIVES OF *STREET ANGEL* (1928), EVEN THOUGH IT WAS ONE OF FOX'S MOST POPULAR LATE SILENTS. *LUCKY STAR* (1929) WAS THOUGHT LOST FOR YEARS UNTIL THE SILENT VERSION WAS DISCOVERED IN THE NETHERLANDS. THE PART-TALKIES' SOUND SCENES HAVE NEVER BEEN FOUND.

His

BORN
Charles Farrell
August 9, 1901
Onset Bay, Massachusetts

DIED
May 6, 1990
Palm Springs, California,
of a heart attack

STAR SIGN
Leo

HEIGHT
6'2"

WIFE
Actress Virginia Valli
(1931–1968, her death)

OFFSCREEN**RELATIONSHIP**

Charles Farrell on his pairing with Janet Gaynor: "Janet Gaynor and I were always receiving wedding-anniversary presents in the mail, care of the studio. The fans didn't even know what date our anniversary fell on, which is logical, since we were never married."

In 1970, Janet Gaynor looked back on her partnership with Charles Farrell: "There can never be a Janet Gaynor and Charles Farrell love team again, because we were not realistic and were far too idealistic for these times. We were romantic and beautiful and innocent. The young people of today have more knowledge of sex, and are far more honest and more advanced than we ever were."

Janet Gaynor was so upset at the poor material she and Charles Farrell had to work with in *High Society Blues*, she swore never to make another musical and took off for a long vacation in Hawaii. Charles Farrell had already booked passage on the same ship Janet Gaynor took for her Hawaiian vacation, but to avoid any hint of an offscreen romance, he canceled his plans.

Janet Gaynor on her relationship with Charles Farrell: "There was nothing in the world I wouldn't have done for Charlie. And I know there is nothing in the world he wouldn't have done for me, but it wasn't the marrying kind of love. No one understands. . . . Anyway, I guess I was too smart to marry an actor. I never have. Actors are terribly attractive, but not to commit your life to."

WILLIAM FOX
Presents

SUNNY SIDE UP

the screens first original all talking, singing, dancing musical comedy

With

JANET GAYNOR and CHARLES FARRELL

SHARON LYNN, FRANK RICHARDSON
EL BRENDEL, MARJORIE WHITE

Original songs, story and dialog by — DE SYLVA, BROWN and HENDERSON

Dances staged by SEYMOUR FELIX
Directed by DAVID BUTLER

SUNNY SIDE UP, 1929

Hers

BORN
Laura Augusta Gainor
October 6, 1906
Philadelphia, Pennsylvania

DIED
September 14, 1984
Palm Springs, California,
of pneumonia

STAR SIGN
Libra

HEIGHT
5'

HUSBANDS AND CHILD
Publicist Jesse Lydell Peck
(1929–1934, divorced)

Costume designer
Gilbert Adrian
(1939–1959, his death)
son, Robin Gaynor

Producer Paul Gregory
(1964–1984, her death)

ESSENTIAL**TEAM-UPS**

SEVENTH HEAVEN (1927, Fox)
In their first film together, Charles Farrell and Janet Gaynor share an idyllic, platonic romance in a seventh-floor walk-up in Paris until World War I comes between them.

STREET ANGEL (1928, Fox)
In their second outing, idealistic painter Farrell helps street-hardened Gaynor, whom he takes in as a model.

SUNNY SIDE UP (1929, Fox)
In their first all-talking, all-singing, all-dancing movie, Gaynor stars as a working girl pretending to be rich to win society boy Farrell's heart.

THE FIRST YEAR (1932, Fox)
After a string of flops, Fox finally recaptured Farrell and Gaynor's magic with this seriocomic tale of newlyweds adjusting to life together.

TESS OF THE STORM COUNTRY (1932, Fox)
Gaynor drew favorable comparisons to Mary Pickford, who had played the same role in 1922—a spirited girl organizing squatters against a New England tycoon while falling for his son (Farrell).

They amiably hoofed their way through a quartet of popular, escapist musicals as Hollywood's Golden Age was drawing to a close.

BETTY GRABLE
DAN DAILEY

Betty Grable would have been the first to tell you that there were better singers, dancers, and actors in Hollywood than she. And Dan Dailey would have immediately pointed out that however talented those others were, they didn't have the unique qualities that audiences saw in the girl with the million-dollar legs. The warmth and generosity of their offscreen friendship shone through their film work. Dailey counseled Grable on her marital problems; she helped him deal with depression and a drinking problem. For all their offscreen crises, onscreen they were as friendly and familiar as the couple next door, the fun pair who could make any party a success. Their musical numbers were just an extension of that. They danced with affection, even in the liveliest routines, and always as equals. In fact, they played married couples in three of their four films together, and estranged spouses in the fourth. Grable had never had a leading man like Dailey before. Most of her costars had been dramatic actors, leaving all of the musical numbers to the most famous pair of legs in movie history. The lack of gifted dance partners didn't limit her—she was already a top box-office star before she worked with Dailey—but it sure wore her out. When 20th Century Fox head Darryl F. Zanuck announced that she would have a dancing costar in 1947's *Mother Wore Tights*, Grable was delighted. Their first choices for the role didn't work out. Warner Bros. wanted too much for James Cagney, while Fred Astaire insisted on rewrites to focus the film on him. When Zanuck proposed Dailey, Grable was appalled at first. He had started his career playing heavies at MGM, most notably as Lana Turner's sadistic boyfriend in *Ziegfeld Girl* (1941), and Grable couldn't picture him in any other role. Dailey had started out as a dancer, however, at the age of six, working his way to Broadway. Zanuck begged Grable to give Dailey a chance and promised she could veto his casting anytime she wanted. After one day's rehearsal, she was sold. MGM was Dailey's home studio at the time, but as soon as Zanuck saw the rushes, he bought his contract. The film was a triumph for both of them. It made Dailey a star and brought Grable her best acting reviews in years. There was even talk of an Oscar nomination. The film made them more than just a popular dancing team; they became friends for life. Both stars begged Zanuck to find another property for them, but that was put on hold when Grable got pregnant. The time apart, however, gave the studio a chance to turn Dailey into one of their most popular leading men. At the same time, Grable's *That Lady in Ermine* (1948), her first film after her maternity leave, flopped colossally. The New York office was threatening Zanuck's job if he didn't revive her career. Reteaming her with Dailey seemed the best option for that. The result, *When My Baby Smiles at Me* (1948), not only scored another hit but even won Dailey an Oscar nomination for Best Actor. By the time they got to their third film, *My Blue Heaven* (1950), Grable was beginning to chafe under her studio workload. When Zanuck wanted her to get straight to work on *Call Me Mister* (1951), her fourth film with Dailey, she took off on a five-day vacation instead of going to her costume fittings. The production was further complicated by Dailey's drinking and growing problems with depression. After the film was finished, he checked himself into a psychiatric center. Although *Call Me Mister* died at the box office, Zanuck was still on the lookout for projects to reunite the team. Grable's demands for some time off between films, however, cost her a role in Dailey's *The Girl Next Door* (1952), which went to June Haver instead. By 1955, Grable had retired from the screen, gladly passing the baton to a new generation of blonde beauties like Marilyn Monroe and Doris Day. Dailey kept at it, but eventually moved into character roles and television. When Grable scored a personal hit touring in *Hello, Dolly!*, there was talk at 20th Century Fox of pairing her with Dailey for the movie version. Sadly, the need for bigger, more current box-office names led the studio to cast Barbra Streisand and Walter Matthau. The nostalgic musical, set in the era of great vaudeville teams like those they had played so memorably in the past, would have been the perfect capper to their partnership, a tribute to the simple, escapist musicals that had made them famous.

WHEN MY BABY SMILES AT ME, 1948

MY BLUE HEAVEN, 1950

BEHINDTHESCENES

BETTY GRABLE'S FIRST FILM WITH DAN DAILEY, *MOTHER WORE TIGHTS* (1947), WAS HER FAVORITE OF ALL HER FILMS.

WHEN BETTY GRABLE AND DAN DAILEY ARE SHOWN DANCING ON TV IN *MY BLUE HEAVEN* (1950), THE SHOT ACTUALLY COMES FROM *MOTHER WORE TIGHTS*.

BETTY GRABLE AND DAN DAILEY WEREN'T THE ONLY TEAM REUNITED FOR *CALL ME MISTER* (1951). DIRECTOR LLOYD BACON AND DANCE DIRECTOR BUSBY BERKELEY HAD NOT WORKED TOGETHER SINCE MAKING *42ND STREET* IN 1933.

AFTER SCORING A FLOP WITH WRITER-DIRECTOR PRESTON STURGES' *THE BEAUTIFUL BLONDE FROM BASHFUL BEND* (1949), BETTY GRABLE ASKED FOR DAN DAILEY AS HER COSTAR ON HER NEXT FILM, *WABASH AVENUE* (1950). HE WAS ALREADY TIED UP WITH ANOTHER FILM, SO SHE GOT ANOTHER NONDANCING COSTAR—VICTOR MATURE. FORTUNATELY, HE WAS FRESH FROM HIS SUCCESS IN *SAMSON AND DELILAH* (1949), AND THE FILM WAS A BIG HIT.

BORN
Daniel James Dailey
December 14, 1913
New York, New York

DIED
October 16, 1978
Los Angeles, California,
of anemia

STAR SIGN
Sagittarius

HEIGHT
6′3″

WIVES AND CHILD
Esther Rodier
(1941–1941, divorced)

Socialite Elizabeth Hofert
(1942–1951, divorced)
son, Dan Dailey III

Gwendolyn Carter O'Connor
(1955–1962, divorced)

Nora Warner
(1968–1972, divorced)

OFFSCREEN**RELATIONSHIP**

Dan Dailey on Betty Grable: "She has never really believed in herself. She always had this thing that put it down to 'good luck' to survive on the little talent she claimed she had. I often had to remind her that although there were admittedly prettier girls around—and some of them were better actresses—it was Betty the customers paid to see."

Betty Grable and Dan Dailey continued to be friends the rest of their lives. She confided in him about her marital problems with bandleader Harry James, and they even did a few television variety shows and limited stage runs together.

When he turned to art therapy at the Menninger center, Dan Dailey sent some of his work to Betty Grable. One note read, "You don't know the satisfaction you can get from just chopping wood. You stand back and look and say, 'I did that!'"

KEY QUOTE

**From *Mother
Wore Tights* (1947)**

Dailey
What's wrong with
a little kiss
between friends?

Grable
It'd be nothing, if we
were friends.

MOTHER WORE TIGHTS, 1947

ESSENTIAL**TEAM-UPS**

MOTHER WORE TIGHTS (1947, 20th Century Fox)
Betty Grable and Dan Dailey set the tone for most of their films together, starring
as a married vaudeville team having trouble with the daughter (Mona Freeman)
they left behind while touring.

WHEN MY BABY SMILES AT ME (1948, 20th Century Fox)
Cast again as a song-and-dance team, Dailey and Grable face marital problems
when he hits the big time and takes up drinking.

MY BLUE HEAVEN (1950, 20th Century Fox)
This time, the vaudeville team played by Grable and Dailey tries to adopt while
breaking into television.

CALL ME MISTER (1951, 20th Century Fox)
For a change of pace, Grable and Dailey play an estranged husband and wife who
reunite when a USO tour takes her to his base in occupied Japan.

The Riviera has never been as glamorous or as sexy as it was when these two went searching for a jewel thief and found romance along the way.

CARY **GRANT**
GRACE **KELLY**
IN *To Catch a Thief*

The fireworks outside the stars' hotel window in *To Catch a Thief*'s (1955) big love scene weren't confined to the sky. They exploded every time Cary Grant and Grace Kelly were onscreen together in one of Alfred Hitchcock's most buoyant thrillers. The connection they shared had Hollywood gossips insisting they must have been having an affair. And when they kissed, it was sheer magic. Kelly was one of the few leading ladies who could match Grant's natural elegance, and was one of the few actresses who could get away with taking the aggressive role in their relationship (Rosalind Russell in 1940's *His Girl Friday* excepted). Whether surprising him with kisses or tempting him with a dazzling diamond necklace and plunging neckline, she never lost her class. Former acrobat Grant was perfectly cast as a one-time cat burglar out to clear his name when another thief starts using his modus operandi. Even at fifty, the star was sleek and sophisticated, whether sneaking across rooftops or lounging in the playgrounds of the rich. And he was so much the definitive image of romantic sophistication that nobody thought to question his pairing with an actress still in her twenties. The film may have been little more than a soufflé, but it was a soufflé made with the perfect ingredients, from Robert Burks's Oscar-winning cinematography to the perfect casting of its stars. Born to a wealthy Philadelphia family, Kelly came to the role of heiress Frances Stevens naturally. She was the definitive Hitchcock leading lady, a cool blonde whose icy exterior masked a passionate soul. Through most of the film, audiences couldn't tell if she wanted to bed Grant or put him in jail. Grant had announced his retirement in 1953, convinced that the influx of Method actors like Marlon Brando rendered his kind of movie star obsolete. It only took one look at the script, however, to get him back to work. Hitchcock had carefully honed the dialogue until almost every line was a double entendre worthy of Mae West. But with the wholesome Kelly delivering speeches like "If you really want to see fireworks, it's better with the lights off," the sex play seemed like good, clean fun. Given the film's box-office returns and the stars' friendship, they could have teamed profitably for several other films had not Kelly left Hollywood in 1956 to marry Prince Rainier of Monaco, where much of the film had been shot. But even though they never worked together again, Grant and Kelly would remain close friends for the rest of her life.

BORN
Archibald Alexander Leach
January 18, 1904
Horfield, Bristol, England

DIED
November 29, 1986
Davenport, Iowa, of a stroke

STAR SIGN
Capricorn

HEIGHT
6'1½"

WIVES AND CHILD
Actress Virginia Cherill
(1934–1935, divorced)

Woolworth heiress
Barbara Hutton
(1942–1945, divorced)

Actress Betsy Drake
(1949–1962, divorced)

Actress Dyan Cannon
(1965–1968, divorced)
daughter, Jennifer

Publicist Barbara Harris
(1981–1986, his death)

OFFSCREEN**RELATIONSHIP**

Cary Grant on Grace Kelly: "Grace acted the way Johnny Weissmuller swam, or Fred Astaire danced. She made it look so easy. Some people said that Grace was just being herself. Well, that's the toughest thing to do if you're an actor."

During filming, Cary Grant received an invitation to party on Aristotle Onassis's yacht and was told to bring along some friends. Grace Kelly was part of the group but, being shy off-camera, kept to the background. She also wore her glasses. When Grant left, Onassis told him to come back any time—"and please bring your secretary along, too."

Director Alfred Hitchcock was so at ease working with Cary Grant and Grace Kelly that he allowed them to improvise on-camera. The two shared a knack for making up dialogue while also getting across all of the key plot points. The most significant of these scenes is the one in which they end up covered in chicken feathers while driving along the Riviera.

Cary Grant considered Grace Kelly the favorite of all his leading ladies because of her tranquility: "Grace had a kind of serenity, a calmness that I hadn't arrived at at that point in my life—and perhaps never will, for all I know. She was so relaxed in front of the camera that she made it look simple. When you played a scene with her, she really listened, she was right there with you. She was Buddha-like in her concentration. She was like Garbo in that respect."

TO CATCH A THIEF, 1955

KEY QUOTE

Kelly

Give up, John. Admit
who you are. Even in this
light I can tell where
your eyes are looking.
Look! Hold them!
Diamonds—the only
thing in the world you
can't resist. . . . Ever
had a better offer
in your whole life? One
with everything! . . .
Just as long
as you're satisfied.

Grant

You know as well
as I do this necklace
is imitation.

Kelly

Well, *I'm* not.

BEHIND THE SCENES

FACED WITH A YOUNGER LEADING LADY, A SCENE IN SWIMMING TRUNKS, AND THE EGO-STROKING POSSIBILITY OF DOING MANY OF HIS OWN STUNTS, CARY GRANT WENT INTO TRAINING BEFORE REPORTING FOR WORK ON *TO CATCH A THIEF*. HE HAD BEGUN TO GO SOFT DURING HIS SELF-IMPOSED RETIREMENT.

ALTHOUGH SHE HATED DRIVING, GRACE KELLY HAD TO PERFORM MUCH OF THE CHASE SCENE ON THE CORNICHES, A SERIES OF TWISTING HILLSIDE ROADS, HERSELF. SOME OF THE TIGHT TURNS AND NEAR CRASHES WERE THE REAL THING, AS WAS THE FEAR IN HER AND CARY GRANT'S FACES. COINCIDENTALLY, IT WAS THE SAME ROAD ON WHICH SHE WOULD HAVE THE CRASH THAT TOOK HER LIFE IN 1982.

Most notably in the classic film noir *Gilda*, they created a surprisingly perverse sizzle, combining glamour with a touch of sadomasochism.

RITA **HAYWORTH**
GLENN **FORD**

Film noir created some great onscreen pairings—Dick Powell and Claire Trevor in *Murder, My Sweet* (1944); Burt Lancaster and Ava Gardner in *The Killers* (1946); Jane Greer and Robert Mitchum in *Out of the Past* (1947)—but few had the erotic charge Rita Hayworth and Glenn Ford brought to the genre. When they got together onscreen, they were as likely to slug each other as to kiss—and more likely to do both. Their best partnerships, in *Gilda* and *Affair in Trinidad* (1952), had them spending as much time at each other's throats as in each other's arms, often commenting on how much they hated each other. Where other noir stars like Humphrey Bogart and Lauren Bacall were knowing, even ironic observers of the genre's twisted tales and romantic obsessions, Ford and Hayworth were caught in the middle of the storm, their conflicting passions reflecting the corruption of their world. When they ventured outside the genre, as in *The Loves of Carmen* (1948), they carried their onscreen love-hate relationship to new extremes, with Ford knifing Hayworth after she destroys his life and casts him aside. The couple first paired in his third film for Columbia, *The Lady in Question* (1940), but though Hayworth worked her seductive wiles on his character, the spark wasn't there. It took time and wartime service to toughen Ford up enough to be a worthwhile match for the sex goddess. Hayworth had already started work on *Gilda* while director Charles Vidor looked for a leading man who could make the warped love story not only believable but also palatable to audiences. After seeing a rough cut of *A Stolen Life* (1946), featuring Ford opposite Bette Davis in his first postwar film, Vidor knew he'd found his man. *Gilda* was a masterpiece of double entendre, none of it unintentional. All of the psychological depths critics would unearth in later years were planted there by Ford, Hayworth, and Vidor, but in a clever fashion that had little trouble getting the most suggestive lines past the censors. Though critics had trouble following the convoluted plot, audiences loved the film, turning it into one of the studio's biggest hits. It created the image fans would always associate with Hayworth, much to her regret. She later told the film's producer, Virginia Van Upp, "Every man I've ever known has fallen in love with Gilda and awakened with me." But the film was also the start of an enduring friendship with Ford. Surprisingly, it was Hayworth, not studio executives, who brought the team back together. Since *The Lady from Shanghai* (1948), her film with husband Orson Welles, was in endless re-edits, Hayworth returned to her sultry roots as one of literature's most notorious temptresses in *The Loves of Carmen*. She asked Ford to take the role of Don José, though he seemed miscast as a Spaniard and as Hayworth's sexual toy. The film was not a hit with critics, but fans lined up around the block to see the picture. Yet it took another career crisis to bring the two together again. After the grueling eighty-one-day shoot for *The Loves of Carmen*, Hayworth insisted on taking a long European vacation, during which she met and married Prince Aly Kahn and retired from the movies. When the marriage broke up, she turned to Ford again for her comeback film, *Affair in Trinidad*. This time they created the same dynamic they had shared in *Gilda*. In fact, the studio had essentially created a carbon copy of the earlier picture, but that didn't hurt the box office, with the picture actually outgrossing the earlier film by $1 million. With the decline of the studio system, it would be more than a decade before the two would team for the fifth and final time, in *The Money Trap* (1966). By then, Hayworth's star was on the wane. She not only had to cede top billing to Ford for the only time, but her role was virtually a cameo, as his former lover. The two shared a bittersweet love scene that reminded more than a few reviewers of their earlier triumph in *Gilda*, when their infatuation had revealed new depths to the corrupt world of film noir.

THE LOVES OF CARMEN, 1943

ON THE SET OF *GILDA*, 1946

BEHINDTHESCENES

DIRECTOR CHARLES VIDOR OFTEN SHOCKED HIS STARS WITH THE SEXUAL UNDERTONES HE WANTED THEM TO PLAY IN *GILDA* (1946). AFTER HE'D DESCRIBED IMAGES NEITHER WOULD EVER REPEAT, HE WOULD FINISH BY ORDERING THEM TO "LOOSEN UP, CHILDREN."

RITA HAYWORTH'S TWO MUSICAL NUMBERS IN *GILDA* WERE ADDED AFTER THE FILM HAD BEEN COMPLETED, WHILE THE STUDIO WAS TRYING TO STRENGTHEN IT WITH RETAKES. THE CLASSIC "PUT THE BLAME ON MAME, BOYS" WAS WRITTEN IN A MATTER OF HOURS, AND HAYWORTH GOT THE MOCK STRIPTEASE IN JUST TWO TAKES.

***GILDA* WAS GLENN FORD'S FAVORITE OF ALL HIS FILMS.**

GLENN FORD MADE *THE LOVES OF CARMEN* (1948) BECAUSE RITA HAYWORTH ASKED FOR HIM. HE LATER CALLED HIS PORTRAYAL OF HER BETRAYED LOVER, DON JOSÉ, "THE MOST LUDICROUS CASTING IN THE HISTORY OF MOTION PICTURES. WHEN IT COMES ON TELEVISION NOW, I PULL THE PLUGS OUT OF ALL THE SETS."

His

BORN
Gwyllyn Samuel Newton Ford
May 1, 1916
Sainte-Christine,
Quebec, Canada

DIED
August 30, 2006
Beverly Hills, California,
of multiple strokes

STAR SIGN
Taurus

HEIGHT
5'11"

WIVES AND CHILD
Dancer/actress Eleanor Powell
(1943–1959, divorced)
son, Peter

Actress Kathryn Hays
(1966–1969, divorced)

Actress Cynthia Hayward
(1977–1984, divorced)

Jeanne Baus
(1993–1994, divorced)

KEY QUOTE

From *Gilda* (1946)

Hayworth

You do hate me,
don't you, Johnny?

Ford

I don't think you have
any idea how much.

Hayworth

Hate is a very exciting
emotion, haven't
you noticed? Very
exciting. I hate you, too,
Johnny. I hate you so
much, I think I'm going
to die from it.

OFFSCREEN **RELATIONSHIP**

Glenn Ford on the success of his work with Rita Hayworth in *Gilda*: "Rita and I were very fond of one another, we became very close friends, and I guess it all came out on the screen."

During the filming of *Gilda*, Rita Hayworth was separated from husband Orson Welles. Studio publicists were quick to invent a romance between her and costar Glenn Ford. By the time the film had been finished, Hayworth and Welles had reconciled, and the publicists had to turn the romance into a friendship.

The one scene that gave Rita Hayworth trouble in *Gilda* was the fight in which she had to slap Glenn Ford four times. When Ford told her to "go all out" she did, knocking out two of his teeth.

Knowing that Columbia Pictures head Harry Cohn had their dressing rooms bugged so he could keep track of his stars, Rita Hayworth and Glenn Ford decided to give him something to worry about while filming *Gilda*. Most days after filming, she would invite Ford to her dressing room for a drink, prompting Cohn to call her every fifteen minutes to demand to know what was going on.

Rita Hayworth lived next door to Glenn Ford late in her life, and the two socialized often.

Glenn Ford's son, Peter, insists that his father always carried a torch for Rita Hayworth. He kept her picture on a table near his bed for most of his life.

THE MONEY TRAP, 1966

Hers

BORN
Margarita Carmen Cansino
October 17, 1918
Brooklyn, New York

DIED
May 14, 1987
New York, New York,
of Alzheimer's disease

STAR SIGN
Libra

HEIGHT
5'6"

HUSBANDS AND CHILDREN
Salesman Edward C. Judson
(1937–1943, divorced)

Actor–director Orson Welles
(1943–1948, divorced)
daughter, Rebecca Welles

Prince Aly Khan
(1949–1953, divorced)
daughter, Princess Yasmin
Khan

Singer Dick Haymes
(1953–1955, divorced)

Producer James Hill
(1958–1961, divorced)

ESSENTIAL TEAM-UPS

THE LADY IN QUESTION (1940, Columbia)
Glenn Ford and Rita Hayworth first worked together in this tale of a jury holdout
(Brian Aherne) who saves a woman from prison only to have her repay him by
driving his son to crime.

GILDA (1946, Columbia)
This twisted tale of desire and betrayal—crooked gambler Ford marries his criminal
boss's widow (Hayworth) only to discover the boss isn't dead—shot both actors to
superstardom.

THE LOVES OF CARMEN (1948, Columbia)
As the tempestuous Gypsy temptress, Hayworth loves and leaves a bewildered Ford.

AFFAIR IN TRINIDAD (1952, Columbia)
Ford heads to the tropics to discover that his brother's widow (Hayworth) is carrying
on with her husband's suspected killer—only to wind up being attracted to her.

THE MONEY TRAP (1966, Columbia)
Elke Sommer may have had the femme-fatale role in this film noir, but Hayworth
and Ford still sparked onscreen as former lovers who reunite while he's trying to
find easy money to support wife Sommer's spending habits.

A unique marriage of beauty and brains reached the screen when Hollywood's greatest maverick placed one of the screen's most iconic sirens at the center of this cinematic hall of mirrors.

RITA HAYWORTH
ORSON WELLES
IN *The Lady from Shanghai*

One of Hollywood's most unexpected real-life couples, boy genius Orson Welles and sex goddess Rita Hayworth created a memorable onscreen pairing in the 1948 film noir *The Lady from Shanghai*. The two first met at a Hollywood party in 1942. Welles, also an avid magician, asked permission to saw her in half during a show for the USO. She agreed to continue to appear with him onstage to benefit the war effort, and their relationship grew. She was enamored of his intelligence and welcomed his efforts to improve her mind. In addition, Welles tried to boost her ego and end her domination by her father and Columbia Pictures head Harry Cohn. Their marriage was strained, however, by Welles's all-consuming film projects and extramarital affairs, which left Hayworth feeling rejected. By the time she made *Gilda* (1946), the two had separated. Although Cohn had opposed their marriage, he was intrigued when Welles offered to film *The Lady from Shanghai* for Columbia in return for an investment in his beleaguered stage version of *Around the World in 80 Days*. Hoping to capitalize on the publicity their marriage had generated, Cohn insisted that Welles cast Hayworth in the female lead. She was thrilled at the prospect, hoping his devotion to the film would bring them back together. In addition, she believed that the role would earn her new respect as a dramatic actress. Determined to present the public with a "new" Rita Hayworth, Welles ordered that her trademark long auburn hair be cut and bleached what publicists called "topaz blonde." Problems with location shooting, an illness that sent Hayworth home for ten days, union troubles, and Welles's own perfectionism put the production behind schedule and over budget. When Welles finally screened his 155-minute cut, Cohn said, "I'll give $1,000 to anyone who can explain the story to me!" Fearing the film would end Hayworth's career, the studio head let it sit on the shelf for more than a year, until Hayworth's next film, *The Loves of Carmen* (1948), with Glenn Ford, had become a box-office winner. By that time, Welles and Hayworth had split for good. The studio finally released *The Lady from Shanghai* after cutting more than an hour out of the picture, including some of the director's favorite moments. The result was panned as incoherent and failed at the box office; Welles wouldn't make another film in Hollywood for ten years. However, *The Lady from Shanghai* is today considered an intriguing marriage of his artistic vision and Hayworth's star persona. Critics now hail her icy-cold portrayal of Elsa Bannister, one of the screen's most irredeemable femmes fatale, as her best performance. Her betrayal of Welles's chivalrous Michael O'Hara still resonates as an image of romantic disillusionment.

BORN
George Orson Welles
May 6, 1915
Kenosha, Wisconsin

DIED
October 10, 1985
Hollywood, California,
of a heart attack

STAR SIGN
Taurus

HEIGHT
6'1½"

WIVES AND CHILDREN
Actress Virginia Nicholson
(1934–1940, divorced)
daughter, Christopher

Actress Rita Hayworth
(1943–1948, divorced)
daughter, Rebecca

Actress Paola Mori
(1955–1985, his death)
daughter, Beatrice

❋
KEY QUOTE

Welles
I'm gonna take you where
there aren't any spies.

Hayworth
Michael, where?

Welles
A long way off. Somewhere
in the far places.

Hayworth
The far places? We're in
one of them now. Anyway,
it doesn't work. I tried it.
Everything's bad, Michael,
everything. You can't
escape it or fight it. You've
got to get along with it. Deal
with it, make terms. You're
such a foolish knight errant,
Michael. You're big and
strong, but you just don't
know how to take care of
yourself. So how could you
take care of me?

❋

OFFSCREEN**RELATIONSHIP**

Rita Hayworth on Orson Welles: "My growing up really started with Orson Welles. He was a brilliant man, a stimulating man, a man with whom I was deeply in love and who was in love with me."

Orson Welles on Rita Hayworth's performance in *The Lady from Shanghai*: "I thought she was great in it, and she was proud to be in it and all that. And then everybody treated her as though she'd been slumming, you know, and so they didn't give her *that* satisfaction!"

The press dubbed Rita Hayworth and Orson Welles "Beauty and the Brain."

Shortly after their marriage, Orson Welles began to withdraw in response to what he saw as Rita Hayworth's emotional neediness. When she accused him of cheating on her, he retaliated by doing just that. Among his affairs was a very public fling with Judy Garland.

As soon as Rita Hayworth learned she would be working with Orson Welles on *The Lady from Shanghai*, she asked her decorator to redo her bedroom to accommodate two people, even though they hadn't reconciled yet.

Rita Hayworth on her reason for divorcing Orson Welles: "I can't take his genius anymore."

WITH DAUGHTER REBECCA WELLES, CIRCA 1945

Hers

BORN
Margarita Carmen Cansino
October 17, 1918
Brooklyn, New York

DIED
May 14, 1987
New York, New York,
of Alzheimer's disease

STAR SIGN
Libra

HEIGHT
5'6"

HUSBANDS AND CHILDREN
Salesman Edward C. Judson
(1937–1943, divorced)

Actor–director Orson Welles
(1943–1948, divorced)
daughter, Rebecca Welles

Prince Aly Khan
(1949–1953, divorced)
daughter, Princess Yasmin
Khan

Singer Dick Haymes
(1953–1955, divorced)

Producer James Hill
(1958–1961, divorced)

BEHIND THE SCENES

THE FIRST SCENES SHOT FOR *THE LADY FROM SHANGHAI* WERE FOR THE FILM'S CENTRAL PARK OPENING. TO CREATE THE ILLUSION THAT RITA HAYWORTH WAS IN A HANSOM CAB DRIVING DOWN A TREE-LINED LANE, STUDIO TECHNICIANS PUSHED PROP TREES ON ROLLERS PAST THE VEHICLE. WHEN THIS LEFT THE OLDER CREWMEMBERS PANTING FOR BREATH, HAYWORTH STARTED GIGGLING DURING THE FIRST TAKE. IT TOOK HER HALF AN HOUR TO REGAIN HER COMPOSURE.

ORSON WELLES QUARRELED WITH RITA HAYWORTH'S MAKEUP MAN, BOB SCHIFFER, ON THE FIRST DAY OF SHOOTING AND FIRED HIM FROM THE FILM. WHEN HAYWORTH LEARNED OF THIS, SHE DIDN'T DISCUSS IT WITH HER HUSBAND. INSTEAD, SHE NOTIFIED THE STUDIO THAT SHE WOULD NOT MAKE THE FILM WITHOUT SCHIFFER AND SECRETLY HIRED HIM BACK. HE HAD TO STAY HIDDEN IN THE DRESSING ROOM AND THEN SEND AN ASSISTANT TO TOUCH HER UP ON THE SET.

THE LADY FROM SHANGHAI'S WORKING TITLES INCLUDED "BLACK IRISH" AND "TAKE THIS WOMAN".

AMONG CHANGES THE PRODUCTION CODE ADMINISTRATION DEMANDED IN ORSON WELLES'S SCRIPT WAS A CHANGE IN HER DEATH SCENE SO THAT SHE WOULD NOT BE SHOWN COMMITTING SUICIDE TO ESCAPE PUNISHMENT FOR HER CRIMES. HAYWORTH'S CHARACTER IS KILLED BY HER HUSBAND (EVERETT SLOANE) IN THE FAMOUS HALL-OF-MIRRORS SCENE, NOW CONSIDERED A STRONGER ENDING TO THE SCRIPT.

THE FILM'S FAMOUS FINALE IN THE HALL OF MIRRORS HAS BEEN IMITATED IN SEVERAL FILMS, INCLUDING *TROUBLE MAN* (1972), STARRING MR. T; *SOMETHING WICKED THIS WAY COMES* (1983); AND WOODY ALLEN'S *MANHATTAN MURDER MYSTERY* (1993), WHICH INCLUDES A CLIP FROM WELLES'S FILM.

They turned the battle of the sexes into good, clean, "come hither" fun in a pair of sparkling romantic comedies.

ROCK **HUDSON**
DORIS **DAY**

Before the '60s started to swing, Doris Day and Rock Hudson paved the way for more permissive times with a pair of popular sex comedies: *Pillow Talk* (1959) and *Lover Come Back* (1961). With Hudson as a wolf on the prowl, Day as a freethinking career girl, and Tony Randall as straight man, the films titillated without ever crossing the bounds of good taste. As Hudson and Day chased each other through these films, they also revitalized their careers and carved a niche in both film and social history. By the late 1950s, women were ready to trade in the image of the pristine housewife, vacuuming in taffeta and pearls, for the sleeker, more independent career girl. Looking chic for the first time onscreen, thanks to designer Jean Louis, Day blossomed in *Pillow Talk*, playing a successful decorator who takes control of her life and her relationships. With his chiseled physique and a sparkle in his eye, Hudson was her perfect foil. *Pillow Talk* remains the film most closely associated with each star and the picture that, despite script references to the contrary, typed Day as the screen's eternal virgin. For Hudson, the film pointed the way to a lighter image that he would continue to mine in television and stage appearances, particularly on his hit television series *MacMillan & Wife*. Although Day and Hudson had been doing well at the late-1950s box office, their fan support was starting to erode. Day's musicals and wholesome comedies were going out of fashion, while Hudson's glossy romantic dramas were beginning to wear thin. Universal Studios' Ross Hunter, who had produced some of Hudson's most successful films, suggested trying a romantic comedy with a bit more sex than usual. Day was more than willing to take the chance, but Hudson actually turned down the project three times. Beyond the fact that he had never done a comedy before, he thought the plot synopsis sounded a little too risqué for his all-American image. The sharp screenplay, however, finally attracted him to the project. And when he met Day, they bonded immediately. Their offscreen relationship created a sense of fun and mutual affection that made their films a sensation—*Pillow Talk* grossed $7.5 million, and Day led the box-office top ten for the first of five consecutive years (still a record). Hudson made it to number two on the list, and the Hollywood Foreign Press named them both "World Film Favorites." It was only natural that the team would want to reunite, which they did in 1961 for *Lover Come Back*. Although a virtual carbon copy of *Pillow Talk*, it was in many ways an improved version, as the two poked gentle fun at the advertising world. With two hit romantic comedies behind them, however, both stars were once again typecast. That worked out better for Day, who found another congenial onscreen partner in James Garner, her costar in *The Thrill of It All* and *Move Over, Darling* (both 1963). Hudson's comedies away from Day were less fortunate, however, leading to a slow decline in his box-office value. Universal hoped another pairing could shore up his appeal, but the result, *Send Me No Flowers* (1964), was the team's one misfire. The main problem was that they tampered with the formula. After two hits in which Hudson wooed Day, they tried to play a married couple. Though profitable, the film didn't do the business their previous pairings had. Instead of looking for another, more suitable vehicle, Day's husband and manager, Martin Melcher, pulled the plug and started pairing Day with other costars. None of them worked, however, and before long Day abandoned features for a hit television series, followed by retirement. The two had one more date, however. When Day launched a cable talk show, *Doris Day's Best Friends*, in 1985, Hudson was the top choice to be her first guest. Although he was already suffering the effects of AIDS, Hudson got through a press conference and two days of taping before going off to Paris for experimental treatments. The announcement a few weeks later that he had AIDS was a shock to Day and his many fans. When the program finally aired following his death, Day closed it with a special tribute to him and sang "My Buddy." The last line, "Your buddy misses you," reflected her feelings and those of their fans, who would never see the two together again.

PILLOW TALK, 1959

CIRCA 1959

BEHIND THE SCENES

DOING MULTIPLE TAKES OF *PILLOW TALK*'S CLIMAX, IN WHICH ROCK HUDSON CARRIES DORIS DAY FROM HER APARTMENT TO HIS, WORE HUDSON OUT. A BIT PLAYER WITH FOUR WORDS TO SAY—"HOW YOU DOING, BRAD?"—KEPT BLOWING THE LINE. FINALLY, THE CREW CONSTRUCTED A SPECIAL SLING THAT DISTRIBUTED DAY'S WEIGHT MORE EVENLY AND ALLOWED HUDSON TO KEEP GOING UNTIL THEY GOT IT RIGHT.

IN 1984, CHILD ACTOR–TURNED-PRODUCER JIMMY HAWKINS CAME UP WITH AN IDEA FOR *PILLOW TALK II*. BOTH ROCK HUDSON AND DORIS DAY LIKED THE IDEA OF A FILM IN WHICH THEIR CHARACTERS, HAVING DIVORCED, REUNITED FOR THEIR DAUGHTER'S WEDDING AND STARTED TO COURT EACH OTHER AGAIN. HUDSON'S DECLINING HEALTH, HOWEVER, MEANT THE PROJECT NEVER GOT BEYOND THE DISCUSSION STAGE.

His

BORN
Roy Harold Scherer Jr.
November 17, 1925
Winnetka, Illinois

DIED
October 2, 1985
Beverly Hills, California,
of AIDS complications

STAR SIGN
Scorpio

HEIGHT
6'4"

WIFE
Secretary Phyllis Gates
(1955–1958, divorced)

OFFSCREEN**RELATIONSHIP**

Doris Day on working with Rock Hudson: "I had never met Rock Hudson before, but the very first day on the set I discovered we had a performing rapport that was remarkable. We played our scenes together as if we had once lived them. Every day on the set was a picnic—sometimes too much of a picnic, in that we took turns at breaking each other up."

Rock Hudson, on his successful work with Doris Day: "I don't really know what makes a movie team . . . I'd say, first of all, the two people have to truly like each other, as Doris and I did, for that shines through the sparkle, the twinkle in the eye as the two people look at each other. Then, too, both parties have to be strong personalities—very important to comedy, so that there's a tug-of-war over who's going to put it over on the other, who's going to get the last word, a fencing match between two adroit opponents of the opposite sex who in the end are going to fall in bed together."

Rock Hudson nicknamed Doris Day "Eunice Blotter," and she called him "Roy Harold." Even when they weren't working together, he would telephone her and say, "Eunice? Is that you?"

Although Rock Hudson's homosexuality was a fairly open secret in Hollywood, both Doris Day and Tony Randall said they knew nothing of it until he announced that he had AIDS. According to Randall, Hudson used to brag about all the starlets he had bedded.

LOVER COME BACK, 1961

Hers

BORN
Doris Mary Ann Von Kappelhoff
April 3, 1924
Cincinnati, Ohio

STAR SIGN
Aries

HEIGHT
5'7"

HUSBANDS AND CHILD
Trombonist Al Jordan
(1941–1943, divorced)
son, Terry

Saxophonist George Weidler
(1946–1949, divorced)

Manager–producer Martin
Melcher (1951–1968, his death)

Restaurant manager Barry
Comden (1976–1981, divorced)

KEY QUOTE

From *Pillow Talk* (1959)

Hudson
Look, I don't know
what's bothering you,
but don't take
your bedroom problems
out on me.

Day
I have no bedroom
problems. There's
nothing in my bedroom
that bothers me.

Hudson
Oh-h-h-h. That's too
bad.

ESSENTIAL**TEAM-UPS**

PILLOW TALK (1959, Universal)
The team kicked things off with this riotous, surprisingly sexy conflict between a successful decorator and a wolfish songwriter forced to share a party line.

LOVER COME BACK (1961, Universal)
A virtual remake of *Pillow Talk*, the film stars Day and Hudson as advertising execs competing to rep a nonexistent product.

SEND ME NO FLOWERS (1964, Universal)
For a change of pace, Day and Hudson are married, with the hypochondriac husband convinced he's dying and planning his wife's next marriage.

When these two blond, baby-faced stars came together onscreen, their scenes were like hot ice, a paradox as baffling and yet thrilling as the plots of their memorable films noir.

ALAN **LADD**
VERONICA **LAKE**

When Alan Ladd shoved Veronica Lake around in *This Gun for Hire* (1942), something electric happened. What seemed like underplaying in their scenes with other actors came across as sexual tension whenever they appeared together, even when they weren't supposed to be romantically matched. Fans simply looked at the two and made the romantic team greater than the sum of its dispassionate parts. Lake and Ladd were the only studio-era costars who were both blonds, and she was the only Ladd leading lady shorter than he was, but their partnership was about more than size or coloring. In their best vehicles together, the writing for their scenes was terse, hard, and muscular, a solid match for their icy looks and icier delivery. But under the surface, each projected a vulnerability that made their teaming poignantly romantic. With Ladd, a tireless craftsman, the effect was carefully calculated. For Lake, who always seemed less serious about her work, it was sheer luck. She had scored a big hit as a siren in *I Wanted Wings* (1941). The way her hair fell in front of one eye triggered a fashion craze and won her the nickname "the peek-a-boo blond." When Preston Sturges' *Sullivan's Travels* (1942) won her more raves, Paramount renegotiated her contract, raising her salary from $75 to $350 a week. They also looked for a vehicle in which to test her star power. The studio had bought the rights to Graham Greene's novel *A Gun for Sale* when it first appeared in 1936. In 1942, the role of a singing magician working undercover for the U.S. government seemed perfect for Lake (even though she couldn't sing or do magic tricks). The story was updated to make the enemy agents Fascists and changed the setting from Europe to Los Angeles. Paramount had Robert Preston under contract to play Lake's police-lieutenant love interest and Laird Cregar for the villain, but nobody seemed right for the baby-faced killer whom Cregar hires and then betrays. Ladd appeared to be an unlikely choice, as he had often been told his height and blond hair would keep him from ever becoming a star. Fortunately, Ladd had a persistent agent, former actress Sue Carol (whom he would later marry), who fought for the role. He impressed director Frank Tuttle—his talent was evident in the first takes in the can, and soon Tuttle started favoring him with shots and giving him extra business. When *This Gun for Hire* (1942) opened, it made Ladd a star. With his fresh face and calculated restraint, his performance as the cold-blooded killer was something raw, creating a new archetype for action pictures. The film that had been planned as a vehicle for Lake became, instead, the introduction of an atypical new screen team. Paramount quickly reunited them. To hedge their bets, they used a story they had filmed profitably once before,

Dashiell Hammett's *The Glass Key*, and gave reliable character actor Brian Donlevy the top-billed role as a political boss in love with Lake. The film's success cemented both actors' positions at the studio. Lake got another new contract, eventually making $4,500 a week, the studio's second-highest star salary. However, Ladd's military service and bad casting kept them apart for three years. By the time they reteamed in 1945, Ladd had top billing and studio executives were beginning to wonder if Lake was worth her salary. Her part in *The Blue Dahlia* (1946) is shorter than those in their earlier pictures together, but both still registered strongly in a feature often ranked among the best films noir. But though they got good reviews and still packed a solid box-office punch, younger film-noir heroines, particularly Lauren Bacall and Lizabeth Scott, were beginning to overshadow Lake. Some critics even compared the Ladd-Lake team to Humphrey Bogart's work with Bacall, with the Bogarts coming out on top. The final Ladd-Lake picture, *Saigon* (1948), was a forgettable action film that gave the studio a chance to exploit Ladd's popularity while just using Lake as window dressing. Within a year, she had left the studio, and quickly sank into obscurity. But the team's best films are far from forgotten, capturing the curious appeal of two stars whose cool demeanor and vulnerable souls heated up film noir.

THE BLUE DAHLIA, 1946

THIS GUN FOR HIRE, 1942

BEHINDTHESCENES

THE ONSCREEN CONNECTION BETWEEN ALAN LADD AND VERONICA LAKE IN *THIS GUN FOR HIRE* (1942) WAS EVIDENTLY SO STRONG THAT AT LEAST ONE REVIEWER ASSUMED THAT LADD'S CHARACTER HAD DIED WITH HIS HEAD IN HER LAP AND EVEN WROTE, "BETTER MEN HAVE DIED WITH THEIR HEADS IN LESS PLEASANT PLACES." IN FACT, HE DIES ON A SOFA, WITH LAKE STANDING WITH HER LOVE INTEREST, ROBERT PRESTON. LAKE EVEN REPEATED THE MISTAKE IN HER MEMOIRS.

THE GLASS KEY (1942) INTRODUCED ANOTHER IMPORTANT PART OF THE ALAN LADD-VERONICA LAKE CHEMISTRY, CHARACTER ACTOR WILLIAM BENDIX, HERE CAST AS A THUG WHO GIVES LADD A VICIOUS BEATING. BENDIX AND LADD WOULD BECOME OFFSCREEN FRIENDS AND COSTAR IN SIX FILMS, INCLUDING *THE BLUE DAHLIA* (1946).

JAPANESE DIRECTOR AKIRA KUROSAWA CITED *THE GLASS KEY* AS A MAJOR INSPIRATION FOR HIS SAMURAI FILM *YOJIMBO* (1961), WHICH IN TURN INSPIRED CLINT EASTWOOD'S FIRST SPAGHETTI WESTERN, *A FISTFUL OF DOLLARS* (1967).

THE BLUE DAHLIA ACHIEVED SOME UNWELCOME NOTORIETY WHEN ITS TITLE INSPIRED THE PRESS'S NAME FOR ELIZABETH SHORT, THE VICTIM OF A GRISLY MURDER THAT HAS NEVER BEEN SOLVED, "THE BLACK DAHLIA."

His

BORN
Alan Walbridge Ladd
September 3, 1913
Hot Springs, Arkansas

DIED
January 29, 1964
Palm Springs, California,
of an alcohol and sedative
overdose

STAR SIGN
Virgo

HEIGHT
5'6"

WIVES AND CHILDREN
Student Marjorie Jane Harrold
(1936–1941, divorced)
son, Alan Jr.

Actress-turned-agent Sue Carol
(1942–1964, his death)
daughter, Alana
son, David

KEY QUOTE

From *This Gun for Hire*
(1942)

Lake

There is something
you can do. Don't kill
anymore. You're just
killing her all over
again. That's all you're
doing. You don't really
want to get Gates.

Ladd

What do you want
me to do? Send him
some candy?

OFFSCREEN **RELATIONSHIP**

Although Paramount's publicity department might have hoped for a romance between Alan Ladd and Veronica Lake to help sell *This Gun for Hire*, there was little likelihood of it and less point in inventing one. Lake was married to MGM art director John Detlie and had just had her first child, while Ladd was hopelessly in love with his married agent, Sue Carol.

Alan Ladd and Veronica Lake rarely socialized. In her memoirs, she described their relationship: "We'd arrive on the set early each morning. Alan would nod and say, 'Good morning, Ronnie.' 'Hi, Alan.' We'd go to wardrobe and makeup, play our scenes together, and go back to our dressing rooms to take off the makeup and wardrobe. 'Night, Ronnie.' 'Night, Alan, see you tomorrow.'"

Veronica Lake on her and Alan Ladd's approach to *The Glass Key*: "Alan and I attacked the project with all the enthusiasm of time-clock employees, a pretty cocky approach for two people without acting credentials and only the instant-star system to thank for your success."

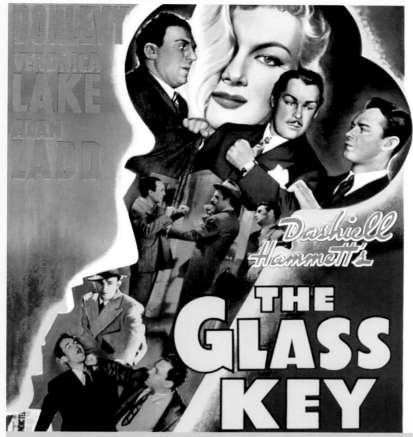

THE GLASS KEY, 1942

Hers

BORN
Constance Frances Marie Ockelman
November 14, 1919
Brooklyn, New York

DIED
July 7, 1973
Burlington, Vermont,
of acute hepatitis

STAR SIGN
Scorpio

HEIGHT
4'11"

HUSBANDS AND CHILDREN
Art director John S. Detlie
(1941–1943, divorced)
daughter, Elaine

Director André De Toth
(1944–1952, divorced)
son, Andre Michael,
daughter, Diana

Music publisher
Joseph H. McCarthy
(1955–1960, divorced)

British sea captain
Robert Carleton-Munro
(1972–1973, her death)

ESSENTIAL**TEAM-UPS**

THIS GUN FOR HIRE (1942, Paramount)
Although Veronica Lake was top-billed as a singing magician trying to ferret out
enemy agents, Alan Ladd stole the show as the baby-faced killer out for revenge
when the spies double-cross him.

THE GLASS KEY (1942, Paramount)
Ladd tries to clear his boss (Brian Donlevy) of a murder charge while fighting his
attraction to another suspect, the boss's girlfriend (Lake), in this moody rendition
of the Dashiell Hammett novel.

DUFFY'S TAVERN (1945, Paramount)
In an all-star variety show, Ladd and Lake spoof their images, playing themselves
in a rehearsal for a violent radio show the hapless Victor Moore thinks is real.

THE BLUE DAHLIA (1946, Paramount)
Veteran Ladd and spurned wife Lake are cynical, hurt, and under suspicion of
killing Ladd's wife in this classic film noir.

Their exuberance and gentle humor, not to mention thrilling vocalizing, brought new life to the operetta and made them America's timeless singing sweethearts.

JEANETTE **MACDONALD** NELSON **EDDY**

Although it has become fashionable in recent years to poke fun at the Jeanette MacDonald–Nelson Eddy musicals, in their day they were more than immensely popular: They were innovative. As much movie stars as they were singers, the pair brought a sense of youthful exuberance to films such as *Naughty Marietta* (1935) and *Rose-Marie* (1936) that had been missing in much of the genre. Although the operetta had been a staple in the early talking era, too much bad acting had driven audiences away. Even critically acclaimed adaptations, like director Ernst Lubitsch's witty pictures with MacDonald and Maurice Chevalier, had fallen out of favor. Nelson Eddy's sincerity helped bring back the romantic side of the genre. MacDonald had the good sense to know when to play it straight and when to insert tongue firmly in cheek. Fans found an escape from the harsh realities of the Depression in soaring duets like "Ah, Sweet Mystery of Life" and "Indian Love Call," while also enjoying the chance to laugh with the stars at their characters. The careful placement of humor also helped MGM get away with the occasional sentimental ending, particularly when MacDonald's and Eddy's youthful spirits were reunited to the tune of "Will You Remember?" in *Maytime* (1937). Astonishingly, the MacDonald–Eddy singing team was paired almost by accident. MGM head Louis B. Mayer had jumped at the chance to sign MacDonald when she left Paramount in 1933. Her ladylike poise was a perfect fit for MGM's image of class and sophistication. But after casting her in *The Merry Widow* (1934), he was having trouble finding the right vehicle for her. When Grace Moore's success in *One Night of Love* (1934) brought the movie operetta back into popularity, Mayer decided to give MacDonald an operetta of her own, *Naughty Marietta*. He wanted Allan Jones as her costar, but the singer couldn't get out of his Broadway contract, so rather than hold up production, Mayer cast Nelson Eddy, who had only small roles in three films. Although the picture was a huge success, with critics lauding the singing stars individually and as a team, there were no immediate plans to reteam them. Eddy was originally slated to costar with Moore in *Rose-Marie*, but a contract dispute forced her to withdraw, and MacDonald took the role. When the notices, box-office receipts, and fan mail started pouring in, Mayer realized he had a potent new screen team on his hands. It helped greatly that their first two films had been directed by W. S. Van Dyke, a fast-working director who filled his pictures with sprightly humor. MacDonald and Eddy's box office soared even further with *Maytime*, a tragic romance that many fans consider their best film. After that, however, Mayer tried splitting the team, arguing that they could produce two hits apart in the time it took them to make one together. When returns weren't as strong as for their films apart, he reunited them in their first contemporary story, *Sweethearts* (1938). The witty Technicolor production would be their last solid hit. By the 1940s, audiences wanted a more contemporary sound to their film musicals. The studio continued to use classical performers in cameos and supporting roles, but gave more emphasis to singers like Judy Garland and June Allyson. MGM couldn't figure out how to update MacDonald's and Eddy's images, nor did they consider letting them play their own ages as they approached middle age. After *I Married an Angel* (1942) flopped, both stars left the studio for concert work and tours with the USO; Eddy eventually signed with Universal. In later years, there was frequent talk of reuniting the two, though it never went beyond a few radio appearances. If anything, the continued professional separation only seemed to burnish their image as the screen's ultimate singing team. Even when MGM tried to create another Nelson and Jeanette, as when they teamed Kathryn Grayson with Mario Lanza or Howard Keel, they couldn't match the success of MacDonald and Eddy. In 1959, a new recording of their greatest duets and solos, *Jeanette MacDonald and Nelson Eddy in HiFi*, sold over a million copies. Although it marked the last time they would work together, the album was a testimony to the popularity of an iconic team whose grace and humor through eight films had truly made them America's singing sweethearts.

NEW MOON, 1940

MAYTIME, 1937

BEHINDTHESCENES

ELEANOR POWELL, WHO COSTARRED WITH NELSON EDDY IN *ROSALIE* (1937), ON THE JEANETTE MACDONALD–NELSON EDDY PARTNERSHIP: "WHEN THEY SANG, THEY LIFTED YOUR SOUL FROM THE ABYSS TO THE HIGHEST FLOATING CLOUD IN THE SKY. TO ME THEY WERE WHAT LYNN FONTANNE AND ALFRED LUNT WERE TO THE SPOKEN WORD AND THE DRAMA OF THE THEATER, THEY WERE WHAT PAVLOVA AND NIJINSKI WERE TO THE DANCE WORLD, THEY WERE THE EPITOME OF PERFECT BLENDING AND PERFECTION."

AS PUBLICITY FOR *ROSE-MARIE* (1936), MGM OFFERED $2,000 TO THE FIRST WOMAN THAT YEAR TO NAME TWIN DAUGHTERS ROSE AND MARIE. THE PRIZE WENT TO MRS. ESKER R. OWENS OF FORT SMITH, ARIZONA.

BECAUSE THEY ENDED UP SIGNING WITH COMPETING RECORD COMPANIES, JEANETTE MACDONALD AND NELSON EDDY ONLY RELEASED FOUR RECORDS OF DUETS DURING THEIR TIME AS MGM STARS.

IN 1963, PRODUCER ROSS HUNTER TRIED TO GET JEANETTE MACDONALD AND NELSON EDDY TO RETURN TO THE SCREEN AS THE OLDER COUPLE EXPECTING A LATE-IN-LIFE BABY IN DORIS DAY'S *THE THRILL OF IT ALL*. THE STARS DECLINED, WITH EDDY EXPLAINING, "WE DECIDED THAT BECAUSE WE HAD HIT THE TOP AND CREATED AN IMAGE FOR ALL TIME, WE WERE NOT GOING TO SIT AROUND AND WATCH THAT IMAGE DESTROYED. AS IT WAS, WE FELT WE COULD HOLD OUR HEADS HIGH, AND IF WE HAD TO GO OUT, WE WOULD GO OUT ON TOP."

IN WOODY ALLEN'S *BANANAS* (1971), A RECORDING FROM *NAUGHTY MARIETTA* (1935) IS USED TO TORTURE A POLITICAL PRISONER.

IN THE 1980 MUSICAL *A DAY IN HOLLYWOOD/A NIGHT IN THE UKRAINE*, THE SONG "OH, NELSON, WHAT YOU'RE PUTTING ME THROUGH" POKES FUN AT THE NELSON EDDY–JEANETTE MACDONALD PARTNERSHIP. IT'S SUNG TO A MANNEQUIN WEARING A CANADIAN MOUNTIE UNIFORM.

His

BORN
Nelson Ackerman Eddy
June 29, 1901
Providence, Rhode Island

DIED
March 6, 1967
Miami Beach, Florida,
of a stroke

STAR SIGN
Cancer

HEIGHT
6'

WIFE
Ann Denitz Franklin
(1939–1967, his death)

OFFSCREEN**RELATIONSHIP**

When Allan Jones was unavailable to make *Naughty Marietta*, MGM head Louis B. Mayer asked Jeanette MacDonald if she would agree to make it with Nelson Eddy even though he had little film experience. Knowing of his success as a concert singer, MacDonald not only agreed but also generously let the studio bill him as her costar.

Jeanette MacDonald on making *Naughty Marietta* with Nelson Eddy: "No question about it, the timbre of our voices blended beautifully, his baritone and my soprano. We liked each other; we enjoyed working together; we were enthusiastic about [*Naughty Marietta*]. Evidently all this came through onscreen."

The only real MacDonald–Eddy feud was between their fan clubs. Each took offense if it thought its star had been given fewer close-ups or musical numbers, and the clubs got so much publicity that their feuding often turned up in newspaper articles.

Nelson Eddy sang "I Love You Truly" at Jeanette MacDonald's 1937 wedding to actor Gene Raymond. He also served as an usher.

Between scenes, Nelson Eddy usually retired to his dressing room to work on sculpture and oil paintings. His most famous work was a portrait of Jeanette MacDonald that he painted during their work on *Bitter Sweet*.

Nelson Eddy on his memories of Jeanette MacDonald: "I play her records, and she is as alive to me as she ever was."

KEY QUOTE
From *New Moon* (1940)

Eddy
Anger makes you very charming, Mademoiselle.

MacDonald
Patronizing makes you very boring, Monsieur.

SWEETHEARTS, 1938

Hers

BORN
Jeanette Anna MacDonald
June 18, 1903
Philadelphia, Pennsylvania

DIED
January 14, 1965
Houston, Texas,
of a heart attack

STAR SIGN
Gemini

HEIGHT
5'4"

HUSBAND
Actor Gene Raymond
(1937–1965, her death)

ESSENTIAL**TEAM-UPS**

NAUGHTY MARIETTA (1935, MGM)
The singing started with this fanciful tale of a runaway bride (Jeanette MacDonald) who falls for a Yankee scout (Nelson Eddy).

ROSE-MARIE (1936, MGM)
MacDonald and Eddy took on the Canadian Rockies in this tale of an opera singer and a Mountie who find love and an "Indian Love Call" while searching for her criminal brother (the young James Stewart).

MAYTIME (1937, MGM)
In their most popular film, the team appear as star-crossed lovers, with singing star MacDonald falling for young musician Eddy after promising to wed her mentor (John Barrymore).

SWEETHEARTS (1938, MGM)
For once, MacDonald and Eddy start out as a married couple, musical stars whose marriage is threatened by a greedy producer who thinks he can make more by splitting them up so they can tour in separate productions of a popular Victor Herbert operetta.

I MARRIED AN ANGEL (1942, MGM)
Though largely panned at the time, the final MacDonald–Eddy film is a surprisingly sophisticated tale of a banker who dreams he has married into a heavenly family.

No audience laughed harder than when the perpetual trickster set his sights on the statuesque, unflappable woman who came to be called "the fifth Marx Brother."

GROUCHO MARX
MARGARET DUMONT

Every clown needs a good straight man or woman. Groucho Marx found his ideal comic foil in Margaret Dumont. She grounded his madcap comedy by taking his bad puns and outlandish schemes seriously, but with a touch of childlike naïveté. At times, his jokes seemed to go right over her head. But even when she fussed at his insults or his gross misbehavior, somewhere deep inside you knew she was tickled that he bothered to go to so much trouble just for her. And best of all, she knew enough to stay out of Groucho's way as he ad-libbed cascades of ever more outrageous jokes. She frequently had to endure verbal and physical assaults from the other Marx Brothers, but it was her interaction with Groucho that audiences remember best. It's little wonder fans assumed they were married offscreen. Even when Groucho shot her out of a cannon at the end of *At the Circus* (1939), you couldn't help wishing they'd find a happily-ever-after. And they always gave the impression that if they ever did get together, they'd have more fun than the often colorless romantic leads in many of their films. Groucho always said that the secret of their success was her seriousness. He claimed that she never understood any of his jokes and even thought of her roles as serious dramatic parts. It made a good story, though in truth she was already an experienced comedienne when playwright-director George S. Kaufman decided to team them for the first time in the stage production of *The Cocoanuts*. She did well enough that she remained with the team for their next play, *Animal Crackers*, and was part of the cast when both productions were filmed by Paramount Pictures in 1929 and 1930, respectively. At that point, however, Groucho decided to take a break from her. Some sources claim he felt she hadn't adjusted successfully to the motion-picture medium. Others say he simply wanted the chance to work with a sexy, younger woman. As a result, his female lead in the next two Marx Brothers films was Thelma Todd. Their scenes were hilarious, but Todd was really more a potential conspirator than a mark in Groucho's perpetual con games. When Dumont rejoined the team for 1933's *Duck Soup*, he realized how much she contributed to the act. Lines like "We're fighting for this woman's honor, which is probably more than she ever did" were just funnier when aimed at the statuesque, dignified Dumont than at a younger woman. When the Marx Brothers moved to MGM, they took her with them for a series of memorable films that started with *A Night at the Opera* (1935). MGM's writers left her out of one film, *Go West* (1940), and her absence was so sorely felt by the brothers and their fans that she was brought back for their next picture, *The Big Store* (1941). Declining box office and growing studio control of their pictures meant that would be their last film at MGM. The Marx Brothers announced their retirement from the screen, and though they would do two more films a few years later, Dumont never teamed with them again. Though she worked opposite such other clowns as Laurel and Hardy, W. C. Fields, Danny Kaye, and Abbott and Costello, she never rose to the comic heights she had scaled with Groucho. She hadn't worked in a year when, for old times' sake, Groucho hired her to reprise her role in *Animal Crackers* (1930) on a 1965 episode of television's *The Hollywood Palace*. She died a few days later, and the show aired posthumously, with no reference to her passing. But that didn't end the team's popularity. When Groucho mentioned her name during concert appearances in later years, the audience always burst into spontaneous applause. In 1974, Groucho received a special Oscar for his contributions to motion-picture comedy. After wishing that his brothers were there to share the honor, he paid tribute to Dumont: "She was a great straight woman, even though she never got any of my jokes."

THE BIG STORE, 1941

A NIGHT AT THE OPERA, 1935

BEHINDTHESCENES

MORRIE RYSKIND, GEORGE S. KAUFMAN'S WRITING PARTNER, ATTEMPTED TO DISPEL THE POPULAR MYTH THAT DUMONT NEVER UNDERSTOOD ANY OF GROUCHO'S JOKES, WRITING, "NO ONE COULD HAVE BEEN A SHOWGIRL FOR AS MANY YEARS AS SHE WAS WITHOUT ACQUIRING AT LEAST A MODICUM OF STREET SAVVY. . . . IF MY THEORY IS CORRECT, THEN SHE SHOULD BE LAUDED FOR THE LONGEST-RUNNING PERFORMANCE IN SHOW BUSINESS HISTORY, FOR SHE NEVER SLIPPED FROM HER CHARACTER UNTIL HER DEATH."

THE MARX BROTHERS' FIRST FILM, *THE COCOANUTS* (1929), WAS SHOT IN PARAMOUNT'S STUDIOS IN ASTORIA, LONG ISLAND. SINCE THE STUDIO WAS NOT SOUNDPROOFED, THE FILM HAD TO BE SHOT IN THE WEE HOURS OF THE MORNING TO REDUCE OUTSIDE TRAFFIC NOISE. THE MARXES AND DUMONT OFTEN CAME DIRECTLY FROM PERFORMANCES OF THEIR STAGE PLAY *ANIMAL CRACKERS*. DESPITE SUCH DEDICATION, THE MARX BROTHERS HATED *THE COCOANUTS* AND ATTEMPTED TO BUY THE FILM FROM PARAMOUNT IN ORDER TO BURN THE NEGATIVE.

WHEN MARGARET DUMONT STARTED WORK ON *A DAY AT THE RACES* (1937), SHE TOLD COSTAR MAUREEN O'SULLIVAN, "IT'S NOT GOING TO BE ONE OF *THOSE* THINGS. I'M HAVING A VERY *SERIOUS* PART THIS TIME."

THE SCREEN ACTORS GUILD VOTED MARGARET DUMONT BEST SUPPORTING ACTRESS OF 1937 FOR HER ROLE IN *A DAY AT THE RACES*.

His

BORN
Julius Henry Marx
October 2, 1890
New York, New York

DIED
August 19, 1977
Los Angeles, California,
of pneumonia

STAR SIGN
Libra

HEIGHT
5'7½"

WIVES AND CHILDREN
Dancer Ruth Johnson
(1920–1942, divorced)
son, Arthur
daughter, Miriam

Actress Kay Marvis
(1945–1951, divorced)
daughter, Melinda

Actress Eden Hartford
(1954–1969, divorced)

OFFSCREEN**RELATIONSHIP**

Margaret Dumont on her first days with the Marx Brothers: "I was told that the Marx Brothers needed an actress with dignity and poise to lend legitimate dramatic balance to their comedy. After three weeks as Groucho's leading lady, I nearly had a nervous breakdown. But I don't regret a minute of it. I just love those boys."

Shortly after beginning work on *The Cocoanuts*, Margaret Dumont realized that there was an unstated dress code if she wanted to survive working with the Marx Brothers. "Chiffons and laces are out," she told an interviewer. "I usually have my dresses made of velvets and gold cloth. They are both very strong, as they have to be when you play one of those love scenes with Groucho."

Though they socialized very little off the set, people thought Groucho Marx and Margaret Dumont were real-life husband and wife. One newspaper even printed that the two were married, and when Groucho found out it threw him into a comic panic. "I have just written an article about my wife," he told her, "and the magazine is running her pictures. When that article comes out, I'll be arrested for bigamy."

The Marx Brothers were inveterate practical jokers, and Margaret Dumont didn't escape them. While they were on the road, one of the brothers got word to hotel security that a prostitute was working out of Dumont's room. Dumont fled and spent the night in the railroad station, only returning to the company after Groucho apologized profusely.

AT THE CIRCUS, 1939

Hers

BORN
Daisy Juliette Baker
October 20, 1882
Brooklyn, New York

DIED
March 6, 1965
Hollywood, California,
of a heart attack

STAR SIGN
Libra

HEIGHT
5'7"

HUSBAND
Sugar heir John Moller Jr.
(1910–1918, his death)

ESSENTIAL**TEAM-UPS**

ANIMAL CRACKERS (1930, Paramount)
Groucho Marx, as African explorer Captain Spaulding, and Margaret Dumont, as society hostess Mrs. Rittenhouse, share their most memorable musical moments, including "Hooray for Captain Spaulding" and "Hello, I Must Be Going."

DUCK SOUP (1933, Paramount)
Wealthy widow Dumont loans her money to cash-strapped Freedonia, then installs Groucho as its new dictator, paving the way for a trenchant satire of war and international relations often hailed as the Marxes' best film.

A NIGHT AT THE OPERA (1935, Paramount)
As the dowager hoping to break into society by financing Groucho's opera company, Dumont gets to bear the brunt of his insults, but also gets to open the door to finish the classic stateroom sequence with a bang.

A DAY AT THE RACES (1937, Paramount)
Quack doctor Groucho tries to get wealthy hypochondriac Dumont to save the sanitarium where he's working illegally.

AT THE CIRCUS (1939, Paramount)
Dumont endures the ultimate indignity at the hands of Groucho when he shoots her out of a cannon at this madcap film's conclusion.

KEY QUOTE

**From *The Big Store*
(1941)**

Dumont
I'm afraid after we're
married a while,
a beautiful young girl
will come along,
and you'll forget all
about me.

Marx
Don't be silly. I'll write
you twice a week.

They became the cult film couple of the ages when they teamed for a pair of devil-may-care films noir as offbeat as their own offscreen personalities.

ROBERT **MITCHUM**
JANE **RUSSELL**

Robert Mitchum and Jane Russell were walking contradictions: the laconic rebel with the soul of a poet and the busty sexpot who led prayer meetings and helped war orphans in her spare time. Their chemistry was a reflection of the buddy relationship they developed offscreen. Although Mitchum always put down his own acting, he and Russell were equals in their dedication to their craft and their refusal to demand star treatment. Russell was apprehensive about her new leading man's drinking and wild ways, but as soon as they started working together, they developed a bond that even the pressures of Hollywood life couldn't threaten. Onscreen, that bond seemed almost too steamy for the conservative climate of the early 1950s. When Mitchum appraised Russell's face and figure through his famously hooded eyes, it created a sexual tension in stark contrast to more innocent screen teams of the day, like Van Johnson and June Allyson, or Betty Grable and Dan Dailey. With dark, thick hair and impressive chests, Russell and Mitchum were an ideal match physically. That they meshed artistically was a bonus that their boss, eccentric tycoon Howard Hughes, didn't anticipate. For him, the equation was simple: Mitchum was RKO Radio Pictures' top box-office draw, and Russell needed some box-office insurance if she was to rise beyond the notoriety of her first film, the sexually charged Western *The Outlaw* (1942). When he teamed them for *His Kind of Woman* (1951) and *Macao* (1952), he wanted to create films on a par with the success of her loan-out to Paramount for the Bob Hope vehicle *The Paleface* (1948). However, Hughes didn't get the profits he wanted, due to his profligate production style. Mitchum's laconic acting was a perfect match for Russell's dry wit and deadpan delivery. Her total lack of pretension made her a unique figure in the film-noir world—a femme fatale with a genuine air of innocence. She seemed, quite believably, to be a nice young lady who'd gotten herself in way over her head. She needed a pair of broad shoulders to lean on, and Mitchum's were just the right size. When *His Kind of Woman* and *Macao* first came out, most critics didn't get the two films. It would take years for the less structured work of Hollywood mavericks like Robert Altman and Francis Ford Coppola to make it clear that pictures like these were far ahead of their time. When historians and cult-film fans started re-evaluating Mitchum's work in terms of what was on the screen, these films found a more appreciative audience. Of course, their plot twists and shifts in style were actually a product of Hughes's peripatetic management. Both pictures sat on the shelf for months while he and his associates tinkered with them. *Macao* was initially directed by Josef von Sternberg, whom Hughes had hoped would work the same magic for Russell that he had for Marlene Dietrich in the 1930s. When preview audiences hated the film, studio executives re-edited it so poorly that Mitchum said his character came through a door for one scene and ran into himself on the other side. Eventually, the film was substantially remade by director Nicholas Ray, with Mitchum himself writing new scenes each morning during conferences with Ray and Russell. *Macao* is recognized as a fascinating variation on the film noir, complete with exotic scenes of Mitchum and Russell fighting in a room full of flying feathers. The film cost so much to shoot twice, however, that it couldn't possibly show much of a profit. That may be the reason Mitchum and Russell only made two films together—Hughes could make more putting the two in separate overproduced films than he could by putting them in one film together. His economy was movie history's loss, as none of their later RKO films generated quite the same heat. Fans were left, however, with warm memories of one of the screen's sexiest and most unconventional screen teams.

MACAO, 1952

WITH DIRECTOR JOSEF VON STERNBERG, 1952

BEHIND THE SCENES

HOWARD HUGHES FIRST CONSIDERED CASTING JANE RUSSELL OPPOSITE ROBERT MITCHUM IN *THE BIG STEAL* (1949), A FILM HE RUSHED INTO PRODUCTION AFTER MITCHUM'S ARREST FOR SMOKING MARIJUANA. WHEN HUGHES HAD SECOND THOUGHTS, FEARING THE TEAMING MIGHT TAINT RUSSELL'S CAREER, HE GAVE THE ROLE TO JANE GREER, A FORMER FLAME HE WANTED TO PUNISH FOR HAVING REJECTED HIM.

WORKING TITLES FOR *HIS KIND OF WOMAN* (1951) INCLUDED "SMILER WITH A GUN" AND "KILLER WITH A SMILE." THE EVENTUAL TITLE CAME FROM ANOTHER SCREENPLAY HUGHES HAD CONSIDERED AS A VEHICLE FOR ROBERT MITCHUM AND JANE RUSSELL IN 1949. THAT SCRIPT WAS NEVER FILMED.

WHEN RKO EXECUTIVES DECIDED THEY DIDN'T WANT TO PAY TO PROVIDE COFFEE AND DONUTS FOR THE CAST AND CREW OF *HIS KIND OF WOMAN* (1951) EVERY MORNING, ROBERT MITCHUM PICKED THEM UP HIMSELF, ON COMPANY TIME. THAT WAS THE ONLY TIME HE WAS EVER LATE FOR HIS CALL. WHEN MANAGEMENT REALIZED THE DELAYS WERE COSTING MORE THAN THE SNACKS, THEY RESUMED THE PRACTICE, AND HE STARTED SHOWING UP ON TIME AGAIN.

HOWARD HUGHES RENTED A LARGE BILLBOARD ON WILSHIRE BOULEVARD IN LOS ANGELES ON WHICH TO DISPLAY A PROVOCATIVE POSTER FOR *HIS KIND OF WOMAN* (1951), COMPLETE WITH AN EROTIC PAINTING OF ROBERT MITCHUM AND JANE RUSSELL LOCKED IN AN EMBRACE. HE EVEN HAD IT SURROUNDED WITH FLAMING GAS JETS. AFTER STARING AT IT FOR HOURS IN THE VERY EARLY MORNING, HE ORDERED IT TAKEN DOWN.

DIRECTOR JOSEF VON STERNBERG WOULD LATER COMPLAIN ABOUT THE WAY HOWARD HUGHES AND HIS EXECUTIVES TAMPERED WITH *MACAO* (1952) AFTER IT WAS FINISHED: "INSTEAD OF FINGERS IN THE PIE, HALF A DOZEN CLOWNS IMMERSED VARIOUS PARTS OF THEIR ANATOMY IN IT." IT WOULD BE VON STERNBERG'S LAST FILM IN THE UNITED STATES.

BORN
Robert Charles Durman Mitchum
August 6, 1917
Bridgeport, Connecticut

DIED
July 1, 1997
Santa Barbara, California,
of lung cancer and emphysema

STAR SIGN
Leo

HEIGHT
6'1½"

WIVES AND CHILDREN
Student Dorothy Spencer
(1940–1997, his death)
sons, Jim and Christopher
daughter, Petrine

OFFSCREEN**RELATIONSHIP**

Robert Mitchum and Jane Russell frequently had picnic lunches on the beach set for *His Kind of Woman*, with food brought in by Mitchum's secretary. Whenever Vincent Price was shooting, he was also included in the party. Mitchum also enjoyed entertaining the rest of the cast and crew with drinks and Chinese take-out in his trailer.

In later years, Robert Mitchum and Jane Russell were neighbors in Santa Barbara, California.

When asked to say what one thing about the other would surprise most people, Russell said, "That he's really an intellectual. That he really is well-read . . . I think maybe now they're getting the idea, but I think years ago, they used to think he was Peck's Bad Boy . . . or something." Mitchum said of Russell, "That she is absolutely, totally, flat-out honest. Honest and true. What you see is what you get."

When Robert Mitchum died, Jane Russell helped his widow, Dorothy, scatter his ashes at sea within sight of the Mitchums' Montecito, California, home. She was the only non–family member invited.

KEY QUOTE

From *His Kind of Woman* (1951)

Mitchum
Fools get away with
the impossible.

Russell
That's because they're
the only ones who try it.

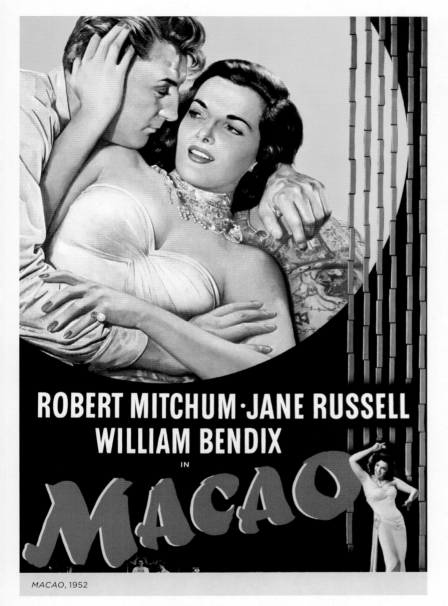

MACAO, 1952

BORN
Ernestine Jane Geraldine Russell
June 21, 1921
Bemidji, Minnesota

STAR SIGN
Gemini

HEIGHT
5'7"

HUSBANDS AND CHILDREN
Football player Bob Waterfield
(1943–1967, divorced)
adopted daughter, Tracy
adopted sons, Tommy
Kavanaugh and Robert John

Actor Roger Barrett
(1968, his death)

Real estate broker
John Calvin Peoples
(1974–1999, his death)

ESSENTIAL**TEAM-UPS**

HIS KIND OF WOMAN (1951, RKO)
Gambler Robert Mitchum and fake heiress Jane Russell come up against a
deported gangster in this free-ranging film noir.

MACAO (1952, RKO)
Mitchum stars as a man on the lam trying to redeem himself by capturing an
international crime lord, with Russell as the sultry (when wasn't she sultry?) singer
who heats up his nights.

Their unrepentant passion, even while still married to others, pervaded the three films made at the height of their romance.

LAURENCE **OLIVIER**
VIVIEN **LEIGH**

They only made three films together, and yet Laurence Olivier and Vivien Leigh have more of an identity as a screen couple than many actors who worked together in twice that number. As with Richard Burton and Elizabeth Taylor in later years, the publicity generated by their love affair and marriage often threatened to overshadow their film work. That it didn't may be because of their tremendous accomplishments as actors. In many ways, their publicity actually fed their identities as consummate professionals, making them more like Broadway's Alfred Lunt and Lynn Fontanne than Liz and Dick. For Olivier and Leigh, acting and love were irretrievably intertwined. Fittingly, their infatuation was born from seeing each other onstage. When producer Alexander Korda teamed them for the first time in *Fire over England* (1937), their love scenes reflected and even deepened their offscreen passion. Soon, the two moved in together, even though they were still married to others. When U.S. producer David O. Selznick announced plans to film *Gone with The Wind* (1939), Olivier tried to help his lover land the role of Scarlett O'Hara, suggesting unsuccessfully that Korda film a test of her in the role and send it to Selznick. After turning down the chance to make her U.S. film debut in *Wuthering Heights* (1939), Leigh followed Olivier to Hollywood. She had an entrée to Selznick through his brother and Olivier's agent, Myron Selznick. Ironically, Leigh didn't really enjoy the stardom brought her by *Gone with The Wind*. Her identification with Scarlett cost her the leading role in *Rebecca* (1940), which she had dearly wanted to play opposite Olivier. Instead, she made *Waterloo Bridge* (1940) opposite Robert Taylor. Olivier finally became her real-life leading man when, freed from their first spouses, they married in 1940. The event pushed the war news off the front pages of most British newspapers. Until 1941, the couple's personal lives and stage work had eclipsed their few films together. They made up for that with *That Hamilton Woman* (1941), a wartime morale booster depicting the doomed romance between the married Lady Emma Hamilton and Lord Admiral Horatio Nelson during the Napoleonic wars. The parallels between Napoleon and Hitler were obvious, but the love story, with Leigh and Olivier bringing all of their real-life passion to the screen, swept viewers away, making the picture a hit in both the United States and the United Kindom. With their lives primarily devoted to stage work in later years, it would be the only film they would make together as man and wife. Theatrical audiences did see the two in a series of renowned Shakespeare productions in the '50s, including *Macbeth* and *Antony and Cleopatra*. But Leigh's increasingly erratic behavior, the result of manic depression, put a tremendous strain on the relationship. In 1949, she told Olivier she only loved him as a brother and embarked on a string of affairs. Olivier responded with extramarital relationships of his own until he found true love, once again, with younger actress Joan Plowright. When he asked Leigh for a divorce, she was devastated. The marriage she clung to was more a question of social position and name by that time, but the loss still hurt, particularly since he had chosen a younger woman at a time when Leigh's legendary beauty had begun to fade. Until her untimely death at the age of 53, she insisted on being addressed as "Lady Olivier."

THAT HAMILTON WOMAN, 1941

LEIGH, SIR VICTOR SASSOON, AND OLIVIER ON THE SET OF *PRIDE AND PREJUDICE*, 1940

BEHINDTHESCENES

THAT HAMILTON WOMAN (1941) WAS WINSTON CHURCHILL'S FAVORITE FILM. LEGEND HAS IT THAT HE MAY ACTUALLY HAVE GHOSTWRITTEN SOME OF THE SCRIPT, CONTRIBUTING SOME OF THE MORE PATRIOTIC SPEECHES. HE CLAIMED TO HAVE SEEN IT EIGHTY-THREE TIMES, AND SCREENED IT FOR PRESIDENT FRANKLIN ROOSEVELT BEFORE THE UNITED STATES' ENTRY INTO WORLD WAR II.

LAURENCE OLIVIER WANTED TO CAST VIVIEN LEIGH IN HIS FILM VERSION OF *HENRY V* (1945) AS THE FRENCH PRINCESS, A ROLE SHE HAD PLAYED OPPOSITE HIM IN TOURS OF BRITISH MILITARY BASES DURING WORLD WAR II. FEELING THE TWO-SCENE ROLE WAS TOO SMALL FOR THE STAR OF *GONE WITH THE WIND* (1939), HOWEVER, PRODUCER DAVID O. SELZNICK, WHO STILL HAD A CONTRACT WITH HER, REFUSED TO ALLOW HER TO MAKE THE FILM.

THAT HAMILTON WOMAN WAS RUSHED THROUGH PRODUCTION IN A MERE FIVE WEEKS BECAUSE OF WARTIME ECONOMIC PROBLEMS IN ENGLAND. THE BUDGET WAS SO TIGHT THAT IN SOME TWO-SHOTS ONLY THE SIDE OF LEIGH'S FACE ON CAMERA WAS FULLY MADE UP.

LAURENCE OLIVIER'S INVOLVEMENT IN THE FILM VERSION OF *HAMLET* (1948), WHICH HE DIRECTED AND STARRED IN, PREVENTED HIM AND VIVIEN LEIGH FROM ACCEPTING AN OFFER TO COSTAR IN A HOLLYWOOD PRODUCTION OF *CYRANO DE BERGERAC*.

BORN
Laurence Kerr Olivier
May 22, 1907
Dorking, Surrey, England

DIED
July 11, 1989
Steyning, West Sussex, England,
of complications from
a muscle disorder

STAR SIGN
Gemini

HEIGHT
5'10½"

WIVES AND CHILDREN
Actress Jill Esmond
(1930–1940, divorced)
son, Tarquin

Actress Vivien Leigh
(1940–1960, divorced)

Actress Joan Plowright
(1961–1989, his death)
son, Richard Kerr,
daughters, Agnes Margaret
and Julie Kate

OFFSCREEN**RELATIONSHIP**

Vivien Leigh first met Laurence Olivier after seeing him in the British production of *The Royal Family*, George S. Kaufman and Edna Ferber's satire of the Barrymores. She went backstage to meet him and planted a kiss on his shoulder as he sat at his makeup mirror.

Laurence Olivier, on his first sight of Vivien Leigh onstage as she performed in *The Mask of Virtue*, the 1935 play that made her name: "Apart from her looks, which were magical, she possessed beautiful poise; her neck looked almost too fragile to support her head and bore it with a sense of surprise, and something of the pride of the master juggler who can make a brilliant maneuver appear almost accidental."

Vivien Leigh begged producer Alexander Korda to cast her in a secondary role in *Fire over England* so she could work with Laurence Olivier. They quickly became lovers early in production.

Laurence Olivier's affair with Vivien Leigh was an open secret on the set of *Fire over England*. When they finally opened up about the relationship to producer Alexander Korda, he just laughed, "Don't be silly—everybody knows that. I've known it for weeks and weeks."

Vivien Leigh and Laurence Olivier were married at San Ysidro Ranch in Santa Barbara, California, with writer-director Garson Kanin as best man and Kanin's close friend Katharine Hepburn as maid of honor. They honeymooned on actor Ronald Colman's yacht. The wedding was such a secret that Kanin didn't even know why he had been asked to join them at the ranch until the ceremony.

FIRE OVER ENGLAND, 1937

BORN
Vivian Mary Hartley
November 5, 1913
Darjeeling, West Bengal,
British India (now India)

DIED
July 7, 1967
London, England,
of chronic tuberculosis

STAR SIGN
Scorpio

HEIGHT
5'3"

HUSBANDS AND CHILD
Attorney Herbert Leigh Holman
(1932–1940, divorced)
daughter, Suzanne

Actor Laurence Olivier
(1940–1960, divorced)

KEY QUOTE

From *That Hamilton Woman* (1941)

Olivier
You shouldn't have
come—people will see
you, they'll talk.

Leigh
Let them talk,
I don't care, do you?
Are you sorry?

Olivier
I'm only sorry for all the
wasted years I've been
without you. For all
the years I shall have to
be without you.

ESSENTIAL**TEAM-UPS**

FIRE OVER ENGLAND (1937, London Film Productions)
Laurence Olivier and Vivien Leigh fell in love while making this impressive adventure, with Olivier as a British spy doing undercover work in Spain before the sailing of the Armada, and Leigh as the Elizabethan lady-in-waiting he loves.

21 DAYS TOGETHER (1940, London Film Productions)
Illicit lovers Leigh and Olivier have three weeks of happiness left before he has to turn himself in for having murdered her blackmailing husband.

THAT HAMILTON WOMAN (1941, London Film Productions)
Leigh and Olivier star as the common-born noblewoman and the British admiral whose affair shocked a nation.

The ethereal waif and the all-American Joe, they played out the perfect opposites-attract courtship in a tragi-comic whirlwind romance against the backdrop of the Eternal City.

GREGORY PECK
AUDREY HEPBURN
IN *Roman Holiday*

It was the perfect fairy tale: A princess escapes from her keepers and finds love with a commoner during a twenty-four-hour tour of Rome. And even if they couldn't share a final clinch, they had changed each other deeply, each coming out of the relationship more mature, better able to face the adult challenges of their social roles. And the timing couldn't have been better. In the early 1950s, the world was gaga for royalty. Princess Elizabeth's marriage had already inspired an MGM musical: *Royal Wedding* (1951). Her sister Margaret's doomed love affair with an army officer had ruled the headlines for months. But with all that going for it, what finally made *Roman Holiday* (1953) a hit was the pairing of lanky, robust Gregory Peck, making his comedy debut as the cynical journalist who originally sees his royal playmate as just another story, and newcomer Audrey Hepburn, shooting to stardom as the impressionable Princess Anne, a tabula rasa waiting for the world to write its lessons on her. The Dalton Trumbo story had initially been planned for Cary Grant and Elizabeth Taylor, with Frank Capra directing. When Paramount balked at the estimated $1.5 million budget, Capra walked. William Wyler came on board and managed to convince the studio to pony up the money for a location shoot. By that point, Grant had left, too, concerned about romancing the much-younger female lead. Fortunately, Gregory Peck was looking to expand into comedy after a decade of dramatic hits. Elizabeth Taylor was tied up with other projects, as was second choice Jean Simmons. So Wyler went on a talent search to find a new girl and unearthed one of the screen's greatest treasures, Audrey Hepburn. During a hot summer of filming in Rome, the two made onscreen magic, so much so that Hepburn won the Oscar for Best Actress for her first leading role. Their perfect teamwork has continued to delight audiences in the United States and overseas. The film became a hit in Moscow as part of a U.S. cultural exchange program in 1960. In Japan, it is consistently voted the most popular American film ever made, thanks to the adoration of female fans enthralled with the Peck-Hepburn romance.

BORN
Eldred Gregory Peck
April 5, 1916
La Jolla, California

DIED
June 12, 2003
Los Angeles, California,
of natural causes

STAR SIGN
Aries

HEIGHT
6'3"

WIVES AND CHILDREN
Hairdresser and
makeup artist Greta Konen
(1942–1954, divorced)
sons, Jonathan, Stephen,
and Carey Paul

Journalist Veronique Passani
(1955–2003, his death)
son, Anthony
daughter, Cecilia

KEY QUOTE

Hepburn
Then at midnight
I'll turn into a pumpkin
and drive away in my
glass slipper.

Peck
And that'll be the end
of the fairy tale.

OFFSCREEN**RELATIONSHIP**

Audrey Hepburn on Gregory Peck: "I am enchanted with Greg. He's so marvelously normal, so genuine, so downright *real*! There's nothing of the 'behaving-like-a-star' routine, no phoniness. He's a dear!"

Gregory Peck on Audrey Hepburn: "Audrey is not the type who, bit by bit, turns to granite and becomes a walking career. She's modest and as lovable as an overstrung tennis racket."

For the scene at the "Mouth of Truth," Gregory Peck and director William Wyler agreed to play a trick on Audrey Hepburn. When Peck stuck his hand into the mouth—which, according to legend, devours the hand of any liar foolish enough to do so—he was supposed to pretend it was holding him tight. During the take, however, he removed his arm to reveal no hand, prompting unrehearsed screams from Hepburn, followed by peals of laughter when she realized he had simply pulled his coat sleeve over his hand.

Because she was tied up with the stage version of *Gigi*, Audrey Hepburn didn't get to meet Gregory Peck until she arrived on location in Rome. During a cocktail party for the international press, they finally were introduced. At the sight of her famous leading man, the young actress became just another speechless fan.

Gregory Peck's contract gave him approval of billing. Originally, he was to have had sole billing above the title, with Audrey Hepburn listed after the title with a special "introducing" credit. Two weeks into filming, he called his agent to insist that she be billed above the title, too. Paramount's executives thought he was insane, but the publicity department agreed that it was the only choice, given the quality of her performance.

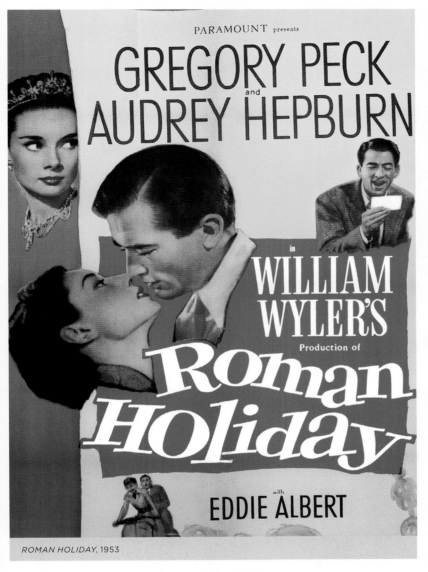

ROMAN HOLIDAY, 1953

Hers

BORN
Audrey Kathleen Hepburn–Ruston
May 4, 1929
Brussels, Belgium

DIED
January 20, 1993
Tolochenaz, Switzerland,
of stomach cancer

STAR SIGN
Taurus

HEIGHT
5'7"

HUSBANDS AND CHILDREN
Actor-director Mel Ferrer
(1954–1968, divorced)
son, Sean

Italian psychiatrist Andrea Dotti
(1969–1982, divorced)
son, Luca

BEHIND THE SCENES

AT THE HEIGHT OF THE CUBAN MISSILE CRISIS, PRESIDENT JOHN KENNEDY ASKED TO SCREEN *ROMAN HOLIDAY* TO KEEP HIMSELF CALM WHILE WAITING FOR THE SOVIET RESPONSE TO HIS ULTIMATUM.

ALTHOUGH THEY HAD GREATLY ENJOYED WORKING TOGETHER ON *ROMAN HOLIDAY*, AUDREY HEPBURN AND GREGORY PECK NEVER GOT TO TEAM UP AGAIN. HEPBURN TRIED TO GET HIM CAST AS HER LEADING MAN IN *WAR AND PEACE* (1956), BUT HE WAS UNAVAILABLE, AND THE PART WENT TO HENRY FONDA. YEARS LATER, PECK TRIED UNSUCCESSFULLY TO MOUNT A REMAKE OF SINCLAIR LEWIS'S *DODSWORTH*, WITH HEPBURN AS HIS COSTAR.

They were the king and queen of the all-singing, all-dancing extravaganza, providing the perfect anchors for some of the screen's most elaborate musical displays.

DICK POWELL
RUBY KEELER

At the end of the "Petting in the Park" number in *Gold Diggers of 1933* (1933), Ruby Keeler dons a metal dress to fight off unwanted advances, only to be confronted by Dick Powell with a large can opener. With any other performers, the moment would have been risqué. But with Powell and Keeler, it was all in the name of good, clean fun. In seven musicals at Warner Bros. between 1933 and 1935, they were the embodiment of youth, innocence, and high spirits. In many ways, they were musical versions of Janet Gaynor and Charles Farrell, a pair of working-class babes in the woods. Unlike that screen team and many others, though, their image wasn't shaped by a director, but rather by a choreographer—Busby Berkeley. The dance director's dazzling kaleidoscopic routines and often lewd elaborations on songs like "Shuffle Off to Buffalo" needed Powell and Keeler's enthusiastic naïveté to ground them. Critics sometimes complained about Keeler's habit of watching her feet as she danced (actually a popular style of tap-dancing that didn't translate well to the screen) and his eternal boyishness (he was still playing ingenues at thirty). However, in the context of films like *42nd Street* (1933) and *Gold Diggers of 1933*, their charm helped sell plot turns that were already clichés in the early '30s. By 1933, the musical had become a glut on the market. Audiences were tired of numbers shoehorned into cardboard plots wherever possible and shot with little cinematic technique. Many theaters even had to advertise "Not a Musical" on their marquees to sell tickets. *42nd Street* had originally been planned as a drama about the seamier side of Broadway. But Warner Bros. production chief Darryl F. Zanuck was convinced the musical still had legs. He took an already proven genre, the "women's picture," set it in the world of show business, and added songs. Then he brought in Berkeley to create musical numbers designed for the screen rather than the stage. For the male lead, he cast Powell, a young band singer who had signed with Warner Bros. a year earlier. And as the chorus girl who goes onstage a youngster and comes back a star, he cast Keeler, the wife of Warner's biggest musical star, Al Jolson. The twenty-four-year-old dancer had followed Jolson to Hollywood, where producers considered casting her but never did. But when *42nd Street* was a runaway hit, she was the picture's breakout star. The film triggered a series of backstage musicals with ever more elaborate dance routines from Berkeley and ever larger roles for Powell and Keeler. She played a neon-framed violin in *Gold Diggers of 1933*, swam "By a Waterfall" in *Footlight Parade* (1933), and comprised the entire femme chorus in *Dames* (1934). When that last film didn't score as well at the box office, the studio tried varying the formula with the more family-oriented *Flirtation Walk* (1934). This time it translated a buddy picture into a musical, casting Powell as a young soldier who grows up fast when he gets into

West Point. The film was the team's first without Berkeley, but it gave them the chance to work with director Frank Borzage, who had created memorable films with Charles Farrell and Janet Gaynor. He focused on the pair's growing romance, and the film put them back on top. With time, however, even the new formula began to wear thin. Though Powell's star was still rising, Keeler was being eclipsed by a new female dancer, Ginger Rogers, whose films with Fred Astaire were making her a top musical star. Both stars eventually left the studio, effectively ending the partnership—Powell in search of more varied roles, and Keeler following Jolson when he walked out on his contract. Eventually Powell reinvented himself as a film-noir tough guy and, later, a television producer and director. Keeler, who was more interested in family life by that time, divorced Jolson and retired after remarrying. Powell and Keeler, for their fans, however, remained the starstruck kids who sang and danced their way to stardom on the strength of hard work, talent, and dogged innocence.

DAMES, 1934

GOLD DIGGERS OF 1933, 1933

BEHINDTHESCENES

WHEN *42ND STREET* (1933) WAS BEING PLANNED AS A STRAIGHT DRAMATIC FILM, LORETTA YOUNG WAS PENCILED IN FOR RUBY KEELER'S ROLE.

AT THE OPENING OF *42ND STREET*, RUBY KEELER WAS CONSIDERED A BIGGER STAR THAN DICK POWELL. BUT WITH POWELL MAKING FILM AFTER FILM ON THE STUDIO TREADMILL, WHILE KEELER ONLY APPEARED IN WARNER'S BIGGEST MUSICALS (IN HER FIVE YEARS AT THE STUDIO SHE MADE ONLY NINE FILMS, WHILE POWELL MADE THREE TIMES THAT NUMBER IN THE SAME PERIOD), HE SOON BECAME THE BIGGER STAR. SHE WAS BILLED ABOVE HIM IN THEIR FIRST THREE FILMS, BUT IN *DAMES* (1934) HE WAS BILLED ABOVE HER, A POSITION HE WOULD KEEP FOR THE REST OF THEIR PARTNERSHIP.

WHEN A BOUT WITH PNEUMONIA SEEMED TO BE KEEPING DICK POWELL FROM STARRING IN *FOOTLIGHT PARADE* (1933), THE STUDIO ANNOUNCED STANLEY SMITH FOR THE BOY-SINGER ROLE. AFTER MAIL PROTESTING THE CASTING POURED IN, THE CHARACTER'S SCENES WERE RESCHEDULED SO POWELL COULD PLAY THE ROLE AFTER HIS RECUPERATION.

IN 1971, RUBY KEELER AND CHOREOGRAPHER BUSBY BERKELEY RETURNED TO BROADWAY FOR A POPULAR REVIVAL OF THE '20S MUSICAL *NO, NO, NANETTE*. THE CAST INCLUDED KEELER'S OLD FRIEND AND FORMER WARNER BROS. CLOWN PATSY KELLY. KEELER'S TWO SOLOS—"I WANT TO BE HAPPY" AND "TAKE A LITTLE ONE STEP"—WERE THE SHOW'S HIGHLIGHTS.

BORN
Richard Ewing Powell
November 14, 1904
Mountain View, Arkansas

DIED
January 3, 1963
Los Angeles, California,
of throat cancer

STAR SIGN
Scorpio

HEIGHT
6'

WIVES AND CHILDREN
Maude Maund
(1925–1927, divorced)

Actress Joan Blondell
(1936–1944, divorced)
daughter, Ellen
adopted son, Norman Barnes

Actress June Allyson
(1945–1963, his death)
adopted daughter, Pamela
son, Richard Keith

OFFSCREEN**RELATIONSHIP**

Keeler considered the films she did with Powell as entertainment that was welcomed in the Depression. In a 1968 interview, she stated, ". . . Dick and I hope we brought some sunshine into peoples' lives."

FLIRTATION WALK, 1934

DAMES, 1934

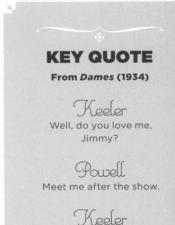

Hers

BORN
Ethel Hilda Keeler
August 25, 1909
Halifax, Nova Scotia, Canada

DIED
February 28, 1993
Rancho Mirage, California,
of cancer

STAR SIGN
Virgo

HEIGHT
5'4"

HUSBANDS AND CHILDREN
Singer Al Jolson
(1928–1939, divorced)
adopted son, Al Jr.

Real estate broker
John Homer Lowe
(1941–1969, his death)
daughters, Kathleen,
Christine, and Theresa
son, John Jr.

ESSENTIAL**TEAM-UPS**

42ND STREET (1933, Warner Bros.)
In the original "putting on a show" musical, Dick Powell is the "Young and Healthy" boy singer, while Ruby Keeler is the newcomer who quickly rises from the chorus to stardom.

GOLD DIGGERS OF 1933 (1933, Warner Bros.)
Songwriter Powell goes "Petting in the Park" with Keeler when she and her showgirl roommates (Joan Blondell and Aline MacMahon) star in his show, but he needs their help to fight off his snobbish relations.

FOOTLIGHT PARADE (1933, Warner Bros.)
Show-biz outsiders Powell and Keeler become the stars of James Cagney's energetic stage productions, including the aquatic ballet "By a Waterfall."

DAMES (1934, Warner Bros.)
This time Keeler's from a posh background and slumming in Powell's show, though nothing onstage can match the dream in which she becomes every member of the chorus in "I Only Have Eyes for You."

FLIRTATION WALK (1934, Warner Bros.)
Powell is a crass young soldier who has to succeed at West Point to win Keeler's love and costar with her in the big end-of-term show.

KEY QUOTE
From *Dames* (1934)

Keeler
Well, do you love me,
Jimmy?

Powell
Meet me after the show.

Keeler
You think I won't?

They made love between quips, insults, and martinis, proving that marriage could be sophisticated, passionate, and fun.

WILLIAM **POWELL**

MYRNA **LOY**

The first time they worked together, in a meet-cute scene set in a cab in *Manhattan Melodrama* (1934), William Powell and Myrna Loy brought out something in each other no other costars had. Where he had been supercilious in previous comic roles and she brittle, together they created something warm and very sexy. Verbal banter became love play, and a truly memorable leading couple was created. With their second film together, *The Thin Man* (1934), the two gave the screen its first genuinely modern marriage. No starry-eyed kids awash in the romance of first love, Powell and Loy played couples that had been around the block. Nor was marriage just a pretext for emotional conflict. They usually portrayed a husband and wife who stuck together because it was fun. Even though the censors kept sleuths Nick and Nora Charles in separate beds, the team made marriage almost irresistibly sexy. Loving insults and private jokes created the sense that these two could take on the world and enjoy every minute of it. For Depression-era couples whose real lives were fraught with concerns about feeding the children and paying the rent, the Powell-Loy movies provided an ideal escape. Contrary to Hollywood legend, the stars were not cast in *The Thin Man* on the strength of their teamwork in *Manhattan Melodrama*. MGM had borrowed Powell from Warner Bros. specifically for the role of Nick Charles, with Loy slated to play his Nora. Delays preparing a suitable script, however, led MGM to move *Manhattan Melodrama* into production first. Director W. S. Van Dyke had to fight to get them cast in *The Thin Man*. Up until that time, Loy had been commonly classified as villainous Asians, and Powell's career had been on a downward turn. The director had to promise to get the film made in two weeks before studio head Louis B. Mayer agreed to the plan. Even beyond the casting, the film itself was a risk. Mixing murder with comedy was still fairly new to Hollywood, and treating marriage so lightly was unprecedented. At the first preview, however, the response was overwhelmingly positive, and the inexpensive film went on to generate huge box office. MGM would make five more *Thin Man* films and team Powell and Loy an additional six times, varying the genres from melodrama (*Evelyn Prentice*, 1934) to screwball comedy (*Libeled Lady*, 1936). When the studio decided to go all-out with an epic biography of Broadway showman Florenz Ziegfeld, they turned him into another incarnation of Powell and brought in Loy—who looked and acted nothing like Ziegfeld's widow, Billie Burke—as box-office insurance. Their thirteen films at MGM (plus one at Universal) are a record for a screen team making major studio pictures. But though *The Thin Man* opened doors for the team, it also became something of a straitjacket. From that point, Loy rarely got to play anything but the perfect wife. And when health problems forced Powell to cut back on screen work through the early '40s, MGM tried to guarantee the success of his limited output by pairing him with Loy on almost every film. He began to wonder if he'd have a career working opposite anyone else.

As he began to tire of his MGM contract, and she became increasingly involved in the war effort and other social causes, their years as a team came to an end. Receipts were down for the final *Thin Man* film, *Song of the Thin Man* (1947). As films grew more realistic after World War II, Nick and Nora's approach to life, love, and murder seemed a frivolous echo of the past. In their last film together, Loy turned up in a cameo as Powell's wife in the final scene of *The Senator Was Indiscreet* (1947). Powell retired in 1955, but Loy kept working for three more decades. For every one of her openings while he was alive, Powell sent her roses with an amusing note. Television and revival screenings helped to keep them in the public eye, and their teamwork was reflected in later generations of happily married big- and small-screen couples. But no matter how popular their followers—from Rock Hudson and Susan St. James in TV's *MacMillan & Wife* to Woody Allen and Diane Keaton in *Manhattan Murder Mystery* (1993)—nobody made marriage as much fun as the original Nick and Nora Charles.

EVELYN PRENTICE, 1934

ON THE SET OF *THE THIN MAN GOES HOME*, 1945

BEHINDTHESCENES

WILLIAM POWELL AND MYRNA LOY WERE SO CONVINCING PLAYING MAN AND WIFE THAT WHEN THEY DID LOCATION SHOOTING IN SAN FRANCISCO FOR *AFTER THE THIN MAN* (1936), THE MANAGEMENT OF THE ST. FRANCIS HOTEL BOOKED THEM INTO A SUITE FOR TWO. POWELL'S OFFSCREEN SWEETHEART, JEAN HARLOW, HAD COME ALONG FOR THE FUN AND SHARED THE SUITE WITH LOY, WHILE HE STAYED A FEW FLOORS BELOW.

ALTHOUGH SEQUELS LIKE *ANOTHER THIN MAN* (1939) AND THE *THIN MAN GOES HOME* (1944) GAVE THE IMPRESSION THAT NICK CHARLES IS THE THIN MAN, THE CHARACTER WAS ACTUALLY THE MISSING SCIENTIST PLAYED BY EDWARD ELLIS IN THE 1934 ORIGINAL.

WHEN A BOUT WITH CANCER KEPT WILLIAM POWELL OFFSCREEN FOR A YEAR, MGM EXECUTIVES CONSIDERED REPLACING HIM IN THE *THIN MAN* FILMS WITH EITHER MELVYN DOUGLAS OR REGINALD GARDINER. LATER, DURING ANOTHER CONTRACT DISPUTE WITH MYRNA LOY, THEY CONSIDERED REPLACING HER WITH MARSHA HUNT.

FOR HER CAMEO APPEARANCE AT THE END OF *THE SENATOR WAS INDISCREET* (1947), IN WHICH SHE'S REVEALED TO BE WILLIAM POWELL'S WIFE, MYRNA LOY WAS PAID A NEW CADILLAC FOR ONE DAY'S WORK.

OFFSCREEN **RELATIONSHIP**

When Myrna Loy showed up for her first scene with William Powell, director W. S. Van Dyke didn't think to introduce them. When Loy forced her way into Powell's cab for their first scene, instead of saying his line, he said, "Miss Loy, I presume?" They both dissolved in laughter, which pretty much set the tone of their working relationship.

According to director W. S. Van Dyke: "They played [Nick and Nora] beautifully, because Powell was just Powell, and Loy was just Loy, both of them wisecracking all the time and clowning right through the picture."

William Powell came in fourth in the popularity poll in 1938 that named Clark Gable and Myrna Loy "King and Queen of Hollywood." On the day of the presentation, he sent Loy the biggest floral box she'd ever seen. Inside was a collection of dead leaves, barren branches, and sour grapes, with a card that read, "With love, from William the Fourth."

Myrna Loy on her partnership with William Powell: "It wasn't a conscious thing. If you heard us talking in a room, you'd hear the same thing. He'd tease me a little, and there was a sort of blending which seemed to please people. Bill is naturally a witty man. He doesn't have to have lines."

William Powell on his partnership with Myrna Loy: "Even my best friends tell me that the smartest thing I ever did was to marry Myrna Loy onscreen. And it was the pleasantest, I might add. . . . When we did a scene together, we forgot about technique, camera angles, and microphones. We weren't acting. We were just two people in perfect harmony."

LOVE CRAZY, 1941

Hers

BORN
Myrna Adele Williams
August 2, 1905
Radersburg, Montana

DIED
December 14, 1993
New York City,
from complications
during surgery

STAR SIGN
Leo

HEIGHT
5'6"

HUSBANDS
Producer Arthur Hornblow Jr.
(1936–1942, divorced)

Rental-car magnate
John Hertz Jr.
(1942–1944, divorced)

Writer–producer Gene Markey
(1946–1950, divorced)

Diplomat Howland H. Sargeant
(1951–1960, divorced)

ESSENTIAL**TEAM-UPS**

MANHATTAN MELODRAMA (1934, MGM)
This crime drama contains Powell's first scenes with Myrna Loy, as the society woman caught between Clark Gable and Powell.

THE THIN MAN (1934, MGM)
As they make their way through multiple martinis, the antics of the sophisticated and witty Nick and Nora Charles become a new model for modern marriage.

THE GREAT ZIEGFELD (1936, MGM)
The story of the rise and fall of Broadway's greatest showman became another triumph for Powell and Loy.

LIBELED LADY (1936, MGM)
As an heiress and the reporter hired to seduce her to keep her from suing his paper for libel, Loy and Powell are teamed with Spencer Tracy, as Powell's editor, and Jean Harlow, as Tracy's neglected girl Friday.

LOVE CRAZY (1941, MGM)
In their zaniest film together, Loy's groundless jealousy threatens her marriage to Powell, who resorts to a series of madcap ploys, including a drag routine, to win her back.

They were the prettiest screen team in history, a distinction that sometimes was more a curse than a blessing.

TYRONE **POWER**
GENE **TIERNEY**

There was one certain attraction in any film starring Tyrone Power and Gene Tierney— audiences couldn't take their eyes off them. They shared the kind of beauty that only seems to exist in the movies. Their career trajectories didn't quite match, however. Power excelled in adventurous roles, while Tierney was more at home in elegant drawing rooms. The one thing they had in common was a struggle to be taken seriously as actors, rather than just great beauties. Tierney came to Hollywood with a contract guaranteeing her she could spend half of each year doing stage work (an option she never exercised). Power constantly fought with 20th Century Fox head Darryl F. Zanuck for more artistically ambitious films, eventually abandoning Hollywood to stretch his talents on Broadway. Most of the time, however, they were simply treated as studio assets to be deployed as Zanuck thought best. Tierney was still new to the movies, and her image as a sleek sophisticate had not yet been set when they first worked together. The film *Son of Fury* (1942) was made to capitalize on Power's new popularity in swashbuckling roles after his success in *The Mark of Zorro* (1940). When Zanuck decided to expand the film's Polynesian sequence, in which Power's character escapes the intrigues of 18th-century England, the role of island girl Eve became a fitting showcase for rising star Tierney. The two were such a faultless match that nobody in the audience questioned it when Power's character gave up the estate he had fought for throughout the film to return to her at the end. During Power's World War II service, Tierney became the studio's top dramatic actress in the high–society film noir *Laura* (1944). As a result, writer W. Somerset Maugham considered her the ideal choice to play the shallow socialite in love with a World War I veteran who is searching for life's deeper meanings in *The Razor's Edge* (1946). Zanuck had envisioned Gregory Peck as the male lead, but when Power asked for meatier dramatic roles upon his return from military service, the part became his. Larry Darrell's spiritual quest seemed a perfect fit for Power's more mature outlook since the war, and he created a compelling portrait of his character's spiritual convictions. Tierney fared less positively. Critics who had been enthralled by her performance as a neurotic villainess in *Leave Her to Heaven* (1945) were disappointed that, cast as the equally selfish Isabel, she did little more than stand around looking beautiful. Power's first film since the war was highly anticipated, and photos released of the two whetted fans' appetites; the film became one of the year's biggest hits. Nonetheless, the pair once more went their separate ways, Power to the heroic *Captain from Castile* and Tierney to the romantic *The Ghost and Mrs. Muir* (both 1947). When Zanuck decided to give Power a comedy as a change of pace, he recycled one of the star's earlier hits, *Love Is News* (1937), as *That Wonderful Urge* (1948), the story of a brash reporter involved with a haughty society girl. With Power's original costar, Loretta Young, gone from the studio, Zanuck turned to Tierney for what would be her last role with Power. It proved to be one of their best films together, with Power charmingly brash and Tierney proving expert at cutting remarks. By the 1950s, Zanuck seemed to have lost interest in Tierney's career. After a few box–office flops, he moved her into adventure films, but they were lesser projects. Power, however, was still starring in top-budgeted productions. During Tierney's highly publicized bout with depression, which kept her offscreen for seven years, Power died. Their three films together have remained favorites for decades. Their island idyll in *Son of Fury*, their whirlwind tour of Paris in *The Razor's Edge*, and their sparring courtship in *That Wonderful Urge* are among the most romantic sequences in film history, thanks to two stars who gave everything they did a dramatic glamour.

THE RAZOR'S EDGE, 1946

SON OF FURY, 1942

BEHINDTHESCENES

**TO SATISFY THE PRODUCTION CODE, WRITERS HAD TO ADD A TRIBAL RITUAL TO
SON OF FURY (1942) TO SUGGEST THAT TYRONE POWER AND GENE TIERNEY
CONSIDERED THEMSELVES MARRIED BEFORE MOVING IN TOGETHER.**

BECAUSE OF A CLAUSE IN W. SOMERSET MAUGHAM'S CONTRACT STATING
THAT HE WOULD RECEIVE AN ADDITIONAL $50,000 IF *THE RAZOR'S EDGE*
(1946) DID NOT BEGIN FILMING BY FEBRUARY 1946, 20TH CENTURY FOX HEAD
DARRYL F. ZANUCK ORDERED LOCATION WORK DONE IN THE COLORADO
MOUNTAINS, WHICH STOOD IN FOR INDIA, IN 1945. WITH THE FILM STILL
UNCAST, A DOUBLE STOOD IN FOR TYRONE POWER, WHOM ZANUCK WAS
STILL HOPING TO CAST IN THE LEAD.

**BEFORE SETTLING ON GENE TIERNEY AS ISABEL IN *THE RAZOR'S EDGE*,
ZANUCK CONSIDERED COMPETITIVE SISTERS OLIVIA DE HAVILLAND AND
JOAN FONTAINE FOR THE ROLE.**

GENE TIERNEY'S WEDDING GOWN IN *THE RAZOR'S EDGE* WAS THE SAME
DESIGN THAT HUSBAND OLEG CASSINI HAD CREATED FOR THEIR WEDDING.
WHEN THEY DECIDED TO ELOPE, THE GOWN WAS NEVER MADE.

**THE RAZOR'S EDGE WAS THE FIRST 20TH CENTURY FOX FILM TO BE GIVEN
A BIG NEW YORK PREMIERE AFTER WORLD WAR II. THE NOVEMBER 19, 1946,
EVENT COINCIDED WITH GENE TIERNEY'S BIRTHDAY AND ALSO INCLUDED
A BELATED CELEBRATION OF COSTAR CLIFTON WEBB'S BIRTHDAY, WHICH
HAD FALLEN ON NOVEMBER 11.**

THE RAZOR'S EDGE BROUGHT IN MORE THAN $5 MILLION IN PROFITS, MAKING
IT 20TH CENTURY FOX'S TOP-EARNING FILM UP TO THAT TIME.

His

BORN
Tyrone Edmund Power Jr.
May 5, 1913
Cincinnati, Ohio

DIED
November 15, 1958
Madrid, Spain,
of a heart attack

STAR SIGN
Taurus

HEIGHT
5'10"

WIVES AND CHILDREN
Actress Annabella
(1939–1948, divorced)
adopted daughter, Annie Murat

Actress Linda Christian
(1949–1955, divorced)
daughters, Romina Francesca
and Taryn Stephanie

Actress Deborah Ann Minardos
(1958, his death)
son, Tyrone IV

KEY QUOTE

**From *The Razor's Edge*
(1946)**

Tierney
And what about me?
Am I of no importance
to you at all?

Power
You're of great
importance to me,
Isabel. I love you
and I want you to
marry me.

Tierney
When? In ten years?

OFFSCREEN**RELATIONSHIP**

Gene Tierney on Tyrone Power: "Ty was warm and considerate. He had a beautiful face."

Gene Tierney on working with Tyrone Power: "Ty had an impish streak of his own. For a nightclub scene [in *The Razor's Edge*], he persuaded the prop man to fill our glasses with champagne, instead of the usual plain or colored water used in such scenes. After a few takes, we felt quite happy and relaxed. This was the silent sequence, with music over it, showing us doing the town in Paris. We had little if any dialogue, while Russian Gypsies played enchanting music. The scene had a special glow that came out of our champagne glasses."

On Tyrone Power's return from military service in World War II, Gene Tierney gave him a white German shepherd named Olaf. Power brought him to the set of *The Razor's Edge*, where he played with Tierney's German shepherd, Butch.

Gene Tierney was separated from husband Oleg Cassini at the time she filmed *The Razor's Edge*. Cassini was outraged when studio publicists invented a romance between her and Tyrone Power during filming. She later wrote in her memoirs that many on the set were rooting for her to have an affair with her costar.

Tyrone Power and Gene Tierney lunched together often while filming *The Razor's Edge*. One day when she wasn't called, he sent her a note reading, "There is no sunshine on the set today."

During one of Gene Tierney and Tyrone Power's love scenes in *The Razor's Edge*, a set piece caught fire. Crewmembers kidded them after that about their "heated" romance.

TYRONE **POWER**
GENE **TIERNEY** *in*

m–m–m– *that Wonderful URGE*

REGINALD GARDINER
ARLEEN WHELAN

THAT WONDERFUL URGE, 1948

Hers

BORN
Gene Eliza Tierney
November 19, 1920
Brooklyn, New York

DIED
November 6, 1991
Houston, Texas,
of emphysema

STAR SIGN
Scorpio

HEIGHT
5'7"

HUSBANDS AND CHILDREN
Couturier Oleg Cassini
(1941–1952, divorced)
daughters, Daria and
Christina Cassini

Oilman Howard Lee
(1960–1981, his death)

ESSENTIAL**TEAM-UPS**

SON OF FURY (1942, 20th Century Fox)
Having been robbed of his inheritance, 18th–century British nobleman Tyrone
Power escapes to the South Seas to find love with Polynesian beauty Gene Tierney,
even as his honor calls him home.

THE RAZOR'S EDGE (1946, 20th Century Fox)
Social–climbing Tierney stops at nothing to win the heart of Power, whose search
for spiritual answers makes him both unattainable and unbelievably sexy.

THAT WONDERFUL URGE (1948, 20th Century Fox)
Power topped himself in this remake of his 1937 film *Love Is News*, playing a
newspaperman who sets out to expose heiress Tierney and ends up pretending
he's married to her.

The King and the Sex Kitten fired up the screen and struck offscreen sparks in a notorious fling when they joined forces for this classic rock 'n' roll musical.

ELVIS PRESLEY
ANN-MARGRET

IN *Viva Las Vegas*

Elvis Presley rarely sang with anybody else onscreen. In fact, there was a clause in his film contracts stating that nobody else in his pictures could sing without approval from his manager, Colonel Tom Parker. When Parker gave his permission for Ann-Margret to join the King for a pair of high-charged duets in *Viva Las Vegas* (1964), there was no danger of her overshadowing him. In fact, their teamwork only enhanced the King's image. Most of Presley's films had featured conventional leading ladies. Working with the woman nicknamed the "Sex Kitten" reminded fans just how sexy a Presley performance could be. Moreover, with direction by MGM's George Sidney and with sophisticated songs, *Viva Las Vegas* proved just how good Elvis could be with the right showcase and costar. Ann-Margret had been just another girl singer until her searing rendition of "Bachelor in Paradise" at the 1962 Academy Awards. With the breakout success of her third film, *Bye Bye Birdie* (1963), ironically a satire of Presley's stardom, publicists were hailing her as the female version of the King, making an onscreen team-up inevitable. The plot of *Viva Las Vegas*, depicting the romance between a hotshot racer and a domestic-minded swimming instructor, provided plenty of opportunities for comedy and singing. There was also a lot of room for flirtation, and during location shooting Presley and Ann-Margret became an item, despite the fact that he had a fiancée, Priscilla Beaulieu, waiting back home at Graceland. Parker was less enamored. In fact, he was concerned that Sidney was throwing the film Ann-Margret's way. He finally put his foot down with the studio, having one of their duets cut and turning another into an Elvis solo. He needn't have worried. Although critics were quick to praise Ann-Margret as his most able onscreen partner ever, the film was still clearly an Elvis Presley picture. Some would even say it was his best. It was certainly his most successful, bringing in $5 million in box office. But even as gossip columns were blazing with news of the affair, it was starting to cool off. Elvis was too much the good ol' boy to stay involved with a rising star who was not likely to abandon her career for him. Nor did he ever make another picture with a leading lady who could pose a threat to him in the musical department. But for one rocking moment in 1964, he shared the screen with an entertainer who could match him move for move and growl for growl. Vegas never had it so good.

His

BORN
Elvis Aaron Presley
January 8, 1935
Tupelo, Mississippi

DIED
August 16, 1977
Memphis, Tennessee,
of cardiac arrhythmia

STAR SIGN
Capricorn

HEIGHT
6'½"

WIFE AND CHILD
Priscilla Beaulieu
(1967–1973, divorced)
daughter, Lisa Marie

OFFSCREEN**RELATIONSHIP**

Ann-Margret on Elvis Presley: "He's an animal. Definitely an animal. A very interesting animal."

Ann-Margret on her relationship with Elvis Presley: "Music ignited a fiery, pent-up passion inside Elvis and inside me. It was an odd, embarrassing, funny, inspiring, and wonderful sensation. We looked at each other more and saw virtual mirror images."

Elvis Presley on his relationship with Ann-Margret: "In *Viva Las Vegas* with Ann-Margret, we got married. It took us a week to film that wedding scene. It is so real, until you think you're married. It took us two years to figure out we weren't."

Ann-Margret was an immediate hit with Elvis Presley's friends, dubbed the Memphis Mafia, because her love of motorcycles made her just one of the boys. They called her by her character's name, Rusty, though Elvis's nickname for her was "Rusty Ammo."

Although Elvis Presley returned to Graceland after shooting *Viva Las Vegas*, he and Ann-Margret spoke on the phone almost every day.

Until his death, Elvis continued to send a roomful of flowers to Ann-Margret for each of her Vegas openings.

KEY QUOTE

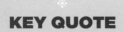

Ann-Margret
Can you check my
motor? It whistles.

Presley
I don't blame it!

CIRCA 1967

Hers

BORN
Ann–Margret Olsson
April 28, 1941
Valsjöbyn, Jämtlands län,
Sweden

STAR SIGN
Taurus

HEIGHT
5'5"

HUSBAND
Actor–personal manager
Roger Smith (1967–)

BEHINDTHESCENES

**WHEN STILLS OF THE WEDDING SCENE AT THE END OF *VIVA LAS VEGAS*
STARTED TURNING UP IN THE PRESS, SOME OF THE TABLOIDS INSISTED THAT
ELVIS PRESLEY AND ANN–MARGRET REALLY HAD GOTTEN MARRIED.**

THE FILM'S EUROPEAN TITLE WAS *LOVE IN LAS VEGAS*. IN BRAZIL, IT WAS
CALLED *LOVE AT HIGH SPEED*.

**DURING THE SHOOTING OF *VIVA LAS VEGAS*, ELVIS PRESLEY ASKED HIS
MANAGER, COLONEL TOM PARKER, TO REPRESENT ANN–MARGRET. KNOWING
BETTER THAN TO ARGUE WITH HIS CLIENT, PARKER AGREED, THEN TOLD HIM
IT WOULD CUT INTO THE TIME HE COULD DEVOTE TO ELVIS. PRESLEY NEVER
BROUGHT THE SUBJECT UP AGAIN.**

In four "backyard musicals" and three Andy Hardy films, they became America's favorite teen couple, creating an idealized image of youthful high spirits.

MICKEY **ROONEY**
JUDY **GARLAND**

On their first onscreen meeting, in *Babes on Broadway* (1941), Mickey Rooney and Judy Garland launched into a rousing rendition of "How About You?"—even breaking into a dance atop a piano. Critics have called it their definitive musical number, capturing the joyful exuberance that made them heirs to the mantle of Dick Powell and Ruby Keeler. They became even more popular than the earlier team, partly thanks to MGM's showmanship but also because their fresh-faced innocence and energy made people feel good about themselves during difficult times. The fact that they were both triple threats—singers, dancers, and actors—with photographic memories and a knack for impressions made them even more valuable to the studio. Although Garland would later complain that MGM's executives didn't want her to grow up, there was something charmingly pristine about her onscreen relationship with Rooney, which remained constant in all their vehicles. They were always more buddies than lovebirds. Mickey was the hyperactive go-getter, while Judy waited for him to realize that he needed her help if he was ever going to succeed, and that she could be more than just his best friend. Instead of conventional love scenes, Mickey and Judy had musical numbers, from her plaintive solos to the pair's peppy duets and a series of over-the-top production numbers staged by Busby Berkeley. Ultimately, the key to their onscreen success was the fact that the two stars genuinely liked each other. Each was the other's greatest fan. On the surface, the films seemed to favor Rooney's manic versatility, but many critics, then and now, have suggested that Garland's quieter support often stole the show. Neither actor was really concerned over who got the better showcase. They were such good friends that they were simply happy for the chance to work together. Initially, Garland was paired with Rooney to build her popularity with audiences, a standard studio practice at the time. He was already establishing himself in a wide variety of roles—from Puck in *A Midsummer Night's Dream* (1935) to Andy Hardy in the series that had started with 1937's *A Family Affair*. Garland had only made two feature films, but her career as a recording artist and radio singer was taking off. Although she was top-billed in their first film together, *Thoroughbreds Don't Cry* (1937), she took a backseat to his role as an ambitious jockey. She did well enough in their second film, *Love Finds Andy Hardy* (1938), to become the only love interest other than Ann Rutherford to return for subsequent Hardy films. When the team's next picture, *Babes in Arms* (1939), became MGM's most profitable film of the year, studio head Louis B. Mayer knew he had a hit. He would reunite them for three more musicals, all produced by Arthur Freed. With their youthful casts and "putting on a show" plots, they were referred to as "backyard musicals." Berkeley had directed their first three, which was hardly a boon for

Garland; his temperamental direction fueled her insecurities, while his insistence on long hours contributed to her problems with prescription drugs. But she and Rooney were such pros that all that came through onscreen were good spirits, in keeping with Mayer's idealized vision of American youth. By the time they made their last vehicle together, *Girl Crazy* (1943), Garland was starting to eclipse Rooney at the box office. While he was away for World War II service, director Vincente Minnelli, who would become her second husband, helped her grow up onscreen in films like *Meet Me in St. Louis* (1944) and *The Clock* (1945). The new Garland was too mature and too much the leading lady to be just a sidekick any more. There was talk of reteaming her with Rooney in *Good News* (1947), but the pair would not appear onscreen together again until *Words and Music* (1948), with Rooney as Broadway lyricist Lorenz Hart and Garland doing two numbers as herself. Their duet to "I Wish I Were in Love Again" would be their last feature-film appearance together. They remained friends until Judy's untimely death. When she launched her TV series *The Judy Garland Show* in 1963, he was immediately booked as a guest. The episode featured an elaborate tribute to their MGM musicals, a reminder of simpler times when putting on a show had been the most exciting thing boys and girls like Rooney and Garland could do together.

ON THE SET OF *THE JUDY GARLAND SHOW*, 1963

ON THE SET OF *BABES ON BROADWAY*, 1941

BEHINDTHESCENES

BABES IN ARMS (1939) WAS THE FIRST FILM FOR WHICH ARTHUR FREED RECEIVED A PRODUCER CREDIT. ITS SUCCESS MADE HIM MGM'S TOP MUSICAL PRODUCER AND MARKED THE BIRTH OF THE LEGENDARY FREED UNIT.

WITH *BABES IN ARMS*, MICKEY ROONEY BECAME THE FIRST TEENAGER (HE WAS NINETEEN) TO WIN AN OSCAR NOMINATION.

MGM BROUGHT IN SOME EXPERTS TO HELP WITH *BABES ON BROADWAY* (1941). CARMEN MIRANDA COACHED MICKEY ROONEY ON HIS IMITATION OF HER, WHILE VAUDEVILLE VETERAN ELSIE JANIS HELPED ROONEY AND GARLAND DEVELOP THE DUCHESS THEATER SEQUENCE, IN WHICH THEY IMITATED SUCH STAGE GREATS AS HARRY LAUDER, WALTER HAMPDEN, FAYE TEMPLETON, AND SARAH BERNHARDT.

ON THE BASIS OF HIS MUSICALS WITH JUDY GARLAND AND THE ANDY HARDY FILMS, MICKEY ROONEY WAS NAMED THE TOP BOX-OFFICE ATTRACTION OF 1939, 1940, AND 1941. GARLAND RANKED NUMBER TEN IN 1940 AND 1941.

MICKEY ROONEY WAS ANNOUNCED TO COSTAR WITH JUDY GARLAND IN *SUMMER STOCK* (1950), BUT WHEN HE LEFT MGM, THE ROLE WENT TO GENE KELLY INSTEAD.

His

BORN
Joe Yule Jr.
September 23, 1920
Brooklyn, New York

STAR SIGN
Virgo

HEIGHT
5'3"

WIVES AND CHILDREN
Actress Ava Gardner
(1942–1943, divorced)

Beauty queen
Betty Jane Rase
(1944–1948, divorced)
sons, Joe Yule Jr. and
Timothy

Actress Martha Vickers
(1949–1952, divorced)
son, Teddy

Model Elaine Mahnken/Devry
(1952–1958, divorced)
son, Jimmy
daughter, Jonelle

Actress Carolyn Mitchell
(1958–1966, her death)
daughters, Kelly Ann,
Kerry, and Kimmy Sue
son, Kyle

Realtor Marge Lane
(1967, divorced)

Secretary Carolyn Hockett
(1969–1974, divorced)

Singer Jan Chamberlin
(1978–)

OFFSCREEN**RELATIONSHIP**

Judy Garland and Mickey Rooney met in the fall of 1933, when both were attending the Lawlor School for Professional Children. The first day they met, he got his comb stuck in his hair, and she helped him disentangle it. They would pass love notes to each other during math class and even appeared in the school's Christmas show.

Before their first scene together in *Love Finds Andy Hardy*, Mickey Rooney took Judy Garland aside and advised her to act the way she sang. She would later say that after she had stumbled through her first few film performances, that was the one bit of coaching that suddenly made everything about acting fall into place for her.

Mickey Rooney on Judy Garland: "Judy has the uncanny ability to get in there and pull it off. When we made *Babes in Arms* and *Strike Up the Band*, she winged some of the numbers without a hell of a lot of rehearsals, and they worked out just fine. It's this spontaneous thing she has that makes her unique."

During their public appearances together, Judy Garland used to slip off her shoes and perform in stockinged feet so she wouldn't be taller than Mickey Rooney.

When Judy Garland was voted a special "juvenile" Oscar for her performance in *The Wizard of Oz*, Mickey Rooney, who had won the same award the previous year, presented it to her. She referred to the miniature statuette as her "Munchkin Award."

Whenever people asked Mickey Rooney why he and Judy Garland never got married, he simply said, "It would be like marrying my sister."

BABES ON BROADWAY, 1941

Hers

BORN
Frances Ethel Gumm
June 10, 1922
Grand Rapids, Michigan

DIED
June 22, 1969
London, England,
of an accidental
barbiturate overdose

STAR SIGN
Gemini

HEIGHT
4'11"

HUSBANDS AND CHILDREN
Composer David Rose
(1941–1945, divorced)

Director Vincente Minnelli
(1945–1951, divorced)
daughter, Liza

Producer Sidney Luft
(1952–1965, divorced)
daughter, Lorna
son, Joseph

Actor Mark Herron
(1965–1966, divorced)

Nightclub manager Mickey
Deans (1969, her death)

ESSENTIAL**TEAM-UPS**

LOVE FINDS ANDY HARDY (1938, MGM)
In her first film as Betsy Booth, who sings "a little," Judy Garland helps Mickey Rooney navigate treacherous romantic waters between girlfriend Ann Rutherford and small-town temptress Lana Turner.

BABES IN ARMS (1939, MGM)
The first "backyard musical" cast Mickey and Judy as vaudeville children putting on their own show to impress their parents.

STRIKE UP THE BAND (1940, MGM)
This time Mickey is out to win a high school swing-band contest, with Judy as his vocalist.

BABES ON BROADWAY (1941, MGM)
Show-biz hopefuls Mickey and Judy team up to raise money for poor children in what most critics consider the best of their films together.

GIRL CRAZY (1943, MGM)
Garland gets to sing a great George Gershwin score—including "Embraceable You" and "But Not for Me"—in this Wild West musical, with Rooney as the party boy sent to an all-boys college to grow up.

KEY QUOTE

From *Babes on Broadway* (1941)

Rooney
Will you sing me a song?

Garland
How do you know I can?

Rooney
Because you sing when you talk, when you walk. Why, your eyes are singing right now.

Garland
They are? Well, I'll be darned.

The delicacy of their onscreen love scenes mirrored one of Hollywood's most famous platonic romances.

MARGARET **SULLAVAN**
JAMES **STEWART**

Art imitated life to glorious effect when Margaret Sullavan and James Stewart shared the screen. Their deep affection for each other gave their teamwork a painful vibrancy. Physically, they were almost totally mismatched. Stewart stood a foot taller than Sullavan, and his angular gawkiness was a sharp contrast to her more reserved sophistication. Even their voices—his hesitant drawl and her husky, hushed delivery—didn't seem to fit. But their emotional openness together gave audiences a privileged look at two souls sharing an intimate connection. That their offscreen relationship never delved into the sexual simply added to the poignancy of their performances. Fittingly, in their four films together, they only got a happy ending once, in Ernst Lubitsch's *The Shop Around the Corner* (1940), a sensitive tale of two lovers who hide their identities from each other. They were rarely at cross-purposes in real life. The pair met in 1931 when Stewart stage-managed a touring play starring Sullavan, and they dated briefly, though they didn't get to act together until they arrived in Hollywood. Sullavan rose to film stardom at Universal Pictures in romantic dramas like *Only Yesterday* (1933). When prior commitments kept Francis Lederer from taking the lead in *Next Time We Love* (1936), Sullavan decided to boost Stewart's fledging screen career by requesting him as her leading man. At the time, he had only played two supporting roles at MGM, where they seemed to have no idea what to do with him. After a few day's shooting on *Next Time We Love*, his inexperience in front of the camera was so obvious that the studio was ready to replace him. Sullavan rehearsed Stewart each night, refining his technique and helping him deliver the first performance that would reveal his talents as an actor to a wider audience. After a return to Broadway to star in *Stage Door*, Sullavan went back to Hollywood with a new husband, agent Leland Hayward, who got her a sweetheart deal, including costar approval, at MGM. The studio had bought the rights to *The Shopworn Angel* (1938), the tale of a hardened showgirl touched by a World War I soldier's devotion, as a vehicle for Jean Harlow. When Harlow died suddenly, Sullavan inherited the role and once again demanded Stewart as her leading man. The film proved he could be a romantic star, and he even started getting amorous mail from female fans. Another love story for the pair was just the ticket, and that's what Lubitsch delivered to MGM when he signed a two-picture deal in 1939. A gentle tale of romance in a small shop in Budapest, *The Shop Around the Corner* required both subtlety and conviction to make the audience accept the stars as lost souls gravitating toward each other. The film may have been too gentle for United States audiences coming out of the hardscrabble days of the Depression, and it failed at the box office. Later generations, however, have found themselves more in tune with the characters' delicate passion and the picture is now considered one of the greatest romantic comedies of all time. *The Shop Around the Corner* had been planned as an antidote to the gloomy news coming from Europe in the early days of World War II. The fourth and final Sullavan–Stewart film, *The Mortal Storm* (1940), put the European situation front and center. Director Frank Borzage, who had helped turn Janet Gaynor and Charles Farrell into a top team at Fox, brought his knack for poignant romance to the tale of lovers torn apart by Hitler's rise to power. The film became particularly timely when France fell to Germany two days after its opening. Despite that, it was the team's second film to lose money, putting a halt to Stewart and Sullavan's work together. When the United States entered World War II a year later, Stewart was one of the first actors to sign up for active duty, leaving Sullavan to finish off her MGM contract without him before returning to Broadway. Even though they were now living on different coasts, the two remained close. When Sullavan began suffering from hearing loss, Stewart, whose hearing had started to decline in the late 1940s, offered his support. Just as she had taught him how to act in movies years before, he tried to teach her how to act in a world of silence. It could have been a moment from one of their movies—two kindred spirits brought together by the pain of life.

ON THE SET OF *THE SHOPWORN ANGEL*, 1938

WITH DIRECTOR ERNST LUBITSCH ON THE SET OF *THE SHOP AROUND THE CORNER*, 1940

BEHIND THE SCENES

JAMES STEWART FELT HE NEEDED TEARS IN HIS EYES FOR THE SCENE IN WHICH HE LEFT HIS WIFE, MARGARET SULLAVAN, AND THEIR INFANT CHILD TO RETURN TO WORK OVERSEAS IN *NEXT TIME WE LOVE* (1938). HE HAD NO PROBLEM ON THE FIRST TAKE, BUT AS THE CHILD ACTOR KEPT RUINING TAKES, HE HAD DIFFICULTY SUSTAINING THE EMOTION. BEFORE THE LAST TAKE, HE WENT BEHIND THE SET, LIT A CIGARETTE, AND HELD IT CLOSE TO HIS EYES TO GET THE RIGHT LOOK.

ACTRESS NORMA SHEARER WAS SO IMPRESSED BY JAMES STEWART'S ROMANTIC PERFORMANCE IN *THE SHOPWORN ANGEL* (1938) THAT SHE SET HER SIGHTS ON HIM. THE AFFAIR REPORTEDLY LASTED SIX WEEKS.

WHEN DIRECTOR ERNST LUBITSCH BROUGHT *THE SHOP AROUND THE CORNER* (1940) TO MGM, THE ONLY ACTORS HE WOULD CONSIDER IN THE LEADING ROLES WERE JAMES STEWART AND MARGARET SULLAVAN. HE EVEN DELAYED PRODUCTION UNTIL AFTER HIS OTHER MGM FILM, *NINOTCHKA* (1939), WAITING FOR BOTH TO BE AVAILABLE.

SINCE MOST OF THE SCENES IN *THE SHOP AROUND THE CORNER* TOOK PLACE IN ONE SET, A GIFT SHOP, DIRECTOR ERNST LUBITSCH SHOT THE FILM IN SEQUENCE. THAT WAS A HUGE BOON TO STAGE-TRAINED STARS JAMES STEWART AND MARGARET SULLAVAN, WHO COULD BUILD THE CHARACTERS AS THEY WOULD HAVE IN A PLAY.

THE SHOP AROUND THE CORNER WAS REMADE TWICE. MGM RELEASED A MUSICAL VERSION, *IN THE GOOD OLD SUMMERTIME*, IN 1949, WITH JUDY GARLAND AND VAN JOHNSON. AN UPDATED VERSION, *YOU'VE GOT MAIL* (1998), HAD RIVAL BOOKSTORE OWNERS TOM HANKS AND MEG RYAN MEETING ONLINE VIA E-MAIL.

WHEN THE NON-ATHLETIC JAMES STEWART FOUND THAT HE HAD TROUBLE CARRYING MARGARET SULLAVAN ACROSS THE BORDER TO FREEDOM AT THE END OF *THE MORTAL STORM* (1940), TECHNICIANS HAD TO CREATE A SPECIAL PULLEY SYSTEM TO SUPPORT HER WEIGHT.

BORN
James Maitland Stewart
May 20, 1908
Indiana, Pennsylvania

DIED
July 2, 1997
Los Angeles, California,
of a pulmonary embolism
following respiratory problems

STAR SIGN
Taurus

HEIGHT
6'3½"

WIFE AND CHILDREN
Former model
Gloria Hatrick McLean
(1949–1994, her death)
daughters, Judy and Kelly,
adopted sons, Ronald
and Michael

KEY QUOTE

**From *The Shop Around
the Corner* (1940)**

Stewart

There might be a lot we
don't know about each
other. You know, people
seldom go to the
trouble of scratching
the surface of things to
find the inner truth.

Sullavan

Well, I really wouldn't
care to scratch your
surface, Mr. Kralik,
because I know exactly
what I'd find. Instead
of a heart, a handbag.
Instead of a soul, a
suitcase. And instead of
an intellect, a cigarette
lighter . . . which
doesn't work.

OFFSCREEN RELATIONSHIP

While at Princeton, James Stewart asked Margaret Sullavan to attend a school reception with him. She would later tell director Josh Logan it was "the longest, slowest, shyest but most sincere invitation" she had ever received.

James Stewart on Margaret Sullavan's acting: "She had great humor. It wasn't mechanical with her. It was a part of her. This was one of the things that made her great. When you'd play a scene with her, you were never quite sure, although she was always letter-perfect in her lines, what was going to happen. She had you just a little bit off-guard, and also the director."

Actor Burgess Meredith on Margaret Sullavan's relationship with James Stewart: "She really treated Jim different to the way she treated other men . . . [b]ut with Jim she was simply affectionate without being predatory. She seemed to want to protect him, to nurture him, to help him become all he could be."

Although James Stewart was notorious for his womanizing ways, most people felt the reason he didn't marry until he was forty-one was his unrequited love for Margaret Sullavan. When Stewart finally married in 1949, few people could miss the resemblance between his wife, former model Gloria McLean, and Sullavan.

Gloria Stewart on her husband's relationship with Margaret Sullavan: "I always knew he was madly in love with Margaret Sullavan, and she was with him. But she was more in love with her career."

THE SHOP AROUND THE CORNER, 1940

Hers

BORN
Margaret Brooke
Sullavan Hancock
May 16, 1911
Norfolk, Virginia

DIED
January 1, 1960
New Haven, Connecticut,
of suicide by drug overdose

STAR SIGN
Taurus

HEIGHT
5'2½"

HUSBANDS AND CHILDREN
Actor Henry Fonda
(1931–1932, divorced)

Director William Wyler
(1934–1936, divorced)

Agent Leland Hayward
(1936–1947, divorced)
daughters, Brooke and Bridget
son, William Leland

British industrialist
Kenneth Wagg
(1950–1960, her death)

ESSENTIAL**TEAM-UPS**

NEXT TIME WE LOVE (1936, Universal)
James Stewart and Margaret Sullavan were so credible as a married couple
torn apart by conflicting careers that few fans noticed how utterly selfish the
characters were.

THE SHOPWORN ANGEL (1938, Universal)
Stewart emerged as a romantic star after Sullavan requested he be cast as the
innocent Texan soldier who wins the heart of a brittle, sophisticated stage star.

THE SHOP AROUND THE CORNER (1940, Universal)
This tale of dueling coworkers who don't realize that each is the other's secret
romantic pen pal may have failed in its initial run, but later generations have
acclaimed it as one of Hollywood's greatest love stories.

THE MORTAL STORM (1940, Universal)
In their last film together, Sullavan and Stewart seek love and security when an
unnamed dictatorship takes over their unidentified European homeland.

They were the screen team for the swinging 1960s, living so large that the headlines about their private lives often eclipsed their eleven films together.

ELIZABETH **TAYLOR**
RICHARD **BURTON**

If Elizabeth Taylor and Richard Burton had left their families for each other in the 1940s, it would have meant career suicide. But by 1963, social mores had loosened so much that instead it made them international stars. After years of postwar austerity, audiences around the world were ready for fun without shame, and that's just what they saw in the couple, who raised stardom to unprecedented levels of glamour and excitement. Whether they were signing film contracts for astronomical sums or spending that money on jewelry, yachts, and whatever else struck their fancy, everything they did was news. And that notoriety sold a lot of movie tickets, often for some very bad films. Their one genuine classic, *Who's Afraid of Virginia Woolf?* (1966), was so unconventional it might not have done as well at the box office without a pair of household names above the title. Good or bad, the fans usually got their money's worth, with love scenes that sizzled with Burton and Taylor's offscreen passion for each other. Taylor connected better with Burton than she had with any other leading man since Montgomery Clift. And Burton was able to show a gentler side to his persona when teamed with his diminutive wife. Publicity and onscreen teamwork turned them into fantasy stand-ins for a world without their talents or money. Over time, however, they couldn't overcome stinkers like *Boom!* (1968) and *Hammersmith Is Out* (1972). Nor could they do much to breathe life into their first film together, 20th Century Fox's notorious *Cleopatra* (1963). The studio paid Taylor the highest salary any actor had ever made for one film (with overtime, she ended up getting about $7 million). It wanted Burton as Antony, but the star was tied up doing *Camelot* on Broadway, so the picture started filming in London in 1960 with Stephen Boyd. When the cold British winter brought on a bout of pneumonia that almost killed Taylor, Boyd had to leave for another film, leaving the role open for the now-available Burton. Before long, director Joseph L. Mankiewicz was having trouble getting the stars to stop their love scenes after he had cried, "Cut." When Taylor admitted to being in love with Burton, her husband, Eddie Fisher, left the location. Burton's wife wasn't far behind, triggering an uproar in the press. That coverage encouraged British producer Anatole de Grunwald to team them as an unhappily married wealthy couple in *The V.I.P.s* (1963). As they hashed through their failed marriage onscreen, fans for the first time wondered if they weren't simply playing themselves. That speculation increased with the screen adaptation of Edward Albee's *Who's Afraid of Virginia Woolf?* But the film was also their greatest triumph. Taylor put on weight and grayed her hair to play the slatternly academic wife, while Burton hid his usually powerful presence under a worn cardigan as they brought Albee's searing truths about love and marriage to life. For a while, critics thought their partnership might turn out for the best after all. But it wasn't to be. Their high-profile lifestyle began taking its toll, and supporting it made them accept the offers carrying the biggest pay rather than the best scripts. They looked tired and bored in *The Comedians* (1967), and sank under the weight of one of Tennessee Williams's worst plays in *Boom!* Their only critical and box-office success after *Virginia Woolf* was *Anne of the Thousand Days* (1969), in which Taylor played a masked courtesan with no lines. The effectiveness of Burton's performance as Henry VIII made reviewers all the more aware of the shoddiness of so much of his work with Taylor. After more pans for the ABC miniseries *Divorce His/Divorce Hers* (1973), they announced a trial separation. Although they would remarry briefly in 1975, they would never make another film together. They did, however, reteam on stage for a 1983 tour of Noel Coward's *Private Lives*, a play about a divorced couple who can't escape their attraction to each other. Taylor was a staunch advocate whenever Burton was nominated for the Oscar and issued blistering statements about the Academy every time he lost (with seven nominations, he is second only to Peter O'Toole in most nominations without a win). When Burton died in 1984, Taylor was devastated. Coverage of his passing made more mention of Taylor than his widow, marking the last time the two would share headlines. Even with two divorces and a mixed filmography behind them, the world still thought of Liz and Dick as the most glamorous couple of their day.

CIRCA 1965

176

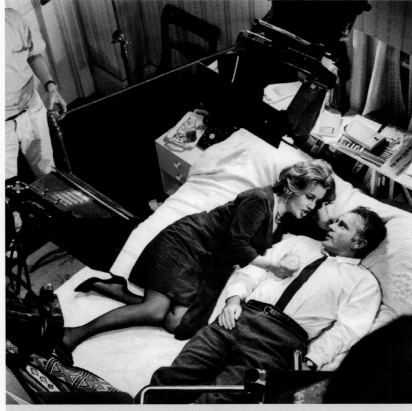

ON THE SET OF *WHO'S AFRAID OF VIRGINIA WOOLF?*, 1966

BEHIND THE SCENES

AT THE HEIGHT OF THE SCANDAL OVER THE RICHARD BURTON–ELIZABETH TAYLOR ROMANCE, LAURENCE OLIVIER SENT BURTON A TELEGRAM READING, "MAKE UP YOUR MIND, DEAR HEART. DO YOU WANT TO BE A GREAT ACTOR OR A HOUSEHOLD WORD?" BURTON ANSWERED WITH ONE WORD: "BOTH."

WANTING TO SUPPORT THE DRAMA SOCIETY OF HIS ALMA MATER, OXFORD UNIVERSITY, RICHARD BURTON TOOK THE HELM AS DIRECTOR FOR THE 1967 FILM VERSION OF THE CLASSIC PLAY *DOCTOR FAUSTUS*. HE AND ELIZABETH TAYLOR ALSO APPEARED IN THE FILM, WORKING FOR SCALE, ABOUT $45 A WEEK. DESPITE SUCH MEAGER EARNINGS AND MISSING OUT ON AN ESTIMATED $2 MILLION IN LOST FILM WORK DURING THIS TIME, BURTON AND TAYLOR WERE MORE THAN HAPPY TO SUPPORT A CAUSE THAT WAS DEAR TO THEM. ALL PROFITS WERE EARMARKED FOR THE SCHOOL'S DRAMA PROGRAM.

IN 1969, RICHARD BURTON OUTBID ARISTOTLE ONASSIS FOR ONE OF THE WORLD'S LARGEST DIAMONDS. THE 244-CARAT SOUTH AFRICAN STONE WAS A GIFT FOR ELIZABETH TAYLOR. OTHER GIFTS FROM BURTON TO TAYLOR INCLUDED THE KRUPP DIAMOND, THE DUCHESS OF WINDSOR DIAMOND BROOCH, THE GRAND DUCHESS OF RUSSIA EMERALDS, AND THE LA PEREGRINA PEARL.

His

BORN
Richard Walter Jenkins
November 10, 1925
Pontrhydyfen, Wales

DIED
August 5, 1984
Céligny, Geneva, Switzerland,
of a cerebral hemorrhage

STAR SIGN
Scorpio

HEIGHT
5'10"

WIVES AND CHILDREN
Actress Sybil Williams
(1949–1963, divorced)
daughters, Kate and Jessica

Actress Elizabeth Taylor
(1964–1974 and 1975–1976,
divorced both times)
adopted daughter, Maria

Susan Hunt
(1976–1982, divorced)

Script girl Sally Hay
(1983–1984, his death)

❋

KEY QUOTE

**From *Who's Afraid
of Virginia Woolf?*
(1966)**

Taylor
I'm going to finish
you before I'm through
with you.

Burton
I warned you not to
go too far.

Taylor
I'm just beginning.

❋

OFFSCREEN**RELATIONSHIP**

Elizabeth Taylor first met Richard Burton in 1951 at a party given by actors Stewart Granger and Jean Simmons. She would later say, "My first impression was that he was rather full of himself. He never stopped talking, and I had given him the cold fish-eye." Burton was perturbed that she spent most of the evening reading but wrote in his diary, "Her breasts were apocalyptic, they would topple empires down before they withered. Indeed, her body was a miracle of construction and the work of an engineer of greatness."

On the first day they worked together, Richard Burton was suffering from a hangover. Elizabeth Taylor had to help him hold his coffee cup steady. When he blew his lines, it brought out her maternal instincts. Within two days, according to crewmembers, they had started their affair.

When she fell in love with Richard Burton, Elizabeth Taylor finally took off her late husband Mike Todd's wedding ring. She had worn it even while married to Eddie Fisher.

Richard Burton on his relationship with Elizabeth Taylor: "Our love is so furious that we burn each other out."

Although the press consistently referred to them as "Liz and Dick", they preferred to be called Elizabeth and Richard.

In the ten years of their marriage, Richard Burton and Elizabeth Taylor earned $88 million and spent $65 million. Besides the jewelry, their biggest purchases included a luxury yacht costing $165,000, a private jet at $1 million, and a $500,000 helicopter.

CLEOPATRA, 1963

Hers

BORN
Elizabeth Rosemond Taylor
February 27, 1932
London, England

STAR SIGN
Pisces

HEIGHT
5'4"

HUSBANDS AND CHILDREN
Hotel heir Conrad "Nicky"
Hilton Jr. (1950–1951, divorced)

Actor Michael Wilding
(1952–1957, divorced)
sons, Christopher and Michael Jr.

Entrepreneur Michael Todd
(1957–1958, his death)
daughter, Liza

Crooner Eddie Fisher
(1959–1964, divorced)

Actor Richard Burton
(1964–1974 and 1975–76,
divorced both times)
adopted daughter, Maria

Senator John W. Warner
(1976–1982, divorced)

Construction worker
Larry Fortensky
(1991–1996, divorced)

ESSENTIAL**TEAM-UPS**

CLEOPATRA (1963, 20th Century Fox)
The scandalous queen of Egypt couldn't hold a candle to the uproar generated when the married Elizabeth Taylor and Richard Burton embarked on an affair while playing one of history's greatest romantic teams.

THE V.I.P.S (1963, 20th Century Fox)
Runaway wife Taylor has to confront Burton, the wealthy husband she's trying to leave, when she's fogged in at Heathrow Airport in this variation on *Grand Hotel*.

THE SANDPIPER (1965, 20th Century Fox)
Married Episcopal priest Burton falls for bohemian artist Taylor in a romance distinguished more by its dazzling photography of the Big Sur region and the Oscar–winning song "The Shadow of Your Smile" than by the stars' performances.

WHO'S AFRAID OF VIRGINIA WOOLF? (1966, Warner Bros)
Burton and Taylor show just how good they could be as they play a fading academic and his slatternly wife out for a night of fun and games in the film adaptation of Edward Albee's acclaimed play.

BOOM! (1968, Universal)
Taylor was too young for the role of a dying millionairess, and Burton is miscast as the charismatic poet who serves as her angel of death, yet the film is almost compulsively watchable.

Neither tragedy nor scandal could upstage two of Hollywood's biggest stars in what would be their only onscreen encounter.

ELIZABETH **TAYLOR**
PAUL **NEWMAN**
IN *Cat on a Hot Tin Roof*

When Elizabeth Taylor proclaimed to Paul Newman in *Cat on a Hot Tin Roof*, (1958) "Maggie the Cat is alive," it marked the first time onscreen that either actor had demonstrated the magnetism that would make them both reigning sex symbols for decades. The plot was one of Hollywood's most controversial to date: For 108 minutes, Taylor's Maggie tries to get her husband (Newman's Brick) to make love to her. There were deeper issues under the surface—the fight to inherit the family estate, the clash between truth and mendacity, and Brick's stunted emotional growth among them— but what pulled fans into seats were the images of Taylor in a slip, curled up on one of history's most provocative brass beds, while a pajama-clad Newman looked on with disdain. The combination of her passionate advances and his smoldering observations made for electrifying entertainment. That there was any inspiration left in Tennessee Williams' Pulitzer Prize–winning play was a testament to the strength of his characterization skills and the cast's talents. From the show's Broadway premiere in 1955, it had seemed a natural for the movies, but also a challenge, due to the subject matter. The central issue, Brick's apprehension about his feelings for his late friend, Skipper, was distinctly verboten under the industry's Production Code. George Cukor had originally been slated to direct but withdrew for fear that censors would cut the guts out of the story. His replacement, Richard Brooks, got the screenplay approved with surprisingly few changes. The sexual implications were still intact, and the combination of scandalous material and MGM's solid production values made the film a critical and box-office winner. In fact, the film would bring Newman his first Oscar nomination and Taylor her second. Both stars would have return dates with author Williams—Newman in *Sweet Bird of Youth* (1962), also directed by Brooks; and Taylor in *Suddenly, Last Summer* (1959), the disastrous *Boom!* (1968), and a television version of *Sweet Bird of Youth* (1989). But none of them packed quite the punch of their first encounter with his material. A rematch for the stars would have seemed logical, but their careers developed in decidedly different directions, particularly after Taylor met Richard Burton and focused most of her efforts on projects with him. Her chemistry with Newman in *Cat on a Hot Tin Roof*, however, has persisted and continues to fascinate generations of moviegoers.

BORN
Paul Leonard Newman
January 26, 1925
Shaker Heights, Ohio

STAR SIGN
Aquarius

HEIGHT
5'9"

WIVES AND CHILDREN
Actress Jackie Witte
(1949–1958, divorced)
son, Scott
daughters, Susan and
Stephanie

Actress Joanne Woodward
(1958–)
daughters, Elinor, Melissa,
and Claire

KEY QUOTE

Newman
I don't have to do
anything I don't
want to! Now, you keep
forgetting the
conditions on which
I agreed to stay on
living with you.

Taylor
I'm not living with you!
We occupy the same
cage, that's all.

OFFSCREEN**RELATIONSHIP**

Paul Newman on *Cat on a Hot Tin Roof*: "This was the first of my pictures, except for the one with Joanne [Woodward, his wife], that I didn't have to carry pretty much on my own. Before that, it had just worked out, somehow, that I'd never played with a star."

Paul Newman on working with Elizabeth Taylor: "She's not afraid to take chances in front of people. Usually stars become very protective of themselves and very self-indulgent, but she's got a lot of guts. She'd go ahead and explore and risk falling on her face."

During rehearsals for *Cat on a Hot Tin Roof*, Paul Newman was concerned that Elizabeth Taylor wasn't fully committed to the role and was giving him nothing to play off. When he spoke to director Richard Brooks about it, Brooks assured him that Taylor, who had grown up on movie sets, would be there once the cameras started rolling. Newman didn't really see it on the set, but when he looked at the rushes, he realized that Taylor's performance was all there onscreen.

Paul Newman was so supportive when Elizabeth Taylor's husband, producer Mike Todd, died in a plane crash during production that it actually motivated her to return to work sooner. She would later say, "Paul Newman is one of the sweetest men I know. He was so unbelievably supportive with his kind words and just being there for me. He helped me through an enormously difficult time in my life, and I will always be grateful."

CIRCA 1958

BEHINDTHESCENES

INITIALLY, MGM BOUGHT THE RIGHTS TO *CAT ON A HOT TIN ROOF* AS A VEHICLE FOR GRACE KELLY. WHEN SHE RETIRED FROM ACTING TO MARRY PRINCE RAINIER OF MONACO, THEY CONSIDERED CASTING LANA TURNER. ELIZABETH TAYLOR WAS DESPERATE TO PLAY THE ROLE, AND HER HUSBAND, PRODUCER MIKE TODD, FINALLY WON IT FOR HER BY AGREEING TO EXTEND HER MGM CONTRACT TO INCLUDE ONE MORE FILM AFTER *CAT*. THIS RESULTED IN HER MAKING *BUTTERFIELD 8* (1960).

MGM AT FIRST TRIED TO CAST MONTGOMERY CLIFT AS BRICK. WHEN RICHARD BROOKS CAME ON BOARD AS DIRECTOR, HE WANTED BEN GAZZARA, WHO HAD PLAYED THE ROLE ON BROADWAY, BUT THE ACTOR TURNED HIM DOWN. MGM THEN PLANNED TO CAST JAMES DEAN BEFORE HE DIED. THEY ALSO CONSIDERED ELVIS PRESLEY FOR THE ROLE, BUT HIS MANAGER, COLONEL TOM PARKER, DECLINED. BY THAT POINT, BROOKS WAS CAMPAIGNING TO CAST PAUL NEWMAN, FEELING THAT THE ACTOR'S ABILITY TO LISTEN ACTIVELY WOULD HELP HIM PLAY THE CHARACTER, WHO WAS PASSIVE FOR MUCH OF THE FILM.

WHEN ELIZABETH TAYLOR'S HUSBAND, PRODUCER MIKE TODD, WAS KILLED IN A PLANE CRASH THREE WEEKS INTO PRODUCTION, THE COMPANY SHOT AROUND HER UNTIL SHE WAS READY TO RETURN TO WORK. FINALLY SHE FORCED HERSELF TO GO BACK, SAYING, "THE ONLY REASON I WANT TO DO IT IS BECAUSE OF MIKE. MIKE LIKED ME IN THIS PICTURE, AND I WANT TO FINISH IT FOR HIM."

They turned the battle of the sexes into high comedy, as the immovable male withstood the spirited attacks of the irresistible female.

SPENCER **TRACY**
KATHARINE **HEPBURN**

Their first meeting set the tone for their onscreen partnership. Running into Tracy with producer and director Joseph L. Mankiewicz, Hepburn looked him up and down and said, "I'm afraid I'm a bit tall for Mr. Tracy." "Don't worry," the producer shot back. "He'll cut you down to size." Indeed, that was the theme of many of their films together, with the stern, unflappable Tracy standing by as Hepburn flitted around him, until he found an opening to shoot her down with a word or a glance. He was the most masculine leading man she had ever had, and his manliness made her more appealing than she had been onscreen since her tomboy performance in *Little Women* (1933). In return, when Hepburn finally melted to his charms, she gave him a sex appeal he had never had before. Their first picture together, *Woman of the Year* (1942), crackles with sexual tension, reflecting their growing attraction to each other. Later films, culminating with *Guess Who's Coming to Dinner* (1967), show an abiding affection few screen teams displayed so persuasively. When writer Garson Kanin was framing the story for *Woman of the Year* in 1941, he had both Hepburn and Tracy in mind for the leading roles. At first Tracy wasn't available, and studio head Louis B. Mayer suggested casting Clark Gable or Water Pidgeon. Then luck stepped in. Tracy's production of *The Yearling* shut down after weeks of disastrous location work in the Florida Everglades, freeing him up to play the role that had been written for him. From their first scene together, the pair were an electric combination, which helped make the film a big hit. Mayer began looking for another property to pair them on, though the only films actually written for them came from outside the MGM writers' wing, when married friends Kanin and Ruth Gordon wrote *Adam's Rib* (1949) and *Pat and Mike* (1952). Through three and a half decades, Tracy and Hepburn built an offscreen relationship that was unique in its tastefulness. Although he had been unfaithful to his wife, Louise, for years, the Catholic-raised Tracy hesitated to ask for a divorce. He also realized the importance of their marriage to Louise's charity work for the deaf (their son, John, was hearing-impaired). Thus, he and Hepburn never appeared together in public or even shared the same living quarters. The press rarely referred to their relationship directly, joining in a gentlemen's agreement to honor the stars' discretion. This may have been encouraged by MGM executives, who realized early on that Hepburn was helping Tracy deal with his drinking. When he went off on a bender, she would often spend the night on the floor outside his hotel room, ready to step in if needed. Beyond that, Hepburn introduced Tracy to her sophisticated friends and got him to take up painting, which she had used as an escape valve since her early days in Hollywood. For his part, Tracy helped Hepburn smooth her rough edges and got her to adopt a less confrontational public image. "Kate the Great," the Hepburn fans grew to love in later years, was really born during their relationship. They weren't together nonstop. Hepburn returned to the stage when she felt she could. During the '50s, their work kept them apart so often that some in the industry thought the relationship was over. But when Tracy's health started to fail and his career seemed to be in trouble, Hepburn returned to care for him, eventually taking five years off from acting to nurse him through a series of illnesses. She even put her salary up as collateral when his health problems made *Guess Who's Coming to Dinner* uninsurable. When Tracy died, Hepburn remained true to the clandestine nature of their relationship. She chose not to attend the funeral but visited the funeral home in the morning and helped load Tracy's coffin onto the hearse. She drove behind it until they came within sight of the church, then turned around and went home. Hepburn would not speak publicly of their relationship until after Tracy's widow died in 1983. By then, of course, it had become a part of Hollywood folklore. Actor Michael Moriarty, Hepburn's costar in a television production of *The Glass Menagerie* (1973), said, "Here's what's most important about Katharine Hepburn: not her career and not her brilliance and not her talent—it was her profound, unconditional love for Spencer Tracy. That was her greatest achievement. She and Spencer were one of the greatest love affairs in the history of America."

ON THE SET OF *STATE OF THE UNION*, 1948

GUESS WHO'S COMING TO DINNER, 1967

BEHINDTHESCENES

WOMAN OF THE YEAR (1942) IS THE ONLY SPENCER TRACY–KATHARINE HEPBURN FILM IN WHICH THEY KISS ROMANTICALLY. IN FACT, HEPBURN SPENDS MORE TIME KISSING IN THE PICTURE THAN IN ALL OF HER EARLIER MOVIES COMBINED. IN THEIR LATER PICTURES, HOWEVER, THEY AVOIDED PHYSICALLY ROMANTIC SCENES, EITHER SUGGESTING THAT IT ALL HAPPENED OFF-CAMERA OR MAKING PHYSICAL CONTACT IN MORE FRIENDLY, LESS ROMANTIC WAYS.

SPENCER TRACY SUGGESTED KATHARINE HEPBURN AS A LAST-MINUTE SUBSTITUTE FOR THE LEAD IN *STATE OF THE UNION* (1948) AFTER CLAUDETTE COLBERT BACKED OUT, TELLING DIRECTOR FRANK CAPRA, "KATE ISN'T HAMMING IT UP RIGHT NOW. ASK HER."

KATHARINE HEPBURN PREFERRED TO WORK ON A CLOSED SET, BUT WHENEVER WORD SPREAD THAT SHE AND SPENCER TRACY WERE SHOOTING A SCENE, ANY ACTORS AT MGM WHO WERE FREE WOULD SNEAK ONTO THE SOUNDSTAGE TO WATCH THEM.

WHEN NO INSURANCE COMPANY WOULD COVER THE AILING SPENCER TRACY DURING THE FILMING OF *GUESS WHO'S COMING TO DINNER*, KATHARINE HEPBURN AND PRODUCER–DIRECTOR STANLEY KRAMER PUT UP THEIR FEES FOR THE FILM AS COLLATERAL IN CASE HE SHOULD BECOME TOO ILL TO FINISH THE PICTURE. AFTER COMPLETING WORK ON THE FILM, HEPBURN ATTENDED THE WRAP PARTY, SOMETHING SHE RARELY DID, SO SHE COULD PERSONALLY THANK THE CREW FOR EVERYTHING THEY HAD DONE TO HELP TRACY GET THROUGH THE PICTURE.

BORN
Spencer Bonaventure Tracy
April 5, 1900
Milwaukee, Wisconsin

DIED
June 10, 1967
Beverly Hills, California,
of a heart attack

STAR SIGN
Aries

HEIGHT
5'10½"

WIFE AND CHILDREN
Actress Louise Treadwell
(1923–1967, his death)
son, John
daughter, Louise "Susie"

OFFSCREEN**RELATIONSHIP**

Katharine Hepburn on Spencer Tracy: "His quality is clear and direct. Ask a question—get an answer. No pause—no fancy thinking—a simple answer. He speaks. He listens. He is not wordy. He is not overemotional. He is simple and totally honest. He makes you believe what he is saying."

Spencer Tracy on acting with Katharine Hepburn: "Well, we just got used to working together. She butts in, and I don't mind, and I pick it up when she leaves off. We just got used to working together, that's all."

In her memoirs, Katharine Hepburn wrote that throughout her relationship with Spencer Tracy, she adapted to his tastes and wishes: "If he didn't like this or that, I changed this and that. They might be qualities which I personally valued. It did not matter. I changed them."

On their first day working together on *Woman of the Year*, Katharine Hepburn was so nervous that she knocked over a glass of water while filming a barroom scene. Instead of stopping the scene, however, Spencer Tracy simply handed her his pocket handkerchief and kept saying his lines. Knowing she was being tested, Hepburn continued with the scene while sopping up the water. When it dripped through to the floor, she simply went under the table and kept cleaning. That was the moment that sealed their rapport as performers.

A few days after Spencer Tracy's death, Katharine Hepburn called his widow, Louise, to offer her friendship and any help she might need adjusting to his passing. Mrs. Tracy's response was, "I thought you were only a rumor."

ADAM'S RIB, 1947

Hers

BORN
Katharine Houghton Hepburn
May 12, 1907
Hartford, Connecticut

DIED
June 29, 2003
Old Saybrook, Connecticut,
of natural causes

STAR SIGN
Taurus

HEIGHT
5'7"

HUSBAND
Businessman
Ludlow Ogden Smith
(1928–1934, divorced)

ESSENTIAL**TEAM-UPS**

WOMAN OF THE YEAR (1942, MGM)
In their first teaming, as a sportswriter and the high-handed political columnist he tames comically, Spencer Tracy and Katharine Hepburn set the tone for their best films together.

ADAM'S RIB (1949, MGM)
Tracy and Hepburn star as married lawyers on opposite sides of a women's-rights case in what many consider their finest film together, taken from an original screenplay written for them by friends Ruth Gordon and Garson Kanin.

PAT AND MIKE (1952, MGM)
Sports are the battleground, with Hepburn as a college professor who turns pro athlete under Tracy's management in another movie written for them by Gordon and Kanin.

DESK SET (1957, MGM)
Hepburn is a research librarian concerned about being replaced by a computer, the recommendation of efficiency expert Tracy in this light comedy, their first color film.

GUESS WHO'S COMING TO DINNER (1967, Columbia Pictures)
For their last film together, Tracy and Hepburn tackled racism as aging liberals whose political views are challenged when their daughter announces her interracial marriage.

KEY QUOTE
From *Adam's Rib* (1949)

Hepburn
No difference between
the sexes. None.
Men, women. The same.

Tracy
They are, huh?

Hepburn
Well, maybe there *is*
a difference. But it's a
little difference.

Tracy
Yeah. Well, as the
French say.

Hepburn
How do they say?

Tracy
Vive la différence!

Hepburn
Which means?

Tracy
Which means: Hurray for
that little difference!

Ads proclaimed "Their Love Was a Flame That Destroyed," a clear reflection of the obsessive and dangerous affair shared onscreen by the pair.

LANA **TURNER**
JOHN **GARFIELD**
IN *The Postman Always Rings Twice*

They shared one of the hottest first meetings in screen history—while retrieving Lana Turner's dropped lipstick, John Garfield looks up from floor level and takes her in, from her white, open-toed heels all the way to her dazzling white turban. From that point, he and the audience were hooked. The 1946 adaptation of James M. Cain's *The Postman Always Rings Twice* raised the heat and raised the bar for onscreen sexuality, thanks largely to the presence of Garfield and Turner. Their characters' romance was like an addiction. Even though she was married to his benefactor (Cecil Kellaway), Garfield couldn't keep his hands off her. Despite the high level of passion onscreen and off, the film never breached standards of good taste, an accomplishment that has to be credited to its stars and director Tay Garnett. It was Garnett who decided to dress Turner entirely in white, providing an image of purity to balance her character's transgressions. Garfield had the skill and the creative intuition to find the vulnerable side of his character, making his fall from grace sympathetically human. In this and other ways, Production Code censorship actually helped the film. MGM had bought the property in 1934, but the Production Code Administration voiced so many objections to the material they let it languish in their story files for over a decade. Finally, with the success of *Double Indemnity* (1944)—another Cain adaptation from a novel nobody thought would get past the censors—they dusted off *The Postman Always Rings Twice* as a vehicle for Turner and came up with a version that could pass the censors. At first, Turner said "No," feeling such an unpleasant character would hurt her fan standing. Studio head Louis B. Mayer convinced her she needed the role to graduate from glamour girl to real actress. MGM had initially offered Garfield the male lead in *The Harvey Girls* (1946), which would have given him the chance to appear in Technicolor and work with Judy Garland, but he turned them down. He was eager to work at the studio, however, and when Joel McCrea decided he didn't want to play drifter Frank Chambers in *The Postman Always Rings Twice*, Garfield was only too happy to become half of one of the screen's hottest couples. Making the passion even stronger was the attraction the stars shared offscreen. It was lust at first sight when they met, which may account for their passionate love scenes. Amazingly, the stars' onscreen sizzle fizzled once the cameras stopped turning. But they remained friends for life and created an erotic charge onscreen that still leaves audiences breathless.

BORN
Jacob Julius Garfinkle
March 4, 1913
New York, New York

DIED
May 21, 1952
New York, New York,
of coronary thrombosis

STAR SIGN
Pisces

HEIGHT
5'7"

WIFE AND CHILDREN
Actress Roberta Siedman
(1935–1952, his death)
daughters, Katharine
and Julie
son, David

KEY QUOTE

Garfield
I've been waiting a long
time for that kiss.

Turner
When we get home,
Frank, then there'll
be kisses, kisses
with dreams in them.
Kisses that come from
life, not death.

OFFSCREEN**RELATIONSHIP**

Lana Turner on working with John Garfield: "He was shy, vibrant, and intelligent. And so ahead of his time. He had terrific magnetism. The lines bounced back and forth between us. It kept a girl on her toes."

Director Tay Garnett on the Turner–Garfield partnership: "There was magic between them. I don't know if they had something going on the side, but sometimes you root for it. John had his fair share of girls, but he had a bad heart, and that might have frightened Lana off. John teased her about sex, which tends to make me believe nothing happened. They sizzled on the screen, though."

Lana Turner always called John Garfield her favorite leading man and Cora her best part, while he considered *The Postman Always Rings Twice* his favorite movie.

John Garfield almost gave up his part in *The Postman Always Rings Twice* in favor of another role: sailor in the U.S. Navy. After years of trying to get into the military to do his duty during World War II, he finally got his orders to report to the Naval induction center just before filming was to start. To his disappointment, he was turned down because of his age. Toward the end of the war, the military wasn't accepting anybody over 30, particularly if, like Garfield, he had a family to support.

CIRCA 1946

BEHIND THE SCENES

TO GET *THE POSTMAN ALWAYS RINGS TWICE* PAST THE PRODUCTION CODE
ADMINISTRATION, PRODUCER CAREY WILSON HAD TO SOFTEN THE
SUGGESTION THAT FRANK AND CORA BECAME LOVERS AS SOON AS THEY MET.
THE MORE SUBTLE APPROACH MADE IT SEEM THAT THE TWO FELL IN LOVE
BEFORE MAKING LOVE, THUS DEEPENING THE SENSE OF TRAGEDY.

JAMES M. CAIN, THE AUTHOR OF *THE POSTMAN ALWAYS RINGS TWICE*, TOOK
LANA TURNER TO LUNCH AND TOLD HER HE HAD HOPED SHE WOULD PLAY
CORA ONE DAY.

The macho man met his match when he teamed with this fiery redhead for five films that were as boisterous as they were romantic.

JOHN **WAYNE**
MAUREEN **O'HARA**

Near the end of *The Quiet Man* (1952), John Wayne, as the boxer Sean Thornton, tracks his rebellious wife to the railroad station and drags her back to their home. Had almost any other actress been cast in the role, the forced return would have been a one-sided scene. With Maureen O'Hara in the role, however, it was a battle of giants, as she scratched, kicked, and dragged against him. That was exactly what made the Wayne–O'Hara pairing so distinctive. He may have been one of the screen's toughest stars, but she was every inch his equal in fighting, loving, drinking, and, at least offscreen, cussing. In four of their five films together, John Wayne and Maureen O'Hara played estranged married couples fighting their way back to each other after years of acrimony, and in *The Quiet Man*, the marriage almost ended as soon as it began. But their reunion in each film was inevitable simply because they were too magnetic a team not to be together. Unlike many leading couples, Wayne and O'Hara were already friends before they made their first film together. They had a mutual friend in director John Ford and had both attended numerous parties at his home and on his yacht. Casting O'Hara opposite Wayne was a form of wish fulfillment for Ford. Friends observed that she seemed to embody many qualities that the director idealized in a woman, and he may even have had a crush on her. The team was essential to Ford's dream project, a film version of the short story "The Quiet Man," whose screen rights he had bought for $10 back in 1933. Ford started assembling the film's cast in 1944, making handshake agreements with Wayne and O'Hara to star in it if it were ever made. After several studios turned the picture down, Wayne got Herbert J. Yates, head of Republic Pictures, to sign a multifilm deal with Ford's Argosy Pictures. Republic specialized in B movies, and Yates was hoping that Ford would move the studio into the big time. Fearing *The Quiet Man* wouldn't be a commercial hit, however, Yates only agreed to make the film if Ford, Wayne, and O'Hara would first deliver a Western. As a result, Ford created *Rio Grande* (1950), the third picture in his Cavalry Trilogy, adapted from the stories of James Warner Bellah. With O'Hara on hand as Wayne's estranged wife, the film brought a new depth to Ford's work that would continue through his films with the team. *Rio Grande* was a financial success, clearing the way for Ford's long-awaited *The Quiet Man*. Once again, Wayne and O'Hara proved themselves as a memorable screen team as newlyweds torn apart by his refusal to fight her brother. The authentic nature of their screen relationship continued with *The Wings of Eagles* (1957), in which they played out the emotionally frustrated marriage of Ford's friend and sometime screenwriter Frank "Spig" Wead. It was O'Hara's last film with Ford, but even without the mentor who had helped shape their onscreen dynamic, she and Wayne remained a potent pair. When he produced *McLintock!* (1963), a Western partly based on Shakespeare's *The Taming of the Shrew*, she was the most obvious choice to play his headstrong wife. Eight years later, Wayne wanted to ensure the box-office success of *Big Jake* (1971), so he turned to O'Hara to play his estranged wife again. The film's success made him the top U.S. box-office star for the fourth and final time, while providing a fitting finale for the team's work together. During the Duke's final years, his relationship with O'Hara was more peaceful than anything they ever portrayed onscreen. In a way, it might have been the relationship their characters might have had if their films had allowed them to mellow into old age. As with so many great screen teams, fans have frequently wondered why the two never got together offscreen. O'Hara always claimed that Wayne knew better than to make a pass at her: "I did judo, I fenced, I played soccer, football. I would've hauled off and hit him." What more could you expect from the woman Wayne dubbed "the greatest guy I ever knew."

McLINTOCK!, 1963

THE QUIET MAN, 1952

BEHINDTHESCENES

IN THE SCENE IN WHICH MAUREEN O'HARA'S CHARACTER LOCKS HER HUSBAND OUT OF THEIR BEDROOM ON THEIR WEDDING NIGHT IN *THE QUIET MAN*, THE ORIGINAL SCRIPT CALLED FOR HIM TO PUT ON HIS BOXING GLOVES WITH AN AIR OF SELF-PITY. JOHN WAYNE DIDN'T THINK THAT WAS RIGHT FOR THE CHARACTER AND, AFTER LENGTHY ARGUMENTS WITH DIRECTOR JOHN FORD, FINALLY ENDED THE SCENE BY KICKING IN THE BEDROOM DOOR. THE SCENE IS NOW CONSIDERED ONE OF THE FILM'S HIGHLIGHTS.

ANGERED BY JOHN WAYNE AND DIRECTOR JOHN FORD'S TEASING ON THE SET, MAUREEN O'HARA REALLY TRIED TO KNOCK THE DUKE OUT WHILE FILMING A FIGHT SCENE FOR *THE QUIET MAN*. WAYNE CAUGHT THE PUNCH, HOWEVER, ACCIDENTALLY BREAKING HER WRIST. SINCE THE INCIDENT OCCURRED EARLY IN THE FILMING, SHE COULDN'T HAVE THE FRACTURE SET. EARLY ON, SHE HID THE SWOLLEN HAND IN THE FOLDS OF HER SKIRT.

DURING THE FILMING OF *MCLINTOCK!* (1963), THE STUNTMEN REFUSED TO SLIDE INTO THE MUD PIT FOR THE FILM'S CLIMACTIC FIGHT SCENE UNLESS THEY GOT HAZARD PAY. THE FIRST MAN WHO HAD TRIED THE STUNT HAD FALLEN IN WRONG AND NEEDED FIFTEEN STITCHES. JOHN WAYNE ANNOUNCED THAT HE AND MAUREEN O'HARA WOULD DO IT FIRST. AFTER CHECKING WITH ONE OF THE STUNTMEN ABOUT HOW TO DO IT RIGHT, SHE NOT ONLY AGREED BUT ALSO JUMPED IN FIRST.

AT THE END OF *THE QUIET MAN*, MAUREEN O'HARA WHISPERS SOMETHING IN JOHN WAYNE'S EAR THAT SHOCKS HIM. DIRECTOR JOHN FORD TOLD HER IN SECRET WHAT TO WHISPER SO THAT WAYNE'S REACTION WOULD BE GENUINE. SHE HAS NEVER REVEALED WHAT SHE UTTERED TO WAYNE.

WHILE FILMING ONE SCENE IN *MCLINTOCK!*, JOHN WAYNE THOUGHT MAUREEN O'HARA WAS HOLDING BACK TO SHARE FOCUS WITH HIM. IN HIS OPINION, IT WAS MEANT TO BE HER SCENE, SO HE TOLD HER, "IT'S YOUR SCENE. STEAL IT," THEN ADDED UNDER HIS BREATH, "IF YOU CAN."

His

BORN
Marion Michael Morrison
May 26, 1907
Winterset, Iowa

DIED
June 11, 1979
Los Angeles, California,
of lung and stomach cancer

STAR SIGN
Gemini

HEIGHT
6'4½"

WIVES AND CHILDREN
Socialite Josephine Saenz
(1933–1945, divorced)
sons, Michael and Patrick
daughters, Antonia Maria
and Melinda Ann

Singer–dancer
Esperanza "Chata" Bauer
(1946–1953, divorced)

Actress Pilar Pallete
(1954–1979, his death)
daughters, Aissa and Marisa
son, John Ethan

OFFSCREEN **RELATIONSHIP**

Maureen O'Hara on working with John Wayne: "So many people think that there was a great romance between Duke and me. There wasn't. We had tremendous respect and love for one another and knew that we were good for each other on the screen."

John Wayne nicknamed Maureen O'Hara "Big Red" and "Herself."

John Wayne was a frequent visitor at the home Maureen O'Hara shared with her third husband, General Charles Blair, in the Virgin Islands. She named the wing in which he stayed the John Wayne Wing.

When word of John Wayne's terminal cancer got out, Senator Barry Goldwater proposed the creation of a special gold medal in his honor. Speaking to the House subcommittee considering the measure, Maureen O'Hara said, "John Wayne is not just an actor. John Wayne is the United States of America." President Carter sent the Duke a letter informing him of the award for his seventy-second birthday, but he had passed on before the medal could be presented.

John Wayne's son and frequent producer, Michael, on the Wayne-O'Hara team: "I think that Maureen was as much woman as my father was man. She was very feminine and just illegally beautiful, but Maureen could be a steamroller. She was just as strong as any guy, although still a lady. But boy, she'd throw the overhand right if things weren't going right, just like a guy would."

Although director John Ford preferred to improvise while shooting fight scenes, Wayne and O'Hara met privately to rehearse every step of their battle in *The Quiet Man*, then pretended all the business painstakingly developed had been spontaneous the day of filming. When they were done, Ford said, "You see, when things aren't rehearsed and they're spontaneous how wonderful they are!"

198

BIG JAKE, 1971

Hers

BORN
Maureen FitzSimons
August 17, 1920
Ranelagh, Dublin, Ireland

STAR SIGN
Leo

HEIGHT
5'8"

HUSBANDS AND CHILD
Production assistant
George Hanley Brown
(1939–1940, annulled)

Writer-director Will Price
(1941–1953, divorced)
daughter, Bronwyn Brigid

U.S. General Charles F. Blair
(1968–1978, his death)

ESSENTIAL**TEAM-UPS**

RIO GRANDE (1950, Republic)
In the third film in director John Ford's Cavalry Trilogy, John Wayne and Maureen
O'Hara play an estranged couple brought together when their son winds up
fighting the Apaches.

THE QUIET MAN (1952, Republic)
Retired prizefighter Wayne tries to recapture his Irish roots, which include winning
the heart of the screen's ultimate colleen, O'Hara, in this rousing folk comedy
considered among Ford's best.

THE WINGS OF EAGLES (1957, MGM)
O'Hara's onscreen relationship with John Wayne, as the husband who keeps leaving
her for military obligations, provides a fittingly bittersweet finish to the team's
collaboration with Ford.

MCLINTOCK! (1963, Batjac Productions)
Rancher Wayne refuses to give up frontier life for city-bred wife O'Hara, fighting
to tame her and their daughter (Stefanie Powers) so they'll accept his rough-and-
tumble life.

BIG JAKE (1971, Batjac Productions)
Nobody but O'Hara could have played the estranged wife who tries to mend
fences with free-spirited westerner Wayne so he can help rescue their grandchild
from kidnappers.

KEY QUOTE

**From *The Quiet Man*
(1952)**

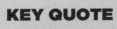

I have a fearful temper.
You might as well know
about it now instead
of findin' out about it
later. We Danahers are
a fightin' people.

I can think of a lot of
things I'd rather do to
one of the Danahers—
Miss Danaher.

They were the screen's first great swingers, turning a studio jungle into the Garden of Eden.

JOHNNY **WEISSMULLER**
MAUREEN **O'SULLIVAN**

Their first love scene in 1932's *Tarzan the Ape Man* was provocative even by pre-Code standards, touching a primal chord as civilization clashed with the primitive world. Johnny Weissmuller's famous Tarzan yell wasn't heard until twenty minutes into the picture, and it was another twenty minutes before he appeared onscreen. But by the time he carried Jane (Maureen O'Sullivan) to his treetop home, the audience was hooked. There had been other Tarzans and Janes on movie screens, and there would be more to come, but no other actors would be as closely identified with the roles as Weissmuller and O'Sullivan. His Olympic training as a swimmer gave him the athleticism of someone raised in the wild. O'Sullivan's cultured accent and fresh-faced look provided her character with a unique combination of sophistication and innocence. Their sincere performances together made the fantastic stories believable and the films top-box-office performers. Although later adaptations would turn the franchise into kiddie matinee fodder, the pair's Tarzan pictures were top-of-the-line product, with impressive sets, strong supporting casts, and an adult approach to the characters' relationship. While other studios might make jungle films on their soundstages, MGM went to Africa for their first big jungle picture, *Trader Horn* (1931). When the film became a hit, studio head Louis B. Mayer wanted a follow-up that would use the leftover location footage. So production chief Irving G. Thalberg optioned writer Edgar Rice Burroughs's characters for two films. They considered casting Clark Gable as Tarzan, but writer Cyril Hume, who was working on the script, noticed Weissmuller swimming at the Hollywood Athletic Club and suggested him for the role. Fox had been grooming O'Sullivan as the next Janet Gaynor, but then they let her go, which turned out to be a blessing when MGM signed her to play Jane two weeks later. To Thalberg's surprise, the role of Tarzan made Weissmuller a sex symbol. MGM carried that as far as possible in the series's second film, *Tarzan and His Mate* (1934), with Weissmuller and O'Sullivan wearing skimpy loincloths and even sharing a nude swim. Although hailed as the rare sequel that was better than the original, it inspired protests from censorship groups. Future films would put the stars in more conservative jungle wear, suggesting that Jane had developed improved tailoring skills. To build excitement, MGM spaced out the Tarzan films, which meant keeping Weissmuller under contract not to make other movies. He had started out with hopes of becoming the next Douglas Fairbanks, but MGM never gave him the chance, for fear of tainting his image. As a result, he and O'Sullivan were the only major screen team to play the same roles in all their films together. The studio didn't impose the same limits on her. In fact, she was making an average of three other movies for each Tarzan picture. Thanks to features like *David Copperfield* and *Anna Karenina* (both 1935), O'Sullivan soon became the studio's top ingenue. But she was also finding her association with the Tarzan films a drawback. Some producers wouldn't consider her for other roles, and she was tired of not always being taken seriously as an actress by her peers. Moreover, with Thalberg's death, MGM began cutting budgets on the Tarzan pictures and targeting a more juvenile market. After the third entry, *Tarzan Escapes* (1936), she tried to get out of the series. Originally, Jane was killed at the end of *Tarzan Finds a Son!* (1939), but negative fan reaction prompted MGM to re-edit the ending. Burroughs was so upset at her onscreen death that he refused to give MGM any more options on the material. Then, with the start of World War II, the international market, a significant portion of the films' revenues, dried up. After their sixth Tarzan picture, *Tarzan's New York Adventure* (1942), the last film permitted by Burroughs, MGM let the series go, thus ending Weissmuller's contract. He moved to RKO, which had picked up rights to the series. Originally O'Sullivan was slated to join him for *Tarzan Triumphs* (1943), but pregnancy kept her from signing. She left the series for good when she asked to be released from her MGM contract so she could nurse her husband, director John Farrow, through a bout of typhus. Ironically, RKO wrote Jane out of the next few Tarzan films, conveniently sending her character back to England, to nurse wounded soldiers during World War II. In 1945, Brenda Joyce took over the role. But neither she nor any of the subsequent Tarzans and Janes could match the appeal of MGM's king and queen of the jungle.

TARZAN ESCAPES, 1936

ON THE SET OF *TARZAN'S NEW YORK ADVENTURE*, 1942

BEHINDTHESCENES

OTHER ACTORS CONSIDERED TO PLAY TARZAN AT MGM WERE CHARLES BICKFORD, JOEL MCCREA, AND JOHNNY MACK BROWN.

JOHNNY WEISSMULLER ON HIS SCREEN TEST TO PLAY TARZAN: "I WENT TO THE BACK LOT AT MGM; THEY GAVE ME A G-STRING AND SAID, 'CAN YOU CLIMB A TREE? CAN YOU PICK UP A GIRL?' I COULD DO ALL THAT, AND I DID ALL MY OWN SWINGING, BECAUSE I HAD BEEN A YMCA CHAMPION ON THE RINGS."

MAUREEN O'SULLIVAN ON CHEETAH: "I COULD NEVER FEEL MUCH SYMPATHY FOR CHEETAH THE CHIMP—WHO WAS REALLY RATHER QUEER, I'M AFRAID. DIDN'T LIKE GIRLS AT ALL. BUT HE ADORED JOHNNY WEISSMULLER AND WAS TERRIBLY JEALOUS OF ME."

JANE'S TOPLESS SCENES IN *TARZAN AND HIS MATE* (1934) WERE CUT AFTER PROTESTS FROM RELIGIOUS GROUPS. THEY WERE DISCOVERED IN THE MGM VAULTS AND RESTORED IN THE LATE '90S. MAUREEN O'SULLIVAN DID NOT DO THE SCENES HERSELF; THEY WERE SUPPLIED BY OLYMPIC GOLD-MEDALIST SWIMMER JOSEPHINE MCKIM.

MAUREEN O'SULLIVAN ON SHOOTING *TARZAN AND HIS MATE*: "I NEVER WAS MORE CONSISTENTLY SICK AND MISERABLE IN MY LIFE . . . [I STOOD] KNEE-DEEP IN WHAT I AM SURE WAS MELTED ICE WATER AND THEN [HEARD] THE SOUNDMAN YELL, 'I CAN HEAR YOUR TEETH CHATTERING, MISS O'SULLIVAN, YOU'LL HAVE TO CONTROL THAT . . . , AND I WAS NEVER, NEVER, NEVER WITHOUT A BITE FROM ONE OF THOSE MONKEYS . . . EVEN LEAVING THE MONKEYS OUT OF IT, I WOULDN'T BE A NUDIST FOR ANYTHING."

MAUREEN O'SULLIVAN GOT CLOSE TO DIRECTOR JOHN FARROW WHILE HE WAS RESHOOTING *TARZAN ESCAPES* (1936), AND THEY WERE MARRIED SHORTLY AFTER.

His

BORN
Janos Weissmuller
June 2, 1904
Freidorf, Banat, Austria-Hungary
(now Romania)

DIED
January 20, 1984
Acapulco, Mexico,
after a series of strokes

STAR SIGN
Gemini

HEIGHT
6′3″

WIVES AND CHILDREN
Actress Bobbe Arnst
(1931–1933, divorced)

Actress Lupe Velez
(1933–1939, divorced)

Socialite Beryl Scott
(1939–1948, divorced)
son, John Scott
daughters, Wendy Ann and
Heidi Elizabeth

Golfer Allene Gates
(1948–1962, divorced)

Maria Brock Mandell Bauman
(1963–1984, his death)

OFFSCREEN**RELATIONSHIP**

Maureen O'Sullivan on working with Johnny Weissmuller:
"I think chemistry's a very strange thing. When you're
working with somebody, maybe you don't know it's there.
I guess Johnny and I must have had good chemistry. I
wasn't aware of it . . . I was very fond of Johnny. He was
a big kid, enjoyed having fun with people, and gave me a
birthday cake."

For publicity purposes, MGM tried to have Johnny
Weissmuller take Maureen O'Sullivan on a date. She was
so tired after a long day shooting that she fell asleep
before he picked her up.

Maureen O'Sullivan on the Tarzan films: "Everybody
cared about the Tarzan pictures, and we all gave our
best. They weren't quickies—it often took a year to make
one—but sometimes we were doing three at a time."

Johnny Weissmuller and Maureen O'Sullivan reunited for
cameo appearances as themselves in *The Phynx* (1970), a
comedy about a rock band.

TARZAN THE APE MAN, 1932

Hers

BORN
Maureen Paula O'Sullivan
May 17, 1911
Boyle, Roscommon, Ireland

DIED
June 23, 1998
Scottsdale, Arizona,
of a heart attack

STAR SIGN
Taurus

HEIGHT
5'3"

HUSBANDS AND CHILDREN
Writer–director John Farrow
(1936–1963, his death)
sons, Michael Damien, Patrick
Joseph, and John Charles
daughters, Maria de Lourdes
(Mia), Prudence, Stephanie
Margarita, and Theresa
Magdalena (Tisa)

Contractor James Cushing
(1983–1998, her death)

ESSENTIAL**TEAM-UPS**

TARZAN THE APE MAN (1932, MGM)
When Maureen O'Sullivan's onscreen father (C. Aubrey Smith) goes off in search of the elephant graveyard, it puts her on a collision course with Johnny Weissmuller's jungle king.

TARZAN AND HIS MATE (1934, MGM)
In the best and most adult of the Tarzan films, Weissmuller once again has to defend the elephant graveyard from O'Sullivan's friends.

TARZAN FINDS A SON! (1939, MGM)
A crashed plane brings Weissmuller and O'Sullivan the only child the censors would let them have, completing the Tarzan family.

TARZAN'S NEW YORK ADVENTURE (1942, MGM)
When Boy (Johnny Sheffield) is kidnapped by a New York circus, Weissmuller and O'Sullivan brave what he calls the "stone jungle" to bring him home.

KEY QUOTE

From *Tarzan the Ape Man* (1932)

O'Sullivan
I'm Jane Parker.
Understand? Jane, Jane.

Weissmuller
Jane, Jane.

O'Sullivan
Yes, Jane. And you? . . .

Weissmuller
Tarzan. Tarzan.

O'Sullivan
Tarzan.

As her blonde allure enslaved his sheer animal power, theirs was the definitive Hollywood version of Beauty and the Beast.

FAY **WRAY**

KING **KONG**

IN *King Kong*

It was an impossible romance. The giant ape from Skull Island and the actress played by Fay Wray were possibly the screen's greatest mismatch. Yet their love story is at the center of the most iconic of monster movies. Of course, what made *King Kong* (1933) great was the fact that it went beyond the monstrous. Special-effects wizard Willis O'Brien turned the animated character of the giant ape into one of the screen's most sympathetic figures. Wray's contribution was just as important. Her pristine blonde beauty, combined with believable reactions to a costar she never really worked with, made their relationship completely credible. Kong was a product of the imagination, the brainchild of producer-director Merian C. Cooper. He had gotten the idea for the film when he became fascinated with gorilla behavior while doing location work in Africa for *The Four Feathers* (1929). When RKO Pictures head David O. Selznick asked Cooper to evaluate O'Brien's work in stop-motion animation, he saw a way to bring his fantasy to life. He and famed mystery writer Edgar Wallace crafted the story of a film company that blunders onto a lost prehistoric world ruled by a giant ape, an ape that falls for its leading lady. Before hiring Wray, who had starred in *The Four Feathers*, Cooper considered Dorothy Jordan, whom he later married, and also Jean Harlow for the role of Ann Darrow. He informed Wray that she was going to have "the tallest, darkest leading man in Hollywood." Wray assumed that he was referring to Cary Grant. To her surprise, he showed her a picture of a giant ape on the side of the Empire State Building and said, "There's your leading man." Connecting with her costar was no picnic. During Kong's fight with the Tyrannosaurus rex, Wray spent hours at the top of a dead tree as special-effects footage was projected on a screen behind her. She had to respond to the action, but at that proximity all she could see was a blur. For the scenes in which Wray squirmed in Kong's grasp, the filmmakers used a giant hand suspended ten feet off the ground. A technician tightened the fingers around her, but as she writhed and screamed for the camera, they gradually loosened. When she thought she was about to fall, she signaled Cooper to stop filming. O'Brien's realistic special effects, coupled with Wray's performance and a top-notch adventure story, made the film the box-office smash that saved RKO Pictures from bankruptcy. The nobility and romance and the talents of both the animators and Wray helped create one of the most recognizable characters in film history and made his relationship with Ann Darrow a most unusual yet very poignant love story.

BORN
Kong (Megaprimatus Kong)
August 1927
Skull Island

DIED
March 7, 1933
New York, New York,
of bullet wounds and a fall

STAR SIGN
Leo

HEIGHT
18'–24'
(depending on the shot)

WIFE AND CHILD
Unknown mate
son

OFFSCREEN**RELATIONSHIP**

Fay Wray remembering Kong: "Every time I'm in New York, I say a little prayer when passing the Empire State Building. A good friend of mine died up there."

When Fay Wray told a French journalist that Kong's death scene always made her tear up, he said, "At last, then, Kong has won!"

Fay Wray always referred to Kong as her "little man."

Five versions of Kong's story have been committed to film. Director Peter Jackson met with Fay Wray while working on plans for his 2005 remake of *King Kong*. He even sought her approval to cast Naomi Watts as Ann Darrow. Before her death, Wray was planning to make a cameo appearance to deliver the film's last line.

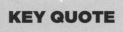

KEY QUOTE

Kong
GRAWWWWRRRR!

Wray
AAAAAAAAH!!!

KING KONG, 1933

FAY WRAY
ROBERT ARMSTRONG
BRUCE CABOT

Hers

BORN
Vina Fay Wray
September 15, 1907
Cardston, Alberta, Canada

DIED
August 8, 2004
New York, New York,
of natural causes

STAR SIGN
Virgo

HEIGHT
5'3"

HUSBANDS AND CHILDREN
Writer John Monk Saunders
(1928–1939, divorced)
daughter, Susan Carey

Writer Robert Riskin
(1942–1955, his death)
son, Robert Jr.
daughter, Victoria

Brain surgeon
Sanford Rothenberg
(1971–1991, his death)

BEHIND THE SCENES

KONG WAS PLAYED BY TWO MINIATURE MODELS, A GIANT HEAD, AND A LIFE-SIZE HAND AND FOOT.

AFTER COMPLETING HER SCENES, FAY WRAY SPENT A DAY IN THE SOUND STUDIO RECORDING A SERIES OF SCREAMS SHE DUBBED HER "ARIA OF THE AGONIES."

KONG'S ROAR WAS CREATED BY PLAYING A LION'S ROAR BACKWARD AND IN SLOW MOTION. THIS WAS THEN OVERDUBBED WITH THE ANIMAL'S HIGH AND LOW NOTES, PLAYED SIMULTANEOUSLY.

FILMOGRAPHIES

ANN-MARGRET

Pocketful of Miracles, 1961
State Fair, 1962
Bye Bye Birdie, 1963
***Viva Las Vegas*, 1964 (with Elvis Presley)**
Kitten with a Whip, 1964
The Pleasure Seekers, 1964
Bus Riley's Back in Town, 1965
Once a Thief, 1965
The Cincinnati Kid, 1965
Made in Paris, 1966
Stagecoach, 1966
The Swinger, 1966
Murderers' Row, 1966
*Il Tigre/*The Tiger and the Pussycat, *1967*
*Il Profeta/*The Prophet, *1968*
Sette uomini e un cervello/
    Criminal Affair, *1968*
Rebus, 1969
R.P.M., 1970
C.C. and Company, 1970
Carnal Knowledge, 1971
*Un homme est mort/*The Outside Man, *1972*
The Train Robbers, 1973
Tommy, 1975
*Folies bourgeoises/*The Twist, *1976*
Joseph Andrews, 1977
The Last Remake of Beau Geste, 1977
The Cheap Detective, 1978
Magic, 1978
The Villain, 1979
Middle Age Crazy, 1980
The Return of the Soldier, 1982
I Ought to Be in Pictures, 1982
Lookin' to Get Out, 1982
Twice in a Lifetime, 1985
52 Pick-Up, 1986
A Tiger's Tale, 1988
A New Life, 1988
Newsies, 1992
Grumpy Old Men, 1993
Grumpier Old Men, 1995
Any Given Sunday, 1999
The Last Producer, 2000
Interstate 60, 2002
Taxi, 2004
The Break-Up, 2006
The Santa Clause 3:
    The Escape Clause, *2006*
Memory, 2006

FRED ASTAIRE

Dancing Lady, 1933
***Flying Down to Rio*, 1933**
    (with Ginger Rogers)
***The Gay Divorcee*, 1934**
    (with Ginger Rogers)
***Roberta*, 1935 (with Ginger Rogers)**
***Top Hat*, 1935 (with Ginger Rogers)**
***Follow the Fleet*, 1936**
    (with Ginger Rogers)
***Swing Time*, 1936 (with Ginger Rogers)**
***Shall We Dance*, 1937 (with Ginger Rogers)**
A Damsel in Distress, 1937
***Carefree*, 1938 (with Ginger Rogers)**
***The Story of Vernon and Irene Castle*, 1939**
    (with Ginger Rogers)
Broadway Melody of 1940, 1940
Second Chorus, 1940
You'll Never Get Rich, 1941
Holiday Inn, 1942
You Were Never Lovelier, 1942
The Sky's the Limit, 1943
Yolanda and the Thief, 1945
Blue Skies, 1946
Easter Parade, 1948
***The Barkleys of Broadway*, 1949**
    (with Ginger Rogers)
Three Little Words, 1950
Let's Dance, 1950
Royal Wedding, 1951
The Belle of New York, 1952
The Band Wagon, 1953
Daddy Long Legs, 1955
Funny Face, 1957
Silk Stockings, 1957
On the Beach, 1959
The Pleasure of His Company, 1961
The Notorious Landlady, 1962
Finian's Rainbow, 1968
Midas Run, 1969
The Towering Inferno, 1974
The Amazing Dobermans, 1976
The Purple Taxi, 1977
Ghost Story, 1981

LAUREN BACALL

***To Have and Have Not*, 1944**
    (with Humphrey Bogart)
Confidential Agent, 1945
***The Big Sleep*, 1946**
    (with Humphrey Bogart)
***Dark Passage*, 1947**
    (with Humphrey Bogart)
***Key Largo*, 1948 (with Humphrey Bogart)**
Young Man with a Horn, 1950
Bright Leaf, 1950
How to Marry a Millionaire, 1953
Woman's World, 1954
The Cobweb, 1955
Blood Alley, 1955
Written on the Wind, 1956
Designing Woman, 1957
The Gift of Love, 1958
North West Frontier, 1959
Shock Treatment, 1964
Sex and the Single Girl, 1964
Harper, 1966
Murder on the Orient Express, 1974
The Shootist, 1976
H.E.A.L.T.H., 1979
The Fan, 1981
Appointment with Death, 1988
Mr. North, 1988
Tree of Hands, 1989
Misery, 1990
All I Want for Christmas, 1991
A Star for Two, 1991
A Foreign Field, 1993
Prêt-à-Porter, 1994
The Mirror Has Two Faces, 1996
My Fellow Americans, 1996
*Le Jour et la nuit/*Day and Night, *1997*
Diamonds, 1999
The Venice Project, 1999
Presence of Mind, 1999
The Limit, 2003
Dogville, 2003
Birth, 2004
Manderlay, 2005
These Foolish Things, 2006
The Walker, 2007

WALLACE BEERY

His Athletic Wife, 1913
Mr. Dippy Dipped, 1913
Sweet Revenge, 1913
The Right of Way, 1913
Love Incognito, 1913
At the Old Maid's Call, 1913
Hello, Trouble, 1913
Smithy's Grandma Party, 1913
The Usual Way, 1913
Their Wives' Indiscretion, 1913
Day by Day, 1913
Dad's Insanity, 1913
A Successful Failure, 1913
Two Dinky Little Dramas
    of a Non-Serious Kind, *1914*
Sweedie Collects for Charity, 1914
Their Cheap Vacation, 1914
Madame Double X, 1914
The Fable of the Bush League
    Lover Who Failed to Qualify, *1914*
Sweedie and the Hypnotist, 1914
A Maid of War, 1914
Sweedie at the Fair, 1914
Countess Sweedie, 1914
The Prevailing Craze, 1914
Three Boiled Down Fables, 1914
Sweedie the Trouble Maker, 1914
Sweedie, the Laundress, 1914
Rivalry and War, 1914
She Landed a Lord, 1914
Sweedie Learns to Swim, 1914
The Fickleness of Sweedie, 1914
Golf Champion "Chick" Evans
    Links with Sweedie, *1914*
Sweedie's Clean-Up, 1914
Sweedie's Skate, 1914
The Plum Tree, 1914
Love and Soda, 1914
Sweedie Springs a Surprise, 1914
Sweedie and the Double Exposure, 1914
Topsy-Turvy Sweedie, 1914

The Fable of the Busy Business
  Boy and the Droppers-In, 1914
In and Out, 1914
The Fable of the Coming Champion
  Who Was Delayed, 1914
Sweedie and the Lord, 1914
The Fable of Higher Education
  That Was Too High for the Old Man, 1914
The Fable of Napoleon and the Bumps, 1914
Sweedie the Swatter, 1914
The Epidemic, 1914
The Fable of the Brash Drummer
  and the Nectarine, 1914
This Is the Life, 1914
Actor Finney's Finish, 1914
Three Little Powders, 1914
Making Him Over—for Minnie, 1914
Curing a Husband, 1914
The Winner, 1914
The Bargain Hunters, 1914
A Queer Quarantine, 1914
Oh, Doctor, 1914
Grass County Goes Dry, 1914
The Girl, the Cop, the Burglar, 1914
Mrs. Manly's Baby, 1914
One-to-Three, 1914
Looking for Trouble, 1914
A Foot of Romance, 1914
Cheering a Husband, 1914
The Ups and Downs, 1914
The Fable of the Roistering Blades, 1915
Education, 1915
The Broken Pledge, 1915
Sweedie's Finish, 1915
The Slim Princess, 1915
Sweedie's Hero, 1915
Sweedie in Vaudeville, 1915
Done in Wax, 1915
The Bouquet, 1915
Sweedie Learns to Ride, 1915
Love and Trouble, 1915
Father's New Maid, 1915
Sweedie's Hopeless Love, 1915
Ain't It the Truth?, 1915
A Pound for a Pound, 1915
The Victor, 1915
Sweedie Goes to College, 1915
The New Teacher, 1915
Two Hearts That Beat as Ten, 1915
Sweedie and Her Dog, 1915
Sweedie's Suicide, 1915
Sweedie and the Sultan's Present, 1915
A Capable Lady Cook, 1916
Sweedie, the Janitor, 1916
Just a Few Little Things, 1916
The Janitor, 1916
A Dash of Courage, 1916
The Janitor's Vacation, 1916
That Night, 1917
Are Waitresses Safe?, 1917
A Clever Dummy, 1917
Cactus Nell, 1917

Teddy at the Throttle, 1917
Maggie's First False Step, 1917
Patria, 1917
Bombs and Banknotes, 1917
Johanna Enlists, 1918
Behind the Door, 1919
Victory, 1919
Soldiers of Fortune, 1919
The Life Line, 1919
The Love Burglar, 1919
The Unpardonable Sin, 1919
A Beach Nut, 1919
Only a Janitor, 1919
The Rookie's Return, 1920
The Last of the Mohicans, 1920
813, 1920
The Round-Up, 1920
The Mollycoddle, 1920
The Virgin of Stamboul, 1920
The Last Trail, 1921
The White Mouse, 1921
The Ne'er to Return Road, 1921
The Policeman and the Baby, 1921
The Golden Snare, 1921
The Northern Trail, 1921
A Tale of Two Worlds, 1921
The Four Horsemen of the Apocalypse, 1921
Patsy, 1921
Sleeping Acres, 1921
Only a Shop Girl, 1922
Robin Hood, 1922
Trouble, Keep Smiling, 1922
Hurricane's Gal, 1922
I Am the Law, 1922
The Man from Hell's River, 1922
The Sagebrush Trail, 1922
Wild Honey, 1922
The Rosary, 1922
White Tiger, 1923
The Drums of Jeopardy, 1923
Richard the Lion-Hearted, 1923
Masters of Women, 1923
The Spanish Dancer, 1923
Three Ages, 1923
Drifting, 1923
Ashes of Vengeance, 1923
Bavu, 1923
Stormswept, 1923
The Flame of Life, 1923
Patsy, 1923
So Big, 1924
Madonna of the Streets, 1924
Dynamite Smith, 1924
The Red Lily, 1924
Another Man's Wife, 1924
The Signal Tower, 1924
The Sea Hawk, 1924
Unseen Hands, 1924
The Pony Express, 1925
Rugged Water, 1925
In the Name of Love, 1925
The Wanderer, 1925
After Five, 1925

Adventure, 1925
Coming Through, 1925
The Great Divide, 1925
The Devil's Cargo, 1925
The Lost World, 1925
Let Women Alone, 1925
Old Ironsides, 1926
We're in the Navy Now, 1926
Volcano, 1926
Behind the Front, 1926
Now We're in the Air, 1927
Fireman, Save My Child, 1927
Casey at the Bat, 1927
Beggars of Life, 1928
The Big Killing, 1928
Partners in Crime, 1928
Wife Savers, 1928
River of Romance, 1929
Stairs of Sand, 1929
Tong War, 1929
Min and Bill, 1930 (with Marie Dressler)
A Lady's Morals, 1930
Way for a Sailor, 1930
Billy the Kid, 1930
The Big House, 1930
Hell Divers, 1931
The Champ, 1931
The Secret Six, 1931
The Slippery Pearls, 1931
Flesh, 1932
Grand Hotel, 1932
The Bowery, 1933
Dinner at Eight, 1933 (with Marie Dressler)
Tugboat Annie, 1933 (with Marie Dressler)
The Mighty Barnum, 1934
Treasure Island, 1934
Viva Villa!, 1934
Ah, Wilderness!, 1935
O'Shaughnessy's Boy, 1935
China Seas, 1935
West Point of the Air, 1935
Old Hutch, 1936
A Message to Garcia, 1936
The Bad Man of Brimstone, 1937
Slave Ship, 1937
The Good Old Soak, 1937
Stablemates, 1938
Port of Seven Seas, 1938
Thunder Afloat, 1939
Sergeant Madden, 1939
Stand Up and Fight, 1939
Wyoming, 1940
20 Mule Team, 1940
Arouse and Beware, 1940
Barnacle Bill, 1941
The Bad Man/Two-Gun Cupid, 1941
Jackass Mail, 1942
The Bugle Sounds, 1942
Salute to the Marines, 1943

Barbary Coast Gent, 1944
Rationing, 1944
This Man's Navy, 1945
Bad Bascomb, 1946
The Mighty McGurk, 1947
A Date with Judy, 1948
Alias a Gentleman, 1948
Big Jack, 1949

INGRID BERGMAN

Munkbrogreven/The Count of the
    Old Monk's Bridge, 1934
Bränningar/The Surf, 1935
Swedenhielms/Swedenhielms Family, 1935
Valborgsmässoafton/Walpurgis Night, 1935
På Solisidan/On the Sunny Side, 1936
Intermezzo, 1936
Dollar, 1938
Die vier Gesellen/
    The Four Companions, 1938
En kvinnas ansikte/A Woman's Face, 1938
En enda natt/One Single Night, 1938
Intermezzo, 1939
Juninatten/A Night in June, 1940
Rage in Heaven, 1941
Adam Had Four Sons, 1941
Dr. Jekyll and Mr. Hyde, 1941
Casablanca, 1942 (with Humphrey Bogart)
For Whom the Bell Tolls, 1943
Gaslight, 1944
Spellbound, 1945
Saratoga Trunk, 1945
The Bells of St. Mary's, 1945
Notorious, 1946
Arch of Triumph, 1948
Joan of Arc, 1948
Under Capricorn, 1949
Stromboli, 1950
Europa '51, 1951
Viaggio in Italia/Journey to Italy, 1953
La paura/Fear, 1954
Giovanna D'Arco al rogo/
    Joan at the Stake, 1954
Elena et les hommes/
    Paris Does Strange Things, 1956
Anastasia, 1956
Indiscreet, 1958
The Inn of the Sixth Happiness, 1958
Goodbye Again, 1961
The Visit, 1964
The Yellow Rolls-Royce, 1965
Stimulantia, 1967
Cactus Flower, 1969
A Walk in the Spring Rain, 1970
From the Mixed-up Files of Mrs. Basil E.
    Frankweiler, 1973
Murder on the Orient Express, 1974
A Matter of Time, 1976
Höstsonaten/Autumn Sonata, 1978

HUMPHREY BOGART

Up the River, 1930
A Devil with Women, 1930
Body and Soul, 1931
The Bad Sister, 1931

A Holy Terror, 1931
Love Affair, 1932
Big City Blues, 1932
Three on a Match, 1932
Midnight, 1934
The Petrified Forest, 1936
Bullets or Ballots, 1936
Two Against the World, 1936
China Clipper, 1936
Isle of Fury, 1936
Black Legion, 1937
The Great O'Malley, 1937
Marked Woman, 1937
Kid Galahad, 1937
San Quentin, 1937
Dead End, 1937
Stand-In, 1937
Swing Your Lady, 1938
Crime School, 1938
Racket Busters, 1938
Men Are Such Fools, 1938
The Amazing Dr. Clitterhouse, 1938
Angles with Dirty Faces, 1938
King of the Underworld, 1939
The Oklahoma Kid, 1939
Dark Victory, 1939
You Can't Get Away with Murder, 1939
The Roaring Twenties, 1939
The Return of Doctor X, 1939
Invisible Stripes, 1939
Virginia City, 1940
It All Came True, 1940
Brother Orchid, 1940
They Drive by Night, 1940
High Sierra, 1941
The Wagons Roll at Night, 1941
The Maltese Falcon, 1941
All Through the Night, 1942
The Big Shot, 1942
Across the Pacific, 1942
Casablanca, 1942 (with Ingrid Bergman)
Action in the North Atlantic, 1943
Sahara, 1943
Passage to Marseille, 1944
To Have and Have Not, 1944
    (with Lauren Bacall)
Conflict, 1945
The Big Sleep, 1946 (with Lauren Bacall)
Dead Reckoning, 1947
The Two Mrs. Carrolls, 1947
Dark Passage, 1947 (with Lauren Bacall)
The Treasure of the Sierra Madre, 1948
Key Largo, 1948 (with Lauren Bacall)
Knock on Any Door, 1949
Tokyo Joe, 1949
Chain Lightning, 1950
In a Lonely Place, 1950
The Enforcer, 1951
Sirocco, 1951
The African Queen, 1951
Deadline—U.S.A., 1952
Battle Circus, 1953

Beat the Devil, 1953
The Caine Mutiny, 1954
Sabrina, 1954
The Barefoot Contessa, 1954
We're No Angels, 1955
The Left Hand of God, 1955
The Desperate Hours, 1955
The Harder They Fall, 1956

CHARLES BOYER

L'homme du large/Man of the Sea, 1920
Chantelouve, 1921
Le grillon du foyer, 1922
La ronde infernale/Infernal Circle, 1927
Le Capitaine Fracasse/
    Captain Fracasse, 1929
La barcarolle d'amour, 1929
Révolte dans la prison/
    Revolt in the Prison, 1930
Le procès de Mary Dugan, 1931
The Magnificent Lie, 1931
Tumultes, 1932
The Man from Yesterday, 1932
Red-Headed Woman, 1932
I.F. 1 ne répond plus/
    F. P. 1 Doesn't Answer, 1932
L'épervier, 1933
Moi et 'l'impératrice/The Only Girl, 1933
Caravane, 1934
Caravan, 1934
Liliom, 1934
La bataille/Thunder in the East, 1934
Le bonheur, 1934
Private Worlds, 1935
Break of Hearts, 1935
Shanghai, 1935
I Loved a Soldier, 1936
Mayerling, 1936
The Garden of Allah, 1936
History Is Made at Night, 1937
Conquest, 1937
Tovarich, 1937
Orage, 1938
Algiers, 1938 (with Hedy Lamarr)
Le corsaire, 1939
Love Affair, 1939
When Tomorrow Comes, 1939
All This, and Heaven Too, 1940
Back Street, 1941
Hold Back the Dawn, 1941
Appointment for Love, 1941
Tales of Manhattan, 1942
The Constant Nymph, 1943
Flesh and Fantasy, 1943
Gaslight, 1944
Together Again, 1944
Confidential Agent, 1945
Cluny Brown, 1946
A Woman's Vengeance, 1948
Arch of Triumph, 1948
The 13th Letter, 1951
The First Legion, 1951
The Happy Time, 1952
Thunder in the East, 1952

Madame de . . . /
The Earrings of Madame de . . . ., 1953
The Cobweb, 1955
Nana, 1955
La fortuna di essere donna/
Lucky to Be a Woman, 1956
Around the World in Eighty Days, 1956
Paris, Palace Hôtel, 1956
La Parisienne, 1957
Maxime, 1958
The Buccaneer, 1958
Fanny, 1961
Les démons de minuit/
Demons at Midnight, 1961
The Four Horseman
of the Apocalypse, 1962
Julia, Du bist zauberhaft/
Adorable Julia, 1962
Love Is a Ball, 1963
A Very Special Favor, 1965
How to Steal a Million, 1966
Paris brûle–t–il?/Is Paris Burning?, 1966
Casino Royale, 1967
Barefoot in the Park, 1967
Le rouble à deux faces/
The Day the Hot Line Got Hot, 1969
The April Fools, 1969
The Madwoman of Chaillot, 1969
Lost Horizon, 1973
Stavisky . . . , 1974
A Matter of Time, 1976

RICHARD BURTON

Now Barabbas, 1949
The Last Days of Dolwyn/
Women of Dolwyn, 1949
The Woman with No Name/
Her Panelled Door, 1950
Waterfront/Waterfront Women, 1950
Green Grow the Rushes, 1951
My Cousin Rachel, 1952
The Robe, 1953
The Desert Rats, 1953
The Rains of Ranchipur, 1955
Prince of Players, 1955
Alexander the Great, 1956
Sea Wife, 1957
Bitter Victory, 1957
Look Back in Anger, 1958
The Bramble Bush, 1960
Ice Palace, 1960
The Longest Day, 1962
***Cleopatra*, 1963 (with Elizabeth Taylor)**
***The V.I.P.s*, 1963 (with Elizabeth Taylor)**
Hamlet, 1964
The Night of the Iguana, 1964
Becket, 1964
The Spy Who Came in from the Cold, 1965
***The Sandpiper*, 1965 (with Elizabeth Taylor)**
***Who's Afraid of Virginia Woolf?*, 1966**
(with Elizabeth Taylor)
***The Comedians*, 1967**
(with Elizabeth Taylor)
***Doctor Faustus*, 1967**
(with Elizabeth Taylor)

***The Taming of the Shrew*, 1967**
(with Elizabeth Taylor)
Candy, 1968
***Boom!*, 1968 (with Elizabeth Taylor)**
Where Eagles Dare, 1968
Anne of the Thousand Days, 1969
Staircase, 1969
Villain, 1971
Raid on Rommel, 1971
***Hammersmith Is Out*, 1972**
(with Elizabeth Taylor)
Bluebeard, 1972
The Assassination of Trotsky, 1972
***Under Milk Wood*, 1972**
(with Elizabeth Taylor)
Rappresaglia/Massacre in Rome, 1973
Sutjeska/The Battle of Sutjeska, 1973
The Klansman, 1974
Il viaggio/The Voyage, 1974
Equus, 1977
Exorcist II: The Heretic, 1977
Absolution, 1978
The Wild Geese, 1978
The Medusa Touch, 1978
Steiner—Das eiserne Kreuz, 2. Teil/
Breakthrough, 1979
Circle of Two, 1980
Summer of the Falcon, 1981
Lovespell, 1981
Nineteen Eighty–Four, 1984

DAN DAILEY

The Mortal Storm, 1940
The Captain Is a Lady, 1940
Dulcy, 1940
Hullabaloo, 1940
Keeping Company, 1940
The Wild Man of Borneo, 1941
Washington Melodrama, 1941
Ziegfeld Girl, 1941
The Get–Away, 1941
Down in San Diego, 1941
Lady Be Good, 1941
Moon Over Her Shoulder, 1941
Mokey, 1942
Sunday Punch, 1942
Timber!, 1942
Panama Hattie, 1942
Give Out, Sisters, 1942
***Mother Wore Tights*, 1947**
(with Betty Grable)
You Were Meant for Me, 1948
Give My Regards to Broadway, 1948
***When My Baby Smiles at Me*, 1948**
(with Betty Grable)
Chicken Every Sunday, 1949
You're My Everything, 1949
When Willie Comes Marching Home, 1950
A Ticket to Tomahawk, 1950
***My Blue Heaven*, 1950 (with Betty Grable)**
***Call Me Mister*, 1951 (with Betty Grable)**
I Can Get It for You Wholesale, 1951

The Pride of St. Louis, 1952
What Price Glory, 1952
Meet Me at the Fair, 1953
Taxi, 1953
The Girl Next Door, 1953
The Kid from Left Field, 1953
There's No Business
Like Show Business, 1954
It's Always Fair Weather, 1955
Meet Me in Las Vegas, 1956
The Best Things in Life Are Free, 1956
The Wings of Eagles, 1957
Oh, Men! Oh, Women!, 1957
The Wayward Bus, 1957
Underwater Warrior, 1958
Pepe, 1960
Hemingway's Adventures
of a Young Man, 1962
Las cuatro noches de la luna llena/
Four Nights of the Full Moon, 1963
The Private Files of J. Edgar Hoover, 1977

DORIS DAY

Romance on the High Seas, 1948
My Dream Is Yours, 1949
It's a Great Feeling, 1949
Young Man with a Horn, 1950
Tea for Two, 1950
The West Point Story, 1950
Storm Warning, 1951
Lullaby of Broadway, 1951
On Moonlight Bay, 1951
I'll See You in My Dreams, 1951
Starlift, 1951
The Winning Team, 1952
April in Paris, 1952
By the Light of the Silvery Moon, 1953
Calamity Jane, 1953
Lucky Me, 1954
Young at Heart, 1954
Love Me or Leave Me, 1955
The Man Who Knew Too Much, 1956
Julie, 1956
The Pajama Game, 1957
Teacher's Pet, 1958
The Tunnel of Love, 1958
It Happened to Jane, 1959
***Pillow Talk*, 1959 (with Rock Hudson)**
Please Don't Eat the Daisies, 1960
Midnight Lace, 1960
***Lover Come Back*, 1961 (with Rock Hudson)**
That Touch of Mink, 1962
Billy Rose's Jumbo, 1962
The Thrill of It All, 1963
Move Over, Darling, 1963
***Send Me No Flowers*, 1964**
(with Rock Hudson)
Do Not Disturb, 1965
The Glass Bottom Boat, 1966
The Ballad of Josie, 1967
Caprice, 1967
Where Were You When
the Lights Went Out?, 1968
With Six You Get Eggroll, 1968

OLIVIA DE HAVILLAND

Alibi Ike, 1935
The Irish in Us, 1935
A Midsummer Night's Dream, 1935
***Captain Blood*, 1935 (with Errol Flynn)**
Anthony Adverse, 1936
***The Charge of the Light Brigade*, 1936
   (with Errol Flynn)**
Call It a Day, 1937
It's Love I'm After, 1937
The Great Garrick, 1937
Gold Is Where You Find it, 1938
***The Adventures of Robin Hood*, 1938
   (with Errol Flynn)**
***Four's a Crowd*, 1938 (with Errol Flynn)**
Hard to Get, 1938
Wings of the Navy, 1939
***Dodge City*, 1939 (with Errol Flynn)**
***The Private Lives of Elizabeth
   and Essex*, 1939 (with Errol Flynn)**
Gone With The Wind, 1939
Raffles, 1940
My Love Came Back, 1940
***Santa Fe Trail*, 1940 (with Errol Flynn)**
The Strawberry Blonde, 1941
Hold Back the Dawn, 1941
***They Died with Their Boots On*, 1941
   (with Errol Flynn)**
The Male Animal, 1942
In This Our Life, 1942
Princess O'Rourke, 1943
Government Girl, 1943
To Each His Own, 1946
Devotion, 1946
The Well-Groomed Bride, 1946
The Dark Mirror, 1946
The Snake Pit, 1948
The Heiress, 1949
My Cousin Rachel, 1953
That Lady, 1955
Not as a Stranger, 1955
The Ambassador's Daughter, 1956
The Proud Rebel, 1958
Libel, 1959
Light in the Piazza, 1962
Lady in a Cage, 1964
Hush . . . Hush, Sweet Charlotte, 1965
The Adventurers, 1970
Pope Joan, 1972
Airport '77, 1977
The Swarm, 1978
The Fifth Musketeer, 1979

MARIE DRESSLER

Tillie's Punctured Romance, 1914
Tillie's Tomato Surprise, 1915
The Scrub Lady, 1917
Fired, 1917
Tillie Wakes Up, 1917
The Red Cross Nurse, 1918
The Agonies of Agnes, 1918
Breakfast at Sunrise, 1927
The Joy Girl, 1927
The Callahans and the Murphys, 1927
The Patsy, 1928

Bringing Up Father, 1928
The Vagabond Lover, 1929
Dangerous Females, 1929
The Divine Lady, 1929
***Min and Bill*, 1930 (with Wallace Beery)**
Let Us Be Gay, 1930
Caught Short, 1930
One Romantic Night, 1930
The Girl Said No, 1930
Anna Christie, 1930
Chasing Rainbows, 1930
Politics, 1931
Reducing, 1931
Prosperity, 1932
Emma, 1932
Christopher Bean, 1933
***Dinner at Eight*, 1933 (with Wallace Beery)**
***Tugboat Annie*, 1933 (with Wallace Beery)**

MARGARET DUMONT

***The Cocoanuts*, 1929 (with Groucho Marx)**
***Animal Crackers*, 1930 (with Groucho Marx)**
The Girl Habit, 1931
Here, Prince, 1932
***Duck Soup*, 1933 (with Groucho Marx)**
Gridiron Flash, 1934
Fifteen Wives, 1934
Kentucky Kernels, 1934
***A Night at the Opera*, 1935
   (with Groucho Marx)**
Gypsy Sweetheart, 1935
Song and Dance Man, 1936
Anything Goes, 1936
Wise Girl, 1937
High Flyers, 1937
Youth on Parole, 1937
The Life of the Party, 1937
***A Day at the Races*, 1937
   (with Groucho Marx)**
Dramatic School, 1938
***At the Circus*, 1939 (with Groucho Marx)**
Never Give a Sucker an Even Break, 1941
***The Big Store*, 1941 (with Groucho Marx)**
For Beauty's Sake, 1941
Rhythm Parade, 1942
About Face, 1942
Sing Your Worries Away, 1942
Born to Sing, 1942
The Dancing Masters, 1943
Bathing Beauty, 1944
Seven Days Ashore, 1944
Up in Arms, 1944
Sunset in El Dorado, 1945
Diamond Horseshoe, 1945
The Horn Blows at Midnight, 1945
Susie Steps Out, 1946
Little Giant, 1946
Stop, You're Killing Me, 1952
3 for Bedroom C, 1952
Shake, Rattle & Rock!, 1956
Zotz!, 1962
What a Way to Go!, 1964

NELSON EDDY

Dancing Lady, 1933
Student Tour, 1934
***Naughty Marietta*, 1935
   (with Jeanette MacDonald)**
***Rose-Marie*, 1936
   (with Jeanette MacDonald)**
Rosalie, 1937
***Maytime*, 1937 (with Jeanette MacDonald)**
***Sweethearts*, 1938
   (with Jeanette MacDonald)**
***The Girl of the Golden West*, 1938
   (with Jeanette MacDonald)**
Balalaika, 1939
Let Freedom Ring, 1939
***Bitter Sweet*, 1940
   (with Jeanette MacDonald)**
***New Moon*, 1940
   (with Jeanette MacDonald)**
The Chocolate Soldier, 1941
***I Married an Angel*, 1942
   (with Jeanette MacDonald)**
Phantom of the Opera, 1943
Knickerbocker Holiday, 1944
Northwest Outpost, 1947

CHARLES FARRELL

Wings of Youth, 1925
The Love Hour, 1925
Clash of the Wolves, 1925
The Freshman, 1925
Old Ironsides, 1926
Sandy, 1926
A Trip to Chinatown, 1926
***Seventh Heaven*, 1927 (with Janet Gaynor)**
The Rough Riders, 1927
Fazil, 1928
***Street Angel*, 1928 (with Janet Gaynor)**
The Red Dance, 1928
The River, 1928
***Lucky Star*, 1929 (with Janet Gaynor)**
Happy Days, 1929
***Sunny Side Up*, 1929 (with Janet Gaynor)**
The Princess and the Plumber, 1930
City Girl, 1930
***High Society Blues*, 1930
   (with Janet Gaynor)**
Liliom, 1930
***The Man Who Came Back*, 1931
   (with Janet Gaynor)**
Body and Soul, 1931
***Merely Mary Ann*, 1931 (with Janet Gaynor)**
Heartbreak, **1931**
***Delicious*, 1931 (with Janet Gaynor)**
After Tomorrow, 1932
***The First Year*, 1932 (with Janet Gaynor)**
Wild Girl, 1932
***Tess of the Storm Country*, 1932
   (with Janet Gaynor)**
Aggie Appleby, Maker of Man, 1933
Girl Without a Room, 1933
The Big Shakedown, 1934
Falling in Love/Trouble Ahead, 1934
***Change of Heart*, 1934 (with Janet Gaynor)**
Fighting Youth, 1935

Forbidden Heaven, 1935
The Flying Doctor, 1936
Midnight Menace/
    Bombs Over London, 1937
Moonlight Sonata, 1937
Flight to Fame, 1938
Just Around the Corner, 1938
Tail Spin, 1939
The Deadly Game, 1941

W. C. FIELDS

His Lordship's Dilemma, 1915
Pool Sharks, 1915
Janice Meredith, 1924
Sally of the Sawdust, 1925
That Royle Girl, 1925
It's the Old Army Game, 1926
So's Your Old Man, 1926
The Potters, 1927
Running Wild, 1927
Two Flaming Youths, 1927
Tillie's Punctured Romance, 1928
Fools for Luck, 1928
The Golf Specialist, 1930
Her Majesty, Love, 1931
Million Dollar Legs, 1932
If I Had a Million, 1932
The Dentist, 1932
The Fatal Glass of Beer, 1933
The Pharmacist, 1933
International House, 1933
The Barber Shop, 1933
Tillie and Gus, 1933
Alice in Wonderland, 1933
Six of a Kind, 1934
You're Telling Me!, 1934
The Old Fashioned Way, 1934
Mrs. Wiggs of the Cabbage Patch, 1934
It's a Gift, 1934
David Copperfield, 1935
Mississippi, 1935
Man on the Flying Trapeze, 1935
Poppy, 1936
The Big Broadcast of 1938, 1938
You Can't Cheat an Honest Man, 1939
My Little Chickadee, 1940 (with Mae West)
The Bank Dick, 1940
Never Give a Sucker an Even Break, 1941

ERROL FLYNN

In the Wake of the Bounty, 1933
Murder at Monte Carlo, 1934
The Case of the Curious Bride, 1935
Don't Bet on Blondes, 1935
**Captain Blood, 1935
    (with Olivia de Havilland)
The Charge of the Light Brigade, 1936
    (with Olivia de Havilland)**
Green Light, 1937
The Prince and the Pauper, 1937
Another Dawn, 1937
The Perfect Specimen, 1937

**The Adventures of Robin Hood, 1938
    (with Olivia de Havilland)
Four's a Crowd, 1938
    (with Olivia de Havilland)**
The Sisters, 1938
The Dawn Patrol, 1938
**Dodge City, 1939 (with Olivia de Havilland)
The Private Lives of Elizabeth and Essex,
    1939 (with Olivia de Havilland)**
Virginia City, 1940
The Sea Hawk, 1940
**Santa Fe Trail, 1940
    (with Olivia de Havilland)**
Footsteps in the Dark, 1941
Dive Bomber, 1941
**They Died with Their Boots On, 1941
    (with Olivia de Havilland)**
Desperate Journey, 1942
Gentleman Jim, 1942
Edge of Darkness, 1943
Northern Pursuit, 1943
Uncertain Glory, 1944
Objective, Burma!, 1945
San Antonio, 1945
Never Say Goodbye, 1946
Cry Wolf, 1947
Escape Me Never, 1947
Silver River, 1948
Adventures of Don Juan, 1948
That Forsyte Woman, 1949
Montana, 1950
Rocky Mountain, 1950
Kim, 1950
Hello God, 1951
Adventures of Captain Fabian, 1951
Mara Maru, 1952
Against All Flags, 1952
The Master of Ballantrae, 1953
Il maestro di Don Giovanni/
    Crossed Swords, 1954
Lilacs in the Spring, 1955
King's Rhapsody, 1955
The Dark Avenger, 1955
Istanbul, 1957
The Big Boodle, 1957
The Sun Also Rises, 1957
Too Much, Too Soon, 1958
The Roots of Heaven, 1958
Cuban Rebel Girls, 1959

GLENN FORD

Night in Manhattan, 1937
My Son Is Guilty, 1939
Heaven with a Barbed Wire Fence, 1939
Blondie Plays Cupid, 1940
**The Lady in Question, 1940
    (with Rita Hayworth)**
Babies for Sale, 1940
Men Without Souls, 1940
Convicted Woman, 1940
Go West, Young Lady, 1941
Texas, 1941
So Ends Our Night, 1941
Flight Lieutenant, 1942
The Adventures of Martin Eden, 1942

Destroyer, 1943
The Desperadoes, 1943
Gallant Journey, 1946
A Stolen Life, 1946
Gilda, 1946 (with Rita Hayworth)
Framed, 1947
The Return of October, 1948
**The Loves of Carmen, 1948
    (with Rita Hayworth)**
The Man from Colorado, 1948
The Mating of Millie, 1948
The Doctor and the Girl, 1949
Mr. Soft Touch, 1949
Lust for Gold, 1949
The Undercover Man, 1949
The Flying Missile, 1950
Convicted, 1950
The White Tower, 1950
The Secret of Convict Lake, 1951
Follow the Sun, 1951
The Redhead and the Cowboy, 1951
**Affair in Trinidad, 1952
    (with Rita Hayworth)**
Young Man with Ideas, 1952
The Green Glove, 1952
Appointment in Honduras, 1953
The Big Heat, 1953
Plunder of the Sun, 1953
The Man from the Alamo, 1953
Time Bomb/Terror on a Train, 1953
Human Desire, 1954
Trial, 1955
Interrupted Melody, 1955
Blackboard Jungle, 1955
The Violent Men, 1955
The Americano, 1955
The Teahouse of the August Moon, 1956
Ransom, 1956
The Fastest Gun Alive, 1956
Jubal, 1956
Don't Go Near the Water, 1957
3:10 to Yuma, 1957
Torpedo Run, 1958
Imitation General, 1958
Stranger with a Gun, 1958
Cowboy, 1958
The Gazebo, 1959
It Started with a Kiss, 1959
Cimarron, 1960
Pocketful of Miracles, 1961
Cry for Happy, 1961
Experiment in Terror, 1962
The Four Horsemen
    of the Apocalypse, 1962
Love Is a Ball, 1963
The Courtship of Eddie's Father, 1963
Dear Heart, 1964
Fate Is the Hunter, 1964
Advance to the Rear, 1964
The Money Trap, 1965 (with Rita Hayworth)
The Rounders, 1965
Rage, 1966

*Paris brûle-t-il?/*Is Paris Burning?, 1966
The Last Challenge, 1967
A Time for Killing, 1967
Day of the Evil Gun, 1968
Heaven with a Gun, 1969
Smith!, 1969
Santee, 1973
Midway, 1976
Superman, 1978
Day of the Assassin, 1979
The Visitor, 1979
*Fukkatsu no hi/*Day of Resurrection, 1980
Happy Birthday to Me, 1981
Casablanca Express, 1989
Border Shootout, 1990
Raw Nerve, 1991

CLARK GABLE

White Man, 1924
North Star, 1925
The Painted Desert, 1931
The Easiest Way, 1931
Dance, Fools, Dance, 1931
The Finger Points, 1931
The Secret Six, 1931 (with Jean Harlow)
Laughing Sinners, 1931
A Free Soul, 1931
Night Nurse, 1931
Sporting Blood, 1931
Susan Lenox (Her Fall and Rise), 1931
Possessed, 1931
Hell Divers, 1931
Polly of the Circus, 1932
Red Dust, 1932 (with Jean Harlow)
No Man of Her Own, 1932
Strange Interlude, 1932
The White Sister, 1933
Hold Your Man, 1933 (with Jean Harlow)
Night Flight, 1933
Dancing Lady, 1933
It Happened One Night, 1934
Men in White, 1934
Manhattan Melodrama, 1934
Chained, 1934
Forsaking All Others, 1934
After Office Hours, 1935
China Seas, 1935 (with Jean Harlow)
The Call of the Wild, 1935
Mutiny on the Bounty, 1935
Wife vs. Secretary, 1936 (with Jean Harlow)
San Francisco, 1936
Cain and Mabel, 1936
Love on the Run, 1936
Parnell, 1937
Saratoga, 1937 (with Jean Harlow)
Test Pilot, 1938
Too Hot to Handle, 1938
Idiot's Delight, 1939
Gone with The Wind, 1939
(with Vivien Leigh)
Strange Cargo, 1940
Boom Town, 1940
Comrade X, 1940

They Met in Bombay, 1941
Honky Tonk, 1941
Somewhere I'll Find You, 1942
Adventure, 1945
The Hucksters, 1947
Homecoming, 1948
Command Decision, 1948
Any Number Can Play, 1949
Key to the City, 1950
To Please a Lady, 1950
Across the Wide Missouri, 1951
Lone Star, 1952
Never Let Me Go, 1953
Mogambo, 1953
Betrayed, 1954
Soldier of Fortune, 1955
The Tall Men, 1955
The King and Four Queens, 1956
Band of Angels, 1957
Run Silent Run Deep, 1958
Teacher's Pet, 1958
But Not for Me, 1959
It Started in Naples, 1960
The Misfits, 1961

GRETA GARBO

*Luffar-Petter/*Peter the Tramp, 1922
Gösta Berlings saga/
    The Saga of Gösta Berling, 1924
Die Freudlose Gasse/
    The Joyless Street, 1925
Torrent, 1926
The Temptress, 1926
Flesh and the Devil, 1926
    (with John Gilbert)
Love, 1927 (with John Gilbert)
The Divine Woman, 1928
The Mysterious Lady, 1928
A Woman of Affairs, 1928
    (with John Gilbert)
Wild Orchids, 1929
The Single Standard, 1929
The Kiss, 1929
Anna Christie, 1930
Romance, 1930
Inspiration, 1931
Susan Lenox (Her Fall and Rise), 1931
Mata Hari, 1931
Grand Hotel, 1932
As You Desire Me, 1932
Queen Christina, 1933 (with John Gilbert)
The Painted Veil, 1934
Anna Karenina, 1935
Camille, 1936 (with Robert Taylor)
Conquest, 1937
Ninotchka, 1939
Two-Faced Woman, 1941

JOHN GARFIELD

Four Daughters, 1938
They Made Me a Criminal, 1939
Blackwell's Island, 1939
Juarez, 1939
Daughters Courageous, 1939
Dust Be My Destiny, 1939

Four Wives, 1939
Castle on the Hudson, 1940
Saturday's Children, 1940
Flowing Gold, 1940
East of the River, 1940
The Sea Wolf, 1941
Out of the Fog, 1941
Dangerously They Live, 1941
Tortilla Flat, 1942
Air Force, 1943
The Fallen Sparrow, 1943
Destination Tokyo, 1943
Between Two Worlds, 1944
Pride of the Marines, 1945
The Postman Always Rings Twice, 1946
    (with Lana Turner)
Nobody Lives Forever, 1946
Humoresque, 1946
Body and Soul, 1947
Gentleman's Agreement, 1947
Force of Evil, 1948
We Were Strangers, 1949
Under My Skin, 1950
The Breaking Point, 1950
He Ran All the Way, 1951

JUDY GARLAND

Pigskin Parade, 1936
Every Sunday, 1936
Broadway Melody of 1938, 1937
Thoroughbreds Don't Cry, 1937
    (with Mickey Rooney)
Everybody Sing, 1938
Love Finds Andy Hardy, 1938
    (with Mickey Rooney)
Listen, Darling, 1938
The Wizard of Oz, 1939
Babes in Arms, 1939 (with Mickey Rooney)
Andy Hardy Meets Debutante, 1940
    (with Mickey Rooney)
Strike Up the Band, 1940
    (with Mickey Rooney)
Little Nellie Kelly, 1940
Ziegfeld Girl, 1941
Life Begins for Andy Hardy, 1941
    (with Mickey Rooney)
Babes on Broadway, 1941
    (with Mickey Rooney)
For Me and My Gal, 1942
Presenting Lily Mars, 1943
Girl Crazy, 1943 (with Mickey Rooney)
Meet Me in St. Louis, 1944
The Clock, 1945
The Harvey Girls, 1946
Ziegfeld Follies, 1946
Till the Clouds Roll By, 1947
Words and Music, 1948
    (with Mickey Rooney)
The Pirate, 1948
Easter Parade, 1948
In the Good Old Summertime, 1949
Summer Stock, 1950

A Star Is Born, 1954
Judgment at Nuremberg, 1961
A Child Is Waiting, 1963
I Could Go On Singing, 1963

GREER GARSON

Goodbye, Mr. Chips, 1939
Remember?, 1939
Pride and Prejudice, 1940
Blossoms in the Dust, 1941
   (with Walter Pidgeon)
When Ladies Meet, 1941
Mrs. Miniver, 1942 (with Walter Pidgeon)
Random Harvest, 1942
The Youngest Profession, 1943
Madame Curie, 1943
   (with Walter Pidgeon)
Mrs. Parkington, 1944
   (with Walter Pidgeon)
The Valley of Decision, 1945
Adventure, 1945
Desire Me, 1947
Julia Misbehaves, 1948
   (with Walter Pidgeon)
That Forsyte Woman, 1949
   (with Walter Pidgeon)
The Miniver Story, 1950
   (with Walter Pidgeon)
The Law and the Lady, 1951
Scandal at Scourie, 1953
   (with Walter Pidgeon)
Julius Caesar, 1953
Her Twelve Men, 1954
Strange Lady in Town, 1955
Sunrise at Campobello, 1960
The Singing Nun, 1966
The Happiest Millionaire, 1967

JANET GAYNOR

The Johnstown Flood, 1926
The Shamrock Handicap, 1926
The Blue Eagle, 1926
The Midnight Kiss, 1926
The Return of Peter Grimm, 1926
Two Girls Wanted, 1927
Seventh Heaven, 1927 (with Charles Farrell)
Sunrise: A Song of Two Humans, 1927
Street Angel, 1928 (with Charles Farrell)
Lucky Star, 1929 (with Charles Farrell)
Four Devils, 1929
Christina, 1929
Sunny Side Up, 1929 (with Charles Farrell)
Happy Days, 1930
High Society Blues, 1930
   (with Charles Farrell)
The Man Who Came Back, 1931
   (with Charles Farrell)
Daddy Long Legs, 1931
Merely Mary Ann, 1931 (with Charles Farrell)
Delicious, 1931 (with Charles Farrell)
The First Year, 1932 (with Charles Farrell)
Tess of the Storm Country, 1932
   (with Charles Farrell)
State Fair, 1933
Adorable, 1933

Paddy the Next Best Thing, 1933
La ciudad de cartón, 1934
Carolina, 1934
Change of Heart, 1934 (with Charles Farrell)
Servants' Entrance, 1934
One More Spring, 1935
The Farmer Takes a Wife, 1935
Small Town Girl, 1936
Ladies in Love, 1936
A Star Is Born, 1937
Three Loves Has Nancy, 1938
The Young in Heart, 1938
Bernardine, 1957

JOHN GILBERT

Bullets and Brown Eyes, 1916
The Phantom, 1916
The Apostle of Vengeance, 1916
Shell 43, 1916
The Sin Ye Do, 1916
The Weaker Sex, 1917
The Bride of Hate, 1917
Princess of the Dark, 1917
The Dark Road, 1917
Happiness, 1917
The Millionaire Vagrant, 1917
The Hater of Men, 1917
The Mother Instinct, 1917
Golden Rule Kate, 1917
The Devil Dodger, 1917
Love or Justice?, 1917
Up or Down?, 1917
Nancy Comes Home, 1918
Shackled, 1918
More Trouble, 1918
One Dollar Bid, 1918
Wedlock, 1918
Doing Their Bit, 1918
The Mask, 1918
Three X Gordon, 1918
The Dawn of Understanding, 1918
The White Heather, 1919
The Busher, 1919
The Man Beneath, 1919
A Little Brother of the Rich, 1919
The Red Viper, 1919
For a Woman's Honor, 1919
Widow by Proxy, 1919
Heart o' the Hills, 1919
Should a Woman Tell?, 1919
The White Circle, 1920
Deep Waters, 1920
The Servant in the House, 1921
Shame, 1921
Ladies Must Live, 1921
Gleam O'Dawn, 1922
Arabian Love, 1922
The Yellow Stain, 1922
Honor First, 1922
Monte Cristo, 1922
Calvert's Valley, 1922
The Love Gambler, 1922
A California Romance, 1922

While Paris Sleeps, 1923
Truxton King, 1923
Madness of Youth, 1923
St. Elmo, 1923
The Exiles, 1923
Cameo Kirby, 1923
Just Off Broadway, 1924
The Wolf Man, 1924
A Man's Mate, 1924
The Lone Chance, 1924
Romance Ranch, 1924
His Hour, 1924
He Who Gets Slapped, 1924
The Snob, 1924
The Wife of the Centaur, 1924
The Merry Widow, 1925
The Big Parade, 1925
La Boheme, 1926
Bardelys the Magnificent, 1926
Flesh and the Devil, 1926
   (with Greta Garbo)
The Show, 1927
Twelve Miles Out, 1927
Man, Woman and Sin, 1927
Love, 1927 (with Greta Garbo)
Four Walls, 1928
The Masks of the Devil, 1928
A Woman of Affairs, 1928
   (with Greta Garbo)
The Cossacks, 1928
Desert Nights, 1929
His Glorious Night, 1929
Redemption, 1930
Way for a Sailor, 1930
Gentleman's Fate, 1931
The Phantom of Paris, 1931
West of Broadway, 1931
Downstairs, 1932
Fast Workers, 1933
Queen Christina, 1933 (with Greta Garbo)
The Captain Hates the Sea, 1934

BETTY GRABLE

Happy Days, 1929
Crashing Hollywood, 1931
Once a Hero, 1931
Lady! Please!, 1932
Hollywood Luck, 1932
Probation, 1932
The Flirty Sleepwalker, 1932
Hollywood Lights, 1932
Hold 'Em Jail, 1932
Child of Manhattan, 1933
What Price Innocence?, 1933
The Sweetheart of Sigma Chi, 1933
Air Tonic, 1933
School for Romance, 1934
Elmer Steps Out, 1934
Love Detectives, 1934
Business Is a Pleasure, 1934
Susie's Affairs, 1934
The Gay Divorcee, 1934
Student Tour, 1934
By Your Leave, 1934
This Band Age, 1935

The Spirit of 1976, 1935
The Nitwits, 1935
A Night at the Biltmore Bowl, 1935
Drawing Rumors, 1935
Old Man Rhythm, 1935
A Quiet Fourth, 1935
Collegiate, 1936
Follow the Fleet, 1936
Don't Turn 'Em Loose, 1936
Pigskin Parade, 1936
This Way Please, 1937
Thrill of a Lifetime, 1937
College Swing, 1938
Give Me a Sailor, 1938
Campus Confessions, 1938
Man About Town, 1939
Million Dollar Legs, 1939
The Day the Bookies Wept, 1939
Down Argentine Way, 1940
Tin Pan Alley, 1940
Moon over Miami, 1941
A Yank in the R.A.F., 1941
I Wake Up Screaming, 1941
Song of the Islands, 1942
Footlight Serenade, 1942
Springtime in the Rockies, 1942
Coney Island, 1943
Sweet Rosie O'Grady, 1943
Pin Up Girl, 1944
Diamond Horseshoe, 1945
The Dolly Sisters, 1945
Hollywood Park, 1946
The Shocking Miss Pilgrim, 1947
Mother Wore Tights, 1947 (with Dan Dailey)
That Lady in Ermine, 1948
**When My Baby Smiles at Me, 1948
   (with Dan Dailey)**
The Beautiful Blonde
   from Bashful Bend, 1949
Wabash Avenue, 1950
My Blue Heaven, 1950 (with Dan Dailey)
Call Me Mister, 1951 (with Dan Dailey)
Meet Me After the Show, 1951
The Farmer Takes a Wife, 1953
How to Marry a Millionaire, 1953
Three for the Show, 1955
How to Be Very, Very Popular, 1955

CARY GRANT

This Is the Night, 1932
Sinners in the Sun, 1932
Merrily We Go to Hell, 1932
Devil and the Deep, 1932
Blonde Venus, 1932
Hot Saturday, 1932
Madame Butterfly, 1932
She Done Him Wrong, 1933
The Woman Accused, 1933
The Eagle and the Hawk, 1933
Gambling Ship, 1933
I'm No Angel, 1933
Alice in Wonderland, 1933
Thirty Day Princess, 1934
Born to Be Bad, 1934

Kiss and Make-Up, 1934
Ladies Should Listen, 1934
Enter Madame, 1935
Wings in the Dark, 1935
The Last Outpost, 1935
Sylvia Scarlett, 1935
The Amazing Quest of Ernest Bliss/
   Romance and Riches, 1936
Big Brown Eyes, 1936
Suzy, 1936
Wedding Present, 1936
When You're in Love, 1937
Topper, 1937
The Toast of New York, 1937
The Awful Truth, 1937
Bringing Up Baby, 1938
Holiday, 1938
Gunga Din, 1939
Only Angels Have Wings, 1939
In Name Only, 1939
His Girl Friday, 1940
My Favorite Wife, 1940
The Howards of Virginia, 1940
The Philadelphia Story, 1940
Penny Serenade, 1941
Suspicion, 1941
The Talk of the Town, 1942
Once Upon a Honeymoon, 1942
Mr. Lucky, 1943
Destination Tokyo, 1943
Once Upon a Time, 1944
None But the Lonely Heart, 1944
Arsenic and Old Lace, 1944
Night and Day, 1946
Notorious, 1946
The Bachelor and the Bobby-Soxer, 1947
The Bishop's Wife, 1947
Mr. Blandings Builds His Dream House, 1948
Every Girl Should Be Married, 1948
I Was a Male War Bride, 1949
Crisis, 1950
People Will Talk, 1951
Room for One More, 1952
Monkey Business, 1952
Dream Wife, 1953
To Catch a Thief, 1955 (with Grace Kelly)
An Affair to Remember, 1957
The Pride and the Passion, 1957
Kiss Them for Me, 1957
Indiscreet, 1958
Houseboat, 1958
North by Northwest, 1959
Operation Petticoat, 1959
The Grass Is Greener, 1960
That Touch of Mink, 1962
Charade, 1963
Father Goose, 1964
Walk Don't Run, 1966

JEAN HARLOW

The Saturday Night Kid, 1929
Hell's Angels, 1930
The Secret Six, 1931 (with Clark Gable)
The Public Enemy, 1931
Iron Man, 1931

Goldie, 1931
Platinum Blonde, 1931
Three Wise Girls, 1932
The Beast of the City, 1932
Red-Headed Woman, 1932
Red Dust, 1932 (with Clark Gable)
Hold Your Man, 1933 (with Clark Gable)
Dinner at Eight, 1933
Bombshell, 1933
The Girl from Missouri, 1934
Reckless, 1935
China Seas, 1935 (with Clark Gable)
Riffraff, 1935
Wife vs. Secretary, 1936 (with Clark Gable)
Suzy, 1936
Libeled Lady, 1936
Personal Property, 1937
Saratoga, 1937 (with Clark Gable)

RITA HAYWORTH

Under the Pampas Moon, 1935
Charlie Chan in Egypt, 1935
Dante's Inferno, 1935
Paddy O'Day, 1935
Dancing Pirate, 1936
Human Cargo, 1936
Meet Nero Wolfe, 1936
Rebellion, 1936
Old Louisiana, 1937
Hit the Saddle, 1937
Trouble in Texas, 1937
Criminals of the Air, 1937
Girls Can Play, 1937
The Game That Kills, 1937
Paid to Dance, 1937
The Shadow, 1937
Who Killed Gail Preston?, 1938
Special Inspector, 1938
Convicted, 1938
Juvenile Court, 1938
The Renegade Ranger, 1939
Homicide Bureau, 1939
The Lone Wolf Spy Hunt, 1939
Only Angels Have Wings, 1939
Music in My Heart, 1940
Blondie on a Budget, 1940
Susan and God, 1940
**The Lady in Question, 1940
   (with Glenn Ford)**
Angels over Broadway, 1940
The Strawberry Blonde, 1941
Affectionately Yours, 1941
Blood and Sand, 1941
You'll Never Get Rich, 1941
My Gal Sal, 1942
Tales of Manhattan, 1942
You Were Never Lovelier, 1942
Cover Girl, 1944
Tonight and Every Night, 1945
Gilda, 1946 (with Glenn Ford)
Down to Earth, 1947

The Lady from Shanghai, **1948**
   (with Orson Welles)
The Loves of Carmen, **1948**
   (with Glenn Ford)
Affair in Trinidad, **1952 (with Glenn Ford)**
Salome, 1952
Miss Sadie Thompson, 1953
Fire Down Below, 1957
Pal Joey, 1957
Separate Tables, 1958
They Came to Cordura, 1959
The Story on Page One, 1959
The Happy Thieves, 1962
Circus World, 1964
The Money Trap, **1966 (with Glenn Ford)**
Poppies Are Also Flowers, 1966
L'avventuriero/The Rover, 1967
I Bastardi, 1969
Road to Salina, 1970
The Naked Zoo, 1970
The Wrath of God, 1972

AUDREY HEPBURN

Laughter in Paradise, 1951
One Wild Oat, 1951
The Lavender Hill Mob, 1951
Young Wives' Tale, 1951
Monte Carlo Baby, 1951
The Secret People, 1952
Nous irons à Monte Carlo/
   We Will All Go to Monte Carlo, 1952
Roman Holiday, **1953 (with Gregory Peck)**
Sabrina, 1954
War and Peace, 1956
Funny Face, 1957
Love in the Afternoon, 1957
Green Mansions, 1959
The Nun's Story, 1959
The Unforgiven, 1960
Breakfast at Tiffany's, 1961
The Children's Hour, 1961
Charade, 1963
Paris—When It Sizzles, 1964
My Fair Lady, 1964
How to Steal a Million, 1966
Two for the Road, 1967
Wait Until Dark, 1967
Robin and Marian, 1976
Bloodline, 1979
They All Laughed, 1981
Always, 1989

KATHARINE HEPBURN

A Bill of Divorcement, 1932
Christopher Strong, 1933
Morning Glory, 1933
Little Women, 1933
Spitfire, 1934
The Little Minister, 1934
Break of Hearts, 1935
Alice Adams, 1935
Sylvia Scarlett, 1935
Mary of Scotland, 1936
A Woman Rebels, 1936
Quality Street, 1937

Stage Door, 1937
Bringing Up Baby, 1938
Holiday, 1938
The Philadelphia Story, 1940
Woman of the Year, **1942**
   (with Spencer Tracy)
Keeper of the Flame, **1942**
   (with Spencer Tracy)
Dragon Seed, 1944
Without Love, **1945 (with Spencer Tracy)**
Undercurrent, 1946
The Sea of Grass, **1947 (with Spencer Tracy)**
Song of Love, 1947
State of the Union, **1948**
   (with Spencer Tracy)
Adam's Rib, **1949 (with Spencer Tracy)**
The African Queen, 1951
Pat and Mike, **1952 (with Spencer Tracy)**
Summertime, 1955
The Rainmaker, 1956
The Iron Petticoat, 1956
Desk Set, **1957 (with Spencer Tracy)**
Suddenly, Last Summer, 1959
Long Day's Journey into Night, 1962
Guess Who's Coming to Dinner, **1967**
   (with Spencer Tracy)
The Lion in Winter, 1968
The Madwoman of Chaillot, 1969
The Trojan Women, 1971
A Delicate Balance, 1973
Rooster Cogburn, 1975
Olly, Olly, Oxen Free, 1978
On Golden Pond, 1981
Grace Quigley, 1984
Love Affair, 1994

ROCK HUDSON

Undertow, 1949
I Was a Shoplifter, 1950
Peggy, 1950
Winchester '73, 1950
The Desert Hawk, 1950
Shakedown, 1950
Tomahawk, 1951
Air Cadet, 1951
The Fat Man, 1951
Bright Victory, 1951
Iron Man, 1951
Bend of the River, 1952
Here Come the Nelsons, 1952
Scarlet Angel, 1952
Has Anybody Seen My Gal?, 1952
Horizons West, 1952
The Lawless Breed, 1953
Seminole, 1953
Sea Devils, 1953
The Golden Blade, 1953
Gun Fury, 1953
Back to God's Country, 1953
Taza, Son of Cochise, 1954
Magnificent Obsession, 1954
Bengal Brigade, 1954

Captain Lightfoot, 1955
One Desire, 1955
All That Heaven Allows, 1955
Never Say Goodbye, 1956
Giant, 1956
Written on the Wind, 1956
Battle Hymn, 1957
Something of Value, 1957
A Farewell to Arms, 1957
The Tarnished Angels, 1958
Twilight for the Gods, 1958
The Earth Is Mine, 1959
Pillow Talk, **1959 (with Doris Day)**
The Last Sunset, 1961
Come September, 1961
Lover Come Back, **1961 (with Doris Day)**
The Spiral Road, 1962
A Gathering of Eagles, 1963
Man's Favorite Sport?, 1964
Send Me No Flowers, **1964 (with Doris Day)**
Strange Bedfellows, 1965
A Very Special Favor, 1965
Blindfold, 1965
Seconds, 1966
Tobruk, 1967
Ice Station Zebra, 1968
Ruba al prossimo tuo/A Fine Pair, 1969
The Undefeated, 1969
Darling Lili, 1970
Hornets' Nest, 1970
Pretty Maids All in a Row, 1971
Showdown, 1973
Embryo, 1976
Avalanche, 1978
The Mirror Crack'd, 1980
The Ambassador, 1984

RUBY KEELER

42nd Street, **1933 (with Dick Powell)**
Gold Diggers of 1933, **1933**
   (with Dick Powell)
Footlight Parade, **1933 (with Dick Powell)**
Dames, **1934 (with Dick Powell)**
Flirtation Walk, **1934 (with Dick Powell)**
Shipmates Forever, **1935 (with Dick Powell)**
Go into Your Dance, 1935
Colleen, **1936 (with Dick Powell)**
Ready, Willing and Able, 1937
Mother Carey's Chickens, 1938
Sweetheart of the Campus, 1941
Beverly Hills Brats, 1989

GRACE KELLY

Fourteen Hours, 1951
High Noon, 1952
Mogambo, 1953
Dial M for Murder, 1954
Rear Window, 1954
The Country Girl, 1954
Green Fire, 1954
The Bridges at Toko-Ri, 1955
To Catch a Thief, **1955 (with Cary Grant)**
The Swan, 1956
High Society, 1956

KING KONG

***King Kong*, 1933 (with Fay Wray)**

Kingu Kongu no gyakushū/
    King Kong Escapes, 1968
King Kong, 1976
King Kong Lives, 1986
King Kong, 2005

ALAN LADD

Hitler—Beast of Berlin, 1939
Rulers of the Sea, 1939
The Light of Western Stars, 1940
In Old Missouri, 1940
Those Were the Days!, 1940
Captain Caution, 1940
Meet the Missus, 1940
Her First Romance, 1940
Petticoat Politics, 1941
The Black Cat, 1941
Paper Bullets, 1941
The Reluctant Dragon, 1941
Joan of Paris, 1942
***This Gun for Hire*, 1942 (with Veronica Lake)**
***The Glass Key*, 1942 (with Veronica Lake)**
Lucky Jordan, 1942
China, 1943
And Now Tomorrow, 1944
Salty O'Rourke, 1945
Two Years Before the Mast, 1946
***The Blue Dahlia*, 1946 (with Veronica Lake)**
O.S.S., 1946
Calcutta, 1947
Wild Harvest, 1947
***Saigon*, 1948 (with Veronica Lake)**
Beyond Glory, 1948
Whispering Smith, 1948
The Great Gatsby, 1949
Chicago Deadline, 1949
Captain Carey, U.S.A., 1950
Branded, 1950
Appointment with Danger, 1951
Red Mountain, 1951
The Iron Mistress, 1952
Thunder in the East, 1952
Botany Bay, 1953
Desert Legion, 1953
Shane, 1953
The Red Beret, 1953
Hell Below Zero, 1954
Saskatchewan, 1954
The Black Knight, 1954
Drum Beat, 1954
Hell on Frisco Bay, 1955
The McConnell Story, 1955
Santiago, 1956
The Big Land, 1957
Boy on a Dolphin, 1957
The Deep Six, 1958
The Proud Rebel, 1958
The Badlanders, 1958
The Man in the Net, 1959
Guns of the Timberland, 1960
All the Young Men, 1960

One Foot in Hell, 1960
Orazi e curiazi/Duel of the Champions, 1961
13 West Street, 1962
The Carpetbaggers, 1964

VERONICA LAKE

All Women Have Secrets, 1939
The Wrong Room, 1939
Young as You Feel, 1940
Sullivan's Travels, 1941
I Wanted Wings, 1941
I Married a Witch, 1942
***This Gun for Hire*, 1942 (with Alan Ladd)**
***The Glass Key*, 1942 (with Alan Ladd)**
So Proudly We Hail!, 1943
The Hour Before the Dawn, 1944
Hold That Blonde, 1945
Out of This World, 1945
Bring on the Girls, 1945
***The Blue Dahlia*, 1946 (with Alan Ladd)**
Miss Susie Slagle's, 1946
Ramrod, 1947
Isn't It Romantic?, 1948
The Sainted Sisters, 1948
***Saigon*, 1948 (with Alan Ladd)**
Slattery's Hurricane, 1949
Stronghold, 1951
Footsteps in the Snow, 1966
Flesh Feast, 1970

HEDY LAMARR

Die Koffer des Herrn O.F./
    The Trunks of Mr. O.F., 1931
Man braucht kein Geld/
    We Need No Money, 1931
Extase/Ecstasy, 1933
***Algiers*, 1938 (with Charles Boyer)**
Lady of the Tropics, 1939
I Take This Woman, 1940
Boom Town, 1940
Comrade X, 1940
Come Live with Me, 1941
Ziegfeld Girl, 1941
H. M. Pulham, Esq., 1940
Tortilla Flat, 1942
Crossroads, 1942
White Cargo, 1942
The Heavenly Body, 1943
The Conspirators, 1944
Experiment Perilous, 1944
Her Highness and the Bellboy, 1945
The Strange Woman, 1946
Dishonored Lady, 1947
Let's Live a Little, 1948
Samson and Delilah, 1949
A Lady Without a Passport, 1950
Copper Canyon, 1950
My Favorite Spy, 1951
L'amante di Paride/
    Loves of Three Queens, 1954
The Story of Mankind, 1957
The Female Animal, 1958

VIVIEN LEIGH

Things Are Looking Up, 1935
The Village Squire, 1935
Gentlemen's Agreement, 1935
Look Up and Laugh, 1935
***Fire over England*, 1937
    (with Laurence Olivier)**
Dark Journey, 1937
Storm in a Teacup, 1937
A Yank at Oxford, 1938
Sidewalks of London, 1938
***Gone with the Wind*, 1939
    (with Clark Gable)**
***21 Days*, 1940 (with Laurence Olivier)**
Waterloo Bridge, 1940
***That Hamilton Woman*, 1941
    (with Laurence Olivier)**
Caesar and Cleopatra, 1946
Anna Karenina, 1948
A Streetcar Named Desire, 1951
The Deep Blue Sea, 1955
The Roman Spring of Mrs. Stone, 1961
Ship of Fools, 1965

MYRNA LOY

What Price Beauty?, 1925
The Caveman, 1926
Why Girls Go Back Home, 1926
The Gilded Highway, 1926
Exquisite Sinner, 1926
So This Is Paris, 1926
Don Juan, 1926
Across the Pacific, 1926
Finger Prints, 1927
Bitter Apples, 1927
The Climbers, 1927
Simple Sis, 1927
The Heart of Maryland, 1927
A Sailor's Sweetheart, 1927
The Girl from Chicago, 1927
If I Were Single, 1927
Ham and Eggs at the Front, 1927
Beware of Married Men, 1928
Turn Back the Hours, 1928
The Crimson City, 1928
Pay As You Enter, 1928
State Street Sadie, 1928
The Midnight Taxi, 1928
Fancy Baggage, 1929
Hardboiled Rose, 1929
The Desert Song, 1929
The Black Watch, 1929
The Squall, 1929
Noah's Ark, 1929
The Great Divide, 1929
Evidence, 1929
The Show of Shows, 1929
Cameo Kirby, 1930
Isle of Escape, 1930
Under a Texas Moon, 1930
Cock o' the Walk, 1930
Bride of the Regiment, 1930
The Last of the Duanes, 1930
The Jazz Cinderella, 1930

The Bad Man, 1930
Renegades, 1930
Rogue of the Rio Grande, 1930
The Truth About Youth, 1930
The Devil to Pay!, 1930
The Naughty Flirt, 1931
Body and Soul, 1931
A Connecticut Yankee, 1931
Hush Money, 1931
Transatlantic, 1931
Rebound, 1931
Skyline, 1931
Consolation Marriage, 1931
Arrowsmith, 1931
Emma, 1932
Vanity Fair, 1932
The Wet Parade, 1932
The Woman in Room 13, 1932
New Morals for Old, 1932
Love Me Tonight, 1932
Thirteen Women, 1932
The Mask of Fu Manchu, 1932
The Animal Kingdom, 1932
Topaze, 1933
The Barbarian, 1933
The Prizefighter and the Lady, 1933
When Ladies Meet, 1933
Penthouse, 1933
Night Flight, 1933
Men in White, 1934
***Manhattan Melodrama*, 1934**
   (with William Powell)
***The Thin Man*, 1934 (with William Powell)**
Stamboul Quest, 1934
***Evelyn Prentice*, 1934 (with William Powell)**
Broadway Bill, 1934
Wings in the Dark, 1935
Whipsaw, 1935
Wife vs. Secretary, 1936
Petticoat Fever, 1936
***The Great Ziegfeld*, 1936**
   (with William Powell)
To Mary—with Love, 1936
***Libeled Lady*, 1936 (with William Powell)**
***After the Thin Man*, 1936**
   (with William Powell)
Parnell, 1937
***Double Wedding*, 1937**
   (with William Powell)
Test Pilot, 1938
Man-Proof, 1938
Too Hot to Handle, 1938
Lucky Night, 1939
The Rains Came, 1939
***Another Thin Man*, 1939**
   (with William Powell)
***I Love You Again*, 1940**
   (with William Powell)
Third Finger, Left Hand, 1940
***Love Crazy*, 1941 (with William Powell)**
***Shadow of the Thin Man*, 1941**
   (with William Powell)

***The Thin Man Goes Home*, 1945**
   (with William Powell)
So Goes My Love, 1946
The Best Years of Our Lives, 1946
The Bachelor and the Bobby-Soxer, 1947
***Song of the Thin Man*, 1947**
   (with William Powell)
***The Senator Was Indiscreet*, 1947**
   (with William Powell)
*Mr. Blandings Builds His
   Dream House*, 1948
The Red Pony, 1949
That Dangerous Age, 1949
Cheaper by the Dozen, 1950
Belles on Their Toes, 1952
The Ambassador's Daughter, 1956
Lonelyhearts, 1958
From the Terrace, 1960
Midnight Lace, 1960
The April Fools, 1969
Airport 1975, 1974
The End, 1978
Just Tell Me What You Want, 1980

JEANETTE MACDONALD
The Love Parade, 1929
Oh, for a Man, 1930
The Lottery Bride, 1930
Monte Carlo, 1930
Let's Go Native, 1930
The Vagabond King, 1930
Annabelle's Affairs, 1931
Don't Bet on Women, 1931
Love Me Tonight, 1932
Une heure près de toi, 1932
One Hour with You, 1932
The Merry Widow, 1934
The Cat and the Fiddle, 1934
La veuve joyeuse, 1934
***Naughty Marietta*, 1935 (with Nelson Eddy)**
San Francisco, 1936
***Rose-Marie*, 1936 (with Nelson Eddy)**
The Firefly, 1937
***Maytime*, 1937 (with Nelson Eddy)**
***Sweethearts*, 1938 (with Nelson Eddy)**
***The Girl of the Golden West*, 1938**
   (with Nelson Eddy)
Broadway Serenade, 1939
***Bitter Sweet*, 1940 (with Nelson Eddy)**
***New Moon*, 1940 (with Nelson Eddy)**
Smilin' Through, 1941
Cairo, 1942
***I Married an Angel*, 1942 (with Nelson Eddy)**
Three Daring Daughters, 1948
The Sun Comes Up, 1949

GROUCHO MARX
Humor Risk, 1926
***The Cocoanuts*, 1929**
   (with Margaret Dumont)
***Animal Crackers*, 1930**
   (with Margaret Dumont)
Monkey Business, 1931
Horse Feathers, 1932
***Duck Soup*, 1933 (with Margaret Dumont)**

***A Night at the Opera*, 1935**
   (with Margaret Dumont)
***A Day at the Races*, 1937**
   (with Margaret Dumont)
Room Service, 1938
***At the Circus*, 1939 (with Margaret Dumont)**
Go West, 1940
***The Big Store*, 1941 (with Margaret Dumont)**
A Night in Casablanca, 1946
Copacabana, 1947
Love Happy, 1949
Double Dynamite, 1951
A Girl in Every Port, 1952
The Story of Mankind, 1957
Skidoo, 1968

ROBERT MITCHUM
Hoppy Serves a Writ, 1943
Border Patrol, 1943
Follow the Band, 1943
Colt Comrades, 1943
We've Never Been Licked, 1943
Lone Star Trail, 1943
Beyond the Last Frontier, 1943
Bar 20, 1943
Doughboys in Ireland, 1943
False Colors, 1943
Minesweeper, 1943
Riders of the Deadline, 1943
Gung Ho!, 1943
Johnny Doesn't Live Here Any More, 1944
When Strangers Marry, 1944
Girl Rush, 1944
Thirty Seconds over Tokyo, 1944
Nevada, 1944
Story of G.I. Joe, 1944
West of the Pecos, 1945
Till the End of Time, 1946
Undercurrent, 1946
The Locket, 1946
Pursued, 1947
Crossfire, 1947
Desire Me, 1947
Out of the Past, 1947
Rachel and the Stranger, 1948
Blood on the Moon, 1948
The Red Pony, 1949
The Big Steal, 1949
Holiday Affair, 1949
Where Danger Lives, 1950
My Forbidden Past, 1951
***His Kind of Woman*, 1951 (with Jane Russell)**
The Racket, 1951
***Macao*, 1952 (with Jane Russell)**
One Minute to Zero, 1952
The Lusty Men, 1952
Angel Face, 1952
White Witch Doctor, 1953
Second Chance, 1953
She Couldn't Say No, 1954
River of No Return, 1954
Track of the Cat, 1954

Not as a Stranger, 1955
The Night of the Hunter, 1955
Man with the Gun, 1955
Foreign Intrigue, 1956
Bandido, 1956
Heaven Knows, Mr. Allison, 1957
Fire Down Below, 1957
The Enemy Below, 1957
Thunder Road, 1958
The Hunters, 1958
The Angry Hills, 1959
The Wonderful Country, 1959
Home from the Hill, 1960
A Terrible Beauty, 1960
The Sundowners, 1960
The Grass Is Greener, 1960
The Last Time I Saw Archie, 1961
Cape Fear, 1962
The Longest Day, 1962
Two for the Seesaw, 1962
Rampage, 1963
The List of Adrian Messenger, 1963
Man in the Middle, 1964
What a Way to Go!, 1964
Mister Moses, 1965
El Dorado, 1966
The Way West, 1967
Villa Rides, 1968
Lo sbarco di Anzio/Anzio, 1968
5 Card Stud, 1968
Secret Ceremony, 1968
Young Billy Young, 1969
The Good Guys and the Bad Guys, 1969
Ryan's Daughter, 1970
Going Home, 1971
The Wrath of God, 1972
The Friends of Eddie Coyle, 1973
The Yakuza, 1975
Farewell, My Lovely, 1975
Midway, 1976
The Last Tycoon, 1976
The Amsterdam Kill, 1977
Matilda, 1978
The Big Sleep, 1978
Steiner—Das eiserne Kreuz, 2. Teil/
    Breakthrough, 1979
Agency, 1980
Nightkill, 1980
That Championship Season, 1983
The Ambassador, 1984
Maria's Lovers, 1984
Mr. North, 1988
Scrooged, 1988
Midnight Ride, 1990
Présumé dangereux, 1990
Cape Fear, 1991
Les sept péchés capitaux/
    The Seven Deadly Sins, 1992
Woman of Desire, 1993
Backfire!, 1995
Dead Man, 1995
Pakten/Waiting for Sunset, 1995

PAUL NEWMAN

The Silver Chalice, 1954
Somebody Up There Likes Me, 1956
The Rack, 1956
The Helen Morgan Story, 1957
Until They Sail, 1957
The Long, Hot Summer, 1958
The Left Handed Gun, 1958
Cat on a Hot Tin Roof, 1958
    (with Elizabeth Taylor)
Rally Round the Flag, Boys!, 1958
The Young Philadelphians, 1959
Exodus, 1960
From the Terrace, 1960
The Hustler, 1961
Paris Blues, 1961
Sweet Bird of Youth, 1962
Hemingway's Adventures
    of a Young Man, 1962
Hud, 1963
A New Kind of Love, 1963
The Prize, 1963
What a Way to Go!, 1964
The Outrage, 1964
Lady L, 1965
Harper, 1966
Torn Curtain, 1966
Hombre, 1967
Cool Hand Luke, 1967
The Secret War of Harry Frigg, 1968
Winning, 1969
Butch Cassidy and the Sundance Kid, 1969
WUSA, 1970
Sometimes a Great Notion, 1971
Pocket Money, 1972
The Life and Times of Judge Roy Bean, 1972
The MacKintosh Man, 1973
The Sting, 1973
The Towering Inferno, 1974
The Drowning Pool, 1975
Buffalo Bill and the Indians,
    or Sitting Bull's History Lesson, 1976
Slap Shot, 1977
Quintet, 1979
When Time Ran Out . . . , 1980
Fort Apache the Bronx, 1981
Absence of Malice, 1981
The Verdict, 1982
Harry & Son, 1984
The Color of Money, 1986
Fat Man and Little Boy, 1989
Blaze, 1989
Mr. & Mrs. Bridge, 1990
The Hudsucker Proxy, 1994
Nobody's Fool, 1994
Twilight, 1998
Message in a Bottle, 1999
Where the Money Is, 2000
Road to Perdition, 2002

MAUREEN O'HARA

My Irish Molly, 1938
Jamaica Inn, 1939
The Hunchback of Notre Dame, 1939
A Bill of Divorcement, 1940

Dance, Girl, Dance, 1940
They Met in Argentina, 1941
How Green Was My Valley, 1941
To the Shores of Tripoli, 1942
Ten Gentlemen from West Point, 1942
The Black Swan, 1942
The Fallen Sparrow, 1943
Immortal Sergeant, 1943
This Land Is Mine, 1943
Buffalo Bill, 1944
The Spanish Main, 1945
Sentimental Journey, 1946
Do You Love Me, 1946
Sinbad the Sailor, 1947
The Homestretch, 1947
Miracle on 34th Street, 1947
The Foxes of Harrow, 1947
Sitting Pretty, 1948
A Woman's Secret, 1949
Brittania Mews/The Forbidden Street, 1949
Father Was a Fullback, 1949
Bagdad, 1949
Comanche Territory, 1950
Rio Grande, 1950 (with John Wayne)
Tripoli, 1950
Flame of Araby, 1952
At Sword's Point, 1952
Kangaroo, 1952
The Quiet Man, 1952 (with John Wayne)
Against All Flags, 1952
The Redhead from Wyoming, 1953
War Arrow, 1954
Malaga/Fire over Africa, 1954
The Long Gray Line, 1955
The Magnificent Matador, 1955
Lady Godiva of Coventry, 1955
Lisbon, 1956
Everything But the Truth, 1956
The Wings of Eagles, 1957
    (with John Wayne)
Our Man in Havana, 1960
The Deadly Companions, 1961
The Parent Trap, 1961
Mr. Hobbs Takes a Vacation, 1962
Spencer's Mountain, 1963
McLintock!, 1963 (with John Wayne)
The Battle of the Villa Fiorita, 1965
The Rare Breed, 1966
How Do I Love Thee?, 1970
Big Jake, 1971 (with John Wayne)
Only the Lonely, 1991

LAURENCE OLIVIER

The Temporary Widow, 1930
Potiphar's Wife, 1931
Friends and Lovers, 1931
The Yellow Ticket, 1931
Westward Passage, 1932
No Funny Business, 1933
Perfect Understanding, 1933
Moscow Nights/I Stand Condemned, 1935
As You Like It, 1936

Fire over England, **1937** (with Vivien Leigh)
The Divorce of Lady X, 1938
Q Planes, 1939
Wuthering Heights, 1939
Conquest of the Air, 1940
21 Days, 1940 (with Vivien Leigh)
Rebecca, 1940
Pride and Prejudice, 1940
That Hamilton Woman, 1941
  (with Vivien Leigh)
49th Parallel, 1941
The Demi-Paradise, 1943
Henry V, 1944
Hamlet, 1948
The Magic Box, 1951
Carrie, 1952
The Beggar's Opera, 1953
Richard III, 1955
The Prince and the Showgirl, 1957
The Devil's Disciple, 1959
The Entertainer, 1960
Spartacus, 1960
Term of Trial, 1962
Uncle Vanya, 1963
Bunny Lake Is Missing, 1965
Othello, 1965
Khartoum, 1966
The Shoes of the Fisherman, 1968
Oh! What a Lovely War, 1969
The Dance of Death, 1969
Battle of Britain, 1969
Three Sisters, 1970
Nicholas and Alexandra, 1971
Lady Caroline Lamb, 1972
Sleuth, 1972
The Rehearsal, 1974
Marathon Man, 1976
The Seven-Per-Cent Solution, 1976
A Bridge too Far, 1977
The Betsy, 1978
The Boys from Brazil, 1978
A Little Romance, 1979
Dracula, 1979
The Jazz Singer, 1980
Inchon, 1981
Clash of the Titans, 1981
The Jigsaw Man, 1983
The Bounty, 1984
Wild Geese II, 1985
War Requiem, 1989

MAUREEN O'SULLIVAN

Princess and the Plumber, 1930
Just Imagine, 1930
Song o' My Heart, 1930
So This Is London, 1930
The Big Shot, 1931
Skyline, 1931
A Connecticut Yankee, 1931
Robbers' Roost, 1932
Strange Interlude, 1932
Payment Deferred, 1932
Skyscraper Souls, 1932
Fast Companions, 1932
The Silver Lining, 1932

Tarzan the Ape Man, **1932**
  (with Johnny Weissmuller)
Okay, America!, 1932
Stage Mother, 1933
Tugboat Annie, 1933
The Cohens and Kellys in Trouble, 1933
The Barretts of Wimpole Street, 1934
Hide-Out, 1934
The Thin Man, 1934
Tarzan and His Mate, 1934
  (with Johnny Weissmuller)
The Bishop Misbehaves, 1935
Anna Karenina, 1935
Woman Wanted, 1935
The Flame Within, 1935
Cardinal Richelieu, 1935
West Point of the Air, 1935
David Copperfield, 1935
Tarzan Escapes, 1936
  (with Johnny Weissmuller)
The Devil-Doll, 1936
The Voice of Bugle Ann, 1936
My Dear Miss Aldrich, 1937
Between Two Women, 1937
The Emperor's Candlesticks, 1937
A Day at the Races, 1937
Spring Madness, 1938
The Crowd Roars, 1938
Port of Seven Seas, 1938
Hold That Kiss, 1938
A Yank at Oxford, 1938
Tarzan Finds a Son!, 1939
  (with Johnny Weissmuller)
Let Us Live!, 1939
Pride and Prejudice, 1940
Sporting Blood, 1940
Tarzan's Secret Treasure, 1941
  (with Johnny Weissmuller)
Maisie Was a Lady, 1941
Tarzan's New York Adventure, 1942
  (with Johnny Weissmuller)
The Big Clock, 1948
Where Danger Lives, 1950
No Resting Place, 1951
Bonzo Goes to College, 1952
Mission over Korea, 1953
All I Desire, 1953
The Steel Cage, 1954
Duffy of San Quentin, 1954
The Tall T, 1957
Wild Heritage, 1958
Never Too Late, 1965
The Phynx, 1970
  (with Johnny Weissmuller)
Mandy's Grandmother, 1978
Too Scared to Scream, 1985
Peggy Sue Got Married, 1986
Hannah and Her Sisters, 1986
Stranded, 1987
Good Old Boy: A Delta Boyhood, 1988

GREGORY PECK

Days of Glory, 1944
The Keys of the Kingdom, 1945
The Valley of Decision, 1945

Spellbound, 1945 *The Yearling*, 1946
Duel in the Sun, 1946
The Macomber Affair, 1947
Gentleman's Agreement, 1947
The Paradine Case, 1947
Yellow Sky, 1949
The Great Sinner, 1949
Twelve O'Clock High, 1949
The Gunfighter, 1950
Captain Horatio Hornblower R.N., 1951
Only the Valiant, 1951
David and Bathsheba, 1951
The Snows of Kilimanjaro, 1952
The World in His Arms, 1952
The Million Pound Note/
  Man with a Million, 1953
Roman Holiday, 1953
  (with Audrey Hepburn)
Night People, 1954
The Purple Plain, 1954
The Man in the Gray Flannel Suit, 1956
Moby Dick, 1956
Designing Woman, 1957
The Bravados, 1958
The Big Country, 1958
Pork Chop Hill, 1959
Beloved Infidel, 1959
On the Beach, 1959
The Guns of Navarone, 1961
Cape Fear, 1962
How the West Was Won, 1962
To Kill a Mockingbird, 1962
Captain Newman, M.D., 1963
Behold a Pale Horse, 1964
Mirage, 1965
Arabesque, 1966
The Stalking Moon, 1969
Mackenna's Gold, 1969
The Chairman, 1969
Marooned, 1969
I Walk the Line, 1970
Shoot Out, 1971
Billy Two Hats, 1974
The Omen, 1976
MacArthur, 1977
The Boys from Brazil, 1978
The Sea Wolves, 1980
Amazing Grace and Chuck, 1987
Old Gringo, 1989
Other People's Money, 1991
Cape Fear, 1991

WALTER PIDGEON

Marriage License?, 1926
Miss Nobody, 1926
Old Loves and New, 1926
The Outsider, 1926
Mannequin, 1926
The Thirteenth Juror, 1927
The Gorilla, 1927
Sumuru, 1927
Heart of Salome, 1927
Melody of Love, 1928
Clothes Make the Woman, 1928
Turn Back the Hours, 1928

Woman Wise, 1928
The Gateway of the Moon, 1928
A Most Immoral Lady, 1929
Her Private Life, 1929
The Voice Within, 1929
Going Wild, 1930
Viennese Nights, 1930
The Gorilla, 1930
Sweet Kitty Bellairs, 1930
Bride of the Regiment, 1930
The Hot Heiress, 1931
Kiss Me Again, 1931
Rockabye, 1932
The Kiss Before the Mirror, 1933
Journal of a Crime, 1934
Fatal Lady, 1936
Big Brown Eyes, 1936
A Girl with Ideas, 1937
My Dear Miss Aldrich, 1937
Saratoga, 1937
As Good as Married, 1937
Girl Overboard, 1937
She's Dangerous, 1937
Listen, Darling, 1938
Too Hot to Handle, 1938
The Shopworn Angel, 1938
The Girl of the Golden West, 1938
Man-Proof, 1938
Nick Carter, Master Detective, 1939
6,000 Enemies, 1939
Stronger Than Desire, 1939
Society Lawyer, 1939
Flight Command, 1940
Sky Murder, 1940
Phantom Raiders, 1940
Dark Command, 1940
It's a Date, 1940
The House Across the Bay, 1940
Design for Scandal, 1941
How Green Was My Valley, 1941
Blossoms in the Dust, 1941
   (with Greer Garson)
Man Hunt, 1941
White Cargo, 1942
Mrs. Miniver, 1942 (with Greer Garson)
Madame Curie, 1943 (with Greer Garson)
Mrs. Parkington, 1944 (with Greer Garson)
Week-End at the Waldorf, 1945
The Secret Heart, 1946
Holiday in Mexico, 1946
American Creed, 1946
If Winter Comes, 1947
Command Decision, 1948
Julia Misbehaves, 1948 (with Greer Garson)
That Forsyte Woman, 1949
   (with Greer Garson)
The Red Danube, 1949
The Miniver Story, 1950 (with Greer Garson)
The Unknown Man, 1951
Calling Bulldog Drummond, 1951
Soldiers Three, 1951
The Bad and the Beautiful, 1952
Million Dollar Mermaid, 1952
The Sellout, 1952
Dream Wife, 1953

Scandal at Scourie, 1953
   (with Greer Garson)
Deep in My Heart, 1954
The Last Time I Saw Paris, 1954
Men of the Fighting Lady, 1954
Executive Suite, 1954
Hit the Deck, 1955
The Rack, 1956
These Wilder Years, 1956
Forbidden Planet, 1956
Voyage to the Bottom of the Sea, 1961
I due colonelli/Two Colonels, 1962
Big Red, 1962
Advise & Consent, 1962
Il giorno più corto/The Shortest Day, 1962
Anniversary, 1963
Warning Shot, 1967
Funny Girl, 1968
A qualsiasi prezzo/The Vatican Affair, 1968
Skyjacked, 1972
The Neptune Factor, 1973
Harry in Your Pocket, 1973
Yellow-Headed Summer, 1974
Two-Minute Warning, 1976
Won Ton Ton, the Dog Who
   Saved Hollywood, 1976
Sextette, 1978

DICK POWELL
Too Busy to Work, 1932
Blessed Event, 1932
42nd Street, 1933 (with Ruby Keeler)
Gold Diggers of 1933, 1933
   (with Ruby Keeler)
Convention City, 1933
College Coach, 1933
Footlight Parade, 1933 (with Ruby Keeler)
The King's Vacation, 1933
The Road Is Open Again, 1933
Just Around the Corner, 1933
Dames, 1934 (with Ruby Keeler)
Flirtation Walk, 1934 (with Ruby Keeler)
Happiness Ahead, 1934
Twenty Million Sweethearts, 1934
Wonder Bar, 1934
Thanks a Million, 1935
Shipmates Forever, 1935 (with Ruby Keeler)
A Midsummer Night's Dream, 1935
Page Miss Glory, 1935
Broadway Gondolier, 1935
Gold Diggers of 1935, 1935
Gold Diggers of 1937, 1936
Stage Struck, 1936
Hearts Divided, 1936
Colleen, 1936 (with Ruby Keeler)
Hollywood Hotel, 1937
Varsity Show, 1937
The Singing Marine, 1937
On the Avenue, 1937
Going Places, 1938
Hard to Get, 1938

Cowboy from Brooklyn, 1938
Naughty But Nice, 1939
Christmas in July, 1940
I Want a Divorce, 1940
In the Navy, 1941
Model Wife, 1941
True to Life, 1943
Riding High, 1943
Happy Go Lucky, 1943
Murder, My Sweet, 1944
Meet the People, 1944
It Happened Tomorrow, 1944
Cornered, 1945
Johnny O'Clock, 1947
Rogues' Regiment, 1948
Station West, 1948
Pitfall, 1948
To the Ends of the Earth, 1948
Mrs. Mike, 1949
Right Cross, 1950
The Reformer and the Redhead, 1950
You Never Can Tell, 1951
The Tall Target, 1951
Cry Danger, 1951
The Bad and the Beautiful, 1952
Susan Slept Here, 1954

WILLIAM POWELL
Sherlock Holmes, 1922
When Knighthood Was in Flower, 1922
Outcast, 1922
The Bright Shawl, 1923
Under the Red Robe, 1923
Dangerous Money, 1924
Romola, 1924
Too Many Kisses, 1925
Faint Perfume, 1925
My Lady's Lips, 1925
The Beautiful City, 1925
White Mice, 1926
Sea Horses, 1926
Desert Gold, 1926
The Runaway, 1926
Aloma of the South Seas, 1926
Beau Geste, 1926
Tin Gods, 1926
The Great Gatsby, 1926
New York, 1927
Love's Greatest Mistake, 1927
Señorita, 1927
Special Delivery, 1927
Time to Love, 1927
Paid to Love, 1927
Nevada, 1927
She's a Sheik, 1927
Beau Sabreur, 1928
The Last Command, 1928
Feel My Pulse, 1928
Partners in Crime, 1928
The Dragnet, 1928
The Vanishing Pioneer, 1928
Forgotten Faces, 1928
Interference, 1928
The Canary Murder Case, 1929
The Four Feathers, 1929

The Greene Murder Case, 1929
Charming Sinners, 1929
Pointed Heels, 1929
Behind the Make-Up, 1930
Street of Chance, 1930
The Benson Murder Case, 1930
Shadow of the Law, 1930
For the Defense, 1930
Man of the World, 1931
Ladies' Man, 1931
The Road to Singapore, 1931
High Pressure, 1932
Jewel Robbery, 1932
One Way Passage, 1932
Lawyer Man, 1933
Private Detective 62, 1933
Double Harness, 1933
The Kennel Murder Case, 1933
Fashions of 1934, 1934
Manhattan Melodrama, 1934
(with Myrna Loy)
The Thin Man, 1934 (with Myrna Loy)
The Key, 1934
Evelyn Prentice, 1934 (with Myrna Loy)
Star of Midnight, 1935
Reckless, 1935
Escapade, 1935
Rendezvous, 1935
The Great Ziegfeld, 1936 (with Myrna Loy)
The Ex-Mrs. Bradford, 1936
My Man Godfrey, 1936
Libeled Lady, 1936 (with Myrna Loy)
After the Thin Man, 1936 (with Myrna Loy)
The Last of Mrs. Cheyney, 1937
The Emperor's Candlesticks, 1937
Double Wedding, 1937 (with Myrna Loy)
The Baroness and the Butler, 1938
Another Thin Man, 1939 (with Myrna Loy)
I Love You Again, 1940 (with Myrna Loy)
Love Crazy, 1941 (with Myrna Loy)
Shadow of the Thin Man, 1941
(with Myrna Loy)
Crossroads, 1942
The Heavenly Body, 1944
The Thin Man Goes Home, 1945
(with Myrna Loy)
Ziegfeld Follies, 1946
The Hoodlum Saint, 1946
Life with Father, 1947
Song of the Thin Man, 1947
(with Myrna Loy)
The Senator Was Indiscreet, 1947
(with Myrna Loy)
Mr. Peabody and the Mermaid, 1948
Take One False Step, 1949
Dancing in the Dark, 1949
It's a Big Country, 1951
The Treasure of Lost Canyon, 1952
The Girl Who Had Everything, 1953
How to Marry a Millionaire, 1953
Mister Roberts, 1955

TYRONE POWER

Tom Brown of Culver, 1932
Girls' Dormitory, 1936
Ladies in Love, 1936
Lloyd's of London, 1936
Love Is News, 1937
Café Metropole, 1937
Thin Ice, 1937
Second Honeymoon, 1937
In Old Chicago, 1938
Alexander's Ragtime Band, 1938
Marie Antoinette, 1938
Suez, 1938
Jesse James, 1939
Rose of Washington Square, 1939
Second Fiddle, 1939
The Rains Came, 1939
Day-Time Wife, 1939
Johnny Apollo, 1940
Brigham Young, 1940
The Mark of Zorro, 1940
Blood and Sand, 1941
A Yank in the R.A.F., 1941
Son of Fury, 1942 (with Gene Tierney)
This Above All, 1942
The Black Swan, 1942
Crash Dive, 1943
The Razor's Edge, 1946 (with Gene Tierney)
Nightmare Alley, 1947
Captain from Castile, 1947
The Luck of the Irish, 1948
That Wonderful Urge, 1948
(with Gene Tierney)
Prince of Foxes, 1949
The Black Rose, 1950
American Guerrilla in the Philippines, 1950
Rawhide, 1951
The House in the Square, 1951
Diplomatic Courier, 1952
Pony Soldier, 1952
The Mississippi Gambler, 1953
King of the Khyber Rifles, 1953
The Long Gray Line, 1955
Untamed, 1955
The Eddy Duchin Story, 1956
Seven Waves Away/Abandon Ship!, 1957
The Sun Also Rises, 1957
Witness for the Prosecution, 1957

ELVIS PRESLEY

Love Me Tender, 1956
Loving You, 1957
Jailhouse Rock, 1957
King Creole, 1958
G. I. Blues, 1960
Flaming Star, 1960
Wild in the Country, 1961
Blue Hawaii, 1961
Girls! Girls! Girls!, 1962
Follow That Dream, 1962
Kid Galahad, 1962
It Happened at the World's Fair, 1963
Fun in Acapulco, 1963
Viva Las Vegas, 1964 (with Ann-Margret)
Roustabout, 1964

Kissin' Cousins, 1964
Harum Scarum, 1965
Tickle Me, 1965
Girl Happy, 1965
Frankie and Johnny, 1966
Paradise, Hawaiian Style, 1966
Spinout, 1966
Easy Come, Easy Go, 1967
Clambake, 1967
Double Trouble, 1967
Stay Away, Joe, 1968
Speedway, 1968
Live a Little, Love a Little, 1968
The Trouble with Girls, 1969
Charro!, 1969
Change of Habit, 1969
Elvis—That's the Way It Is, 1970
Elvis on Tour, 1972

GINGER ROGERS

Young Man of Manhattan, 1930
The Sap from Syracuse, 1930
Queen High, 1930
Office Blues, 1930
Follow the Leader, 1930
Honor Among Lovers, 1931
The Tip-Off, 1931
Suicide Fleet, 1931
Carnival Boat, 1932
The Tenderfoot, 1932
The Thirteenth Guest, 1932
Hat Check Girl, 1932
You Said a Mouthful, 1932
42nd Street, 1933
Broadway Bad, 1933
Gold Diggers of 1933, 1933
Professional Sweetheart, 1933
Don't Bet on Love, 1933
A Shriek in the Night, 1933
Rafter Romance, 1933
Chance at Heaven, 1933
Sitting Pretty, 1933
Flying Down to Rio, 1933
(with Fred Astaire)
Twenty Million Sweethearts, 1934
Upperworld, 1934
Finishing School, 1934
Change of Heart, 1934
The Gay Divorcee, 1934 (with Fred Astaire)
Romance in Manhattan, 1935
Roberta, 1935 (with Fred Astaire)
Star of Midnight, 1935
Top Hat, 1935 (with Fred Astaire)
In Person, 1935
Follow the Fleet, 1936 (with Fred Astaire)
Swing Time, 1936 (with Fred Astaire)
Shall We Dance, 1937 (with Fred Astaire)
Stage Door, 1937
Vivacious Lady, 1938
Having Wonderful Time, 1938
Carefree, 1938 (with Fred Astaire)

The Story of Vernon and Irene Castle, **1939**
  (with Fred Astaire)
Bachelor Mother, 1939
5th Ave Girl, 1939
Primrose Path, 1940
Lucky Partners, 1940
Kitty Foyle, 1940
Tom Dick and Harry, 1941
Roxie Hart, 1942
Tales of Manhattan, 1942
The Major and the Minor, 1942
Once Upon a Honeymoon, 1942
Tender Comrade, 1943
Lady in the Dark, 1944
I'll Be Seeing You, 1945
Week-End at the Waldorf, 1945
Heartbeat, 1946
Magnificent Doll, 1946
It Had to Be You, 1947
The Barkleys of Broadway, **1949**
  (with Fred Astaire)
Perfect Strangers, 1950
Storm Warning, 1951
The Groom Wore Spurs, 1951
We're Not Married!, 1952
Dreamboat, 1952
Monkey Business, 1952
Forever Female, 1953
Black Widow, 1954
Beautiful Stranger, 1954
Tight Spot, 1955
The First Traveling Saleslady, 1956
Teenage Rebel, 1956
Oh, Men! Oh, Women!, 1957
The Confession, 1964
Harlow, 1965

MICKEY ROONEY

Sin's Pay Day, 1932
High Speed, 1932
Fast Companions, 1932
My Pal, the King, 1932
The Big Cage, 1933
The Big Chance, 1933
Broadway to Hollywood, 1933
The World Changes, 1933
The Chief, 1933
Beloved, 1934
The Lost Jungle, 1934
I Like It That Way, 1934
Manhattan Melodrama, 1934
Love Birds, 1934
Hide-Out, 1934
Half a Sinner, 1934
Blind Date, 1934
Death on the Diamond, 1934
The County Chairman, 1935
The Healer, 1935
A Midsummer Night's Dream, 1935
Ah, Wilderness!, 1935
Riffraff, 1936
Little Lord Fauntleroy, 1936
Down the Stretch, 1936

The Devil Is a Sissy, 1936
A Family Affair, 1937
Captains Courageous, 1937
Slave Ship, 1937
Live, Love and Learn, 1937
Thoroughbreds Don't Cry, **1937**
  (with Judy Garland)
You're Only Young Once, 1937
Love Is a Headache, 1938
Judge Hardy's Children, 1938
Hold That Kiss, 1938
Lord Jeff, 1938
Love Finds Andy Hardy, **1938**
  (with Judy Garland)
Boys Town, 1938
Stablemates, 1938
Out West with the Hardys, 1938
The Adventures of Huckleberry Finn, 1939
The Hardys Ride High, 1939
Andy Hardy Gets Spring Fever, 1939
Babes in Arms, **1939 (with Judy Garland)**
Judge Hardy and Son, 1939
Young Tom Edison, 1940
Andy Hardy Meets Debutante, **1940**
  (with Judy Garland)
Strike Up the Band, **1940**
  (with Judy Garland)
Andy Hardy's Private Secretary, 1941
Men of Boys Town, 1941
Life Begins for Andy Hardy, **1941**
  (with Judy Garland)
Babes on Broadway, **1941**
  (with Judy Garland)
The Courtship of Andy Hardy, 1942
A Yank at Eton, 1942
Andy Hardy's Double Life, 1942
The Human Comedy, 1943
Girl Crazy, **1943 (with Judy Garland)**
Andy Hardy's Blonde Trouble, 1944
National Velvet, 1944
Love Laughs at Andy Hardy, 1947
Killer McCoy, 1947
Summer Holiday, 1948
Words and Music, **1948 (with Judy Garland)**
The Big Wheel, 1949
Quicksand, 1950
The Fireball, 1950
He's a Cockeyed Wonder, 1950
My Outlaw Brother, 1951
The Strip, 1951
Sound Off, 1952
Off Limits, 1953
All Ashore, 1953
A Slight Case of Larceny, 1953
Drive a Crooked Road, 1954
The Atomic Kid, 1954
The Bridges at Toko-Ri, 1955
The Twinkle in God's Eye, 1955
The Bold and the Brave, 1956
Francis in the Haunted House, 1956
Magnificent Roughnecks, 1956
Operation Mad Ball, 1957
Baby Face Nelson, 1957
*A Nice Little Bank
  That Should Be Robbed,* 1958

Andy Hardy Comes Home, 1958
The Big Operator, 1959
The Last Mile, 1959
Platinum High School, 1960
The Private Lives of Adam and Eve, 1960
*King of the Roaring 20's—
  The Story of Arnold Rothstein,* 1961
Breakfast at Tiffany's, 1961
Everything's Ducky, 1961
Requiem for a Heavyweight, 1962
It's a Mad Mad Mad Mad World, 1963
The Secret Invasion, 1964
Twenty-Four Hours to Kill, 1965
How to Stuff a Wild Bikini, 1965
L'arcidiavolo/The Devil in Love, 1966
Ambush Bay, 1966
Skidoo, 1968
The Extraordinary Seaman, 1969
The Comic, 1969
80 Steps to Jonah, 1969
Cockeyed Cowboys of Calico County, 1970
The Manipulator, 1971
Pulp, 1972
Richard, 1972
The Godmothers, 1973
Thunder County, 1974
Rachel's Man, 1974
Juego sucio en Panamá/Ace of Hearts, 1975
*Bons baisers de Hong Kong/
  From Hong Kong with Love,* 1975
Find the Lady, 1976
The Domino Principle, 1977
Pete's Dragon, 1977
The Magic of Lassie, 1978
The Black Stallion, 1979
Arabian Adventure, 1979
The Emperor of Peru, 1982
Lightning, the White Stallion, 1986
Erik the Viking, 1989
*My Heroes Have
  Always Been Cowboys,* 1991
La vida láctea/The Milky Life, 1992
*Silent Night, Deadly Night 5:
  The Toy Maker,* 1992
Maximum Force, 1992
The Legend of Wolf Mountain, 1993
Revenge of the Red Baron, 1994
The Outlaws: Legend of O.B. Taggart, 1994
Making Waves, 1994
Killing Midnight, 1997
Boys Will Be Boys, 1997
Animals and the Tollkeeper, 1998
*Michael Kael contre la World News
  Company,* 1998
Sinbad: The Battle of the Dark Nights, 1998
Babe: Pig in the City, 1998
The First of May, 1999
Topa Topa Bluffs, 2002
Paradise, 2003
Night at the Museum, 2006

JANE RUSSELL

The Outlaw, 1943
Young Widow, 1946
The Paleface, 1948
His Kind of Woman, 1951
    (with Robert Mitchum)
Double Dynamite, 1951
The Las Vegas Story, 1952
Macao, 1952 (with Robert Mitchum)
Son of Paleface, 1952
Montana Belle, 1952
Road to Bali, 1953
Gentlemen Prefer Blondes, 1953
The French Line, 1954
Underwater!, 1955
Foxfire, 1955
Gentlemen Marry Brunettes, 1955
The Tall Men, 1955
Hot Blood, 1956
The Revolt of Mamie Stover, 1956
The Fuzzy Pink Nightgown, 1957
Fate Is the Hunter, 1964
Johnny Reno, 1966
Waco, 1966
The Born Losers, 1967
Darker Than Amber, 1970

JAMES STEWART

The Murder Man, 1935
Rose-Marie, 1936
Next Time We Love, 1936
    (with Margaret Sullavan)
Wife vs. Secretary, 1936
Small Town Girl, 1936
Speed, 1936
The Gorgeous Hussy, 1936
Born to Dance, 1936
After the Thin Man, 1936
Seventh Heaven, 1937
The Last Gangster, 1937
Navy Blue and Gold, 1937
Of Human Hearts, 1938
Vivacious Lady, 1938
The Shopworn Angel, 1938
    (with Margaret Sullavan)
You Can't Take It with You, 1938
Made for Each Other, 1939
The Ice Follies of 1939, 1939
It's a Wonderful World, 1939
Mr. Smith Goes to Washington, 1939
Destry Rides Again, 1939
The Shop Around the Corner, 1940
    (with Margaret Sullavan)
The Mortal Storm, 1940
    (with Margaret Sullavan)
No Time for Comedy, 1940
The Philadelphia Story, 1940
Come Live with Me, 1941
Pot o' Gold, 1941
Ziegfeld Girl, 1941
It's a Wonderful Life, 1946
Magic Town, 1947
Call Northside 777, 1948
On Our Merry Way, 1948
Rope, 1948

You Gotta Stay Happy, 1948
The Stratton Story, 1949
Malaya, 1949
Winchester '73, 1950
Broken Arrow, 1950
Harvey, 1950
The Jackpot, 1950
No Highway in the Sky, 1951
The Greatest Show on Earth, 1952
Bend of the River, 1952
Carbine Williams, 1952
The Naked Spur, 1953
Thunder Bay, 1953
The Glenn Miller Story, 1953
Rear Window, 1954
The Far Country, 1954
Strategic Air Command, 1955
The Man from Laramie, 1955
The Man Who Knew Too Much, 1956
The Spirit of St. Louis, 1957
Night Passage, 1957
Vertigo, 1958
Bell, Book and Candle, 1958
Anatomy of a Murder, 1959
The FBI Story, 1959
The Mountain Road, 1960
Two Rode Together, 1961
The Man Who Shot Liberty Valance, 1962
Mr. Hobbs Takes a Vacation, 1962
How the West Was Won, 1962
Take Her, She's Mine, 1963
Cheyenne Autumn, 1964
Dear Brigitte, 1965
Shenandoah, 1965
The Flight of the Phoenix, 1965
The Rare Breed, 1966
Firecreek, 1967
Bandolero!, 1969
The Cheyenne Social Club, 1970
Fools' Parade, 1971
The Shootist, 1976
Airport '77, 1977
The Big Sleep, 1978
The Magic of Lassie, 1978
Afurika monogatari/
    The Green Horizon, 1981

MARGARET SULLAVAN

Only Yesterday, 1933
Little Man, What Now?, 1934
So Red the Rose, 1935
The Good Fairy, 1935
The Moon's Our Home, 1936
Next Time We Love, 1936
    (with James Stewart)
I Loved a Soldier, 1936
The Shining Hour, 1938
Three Comrades, 1938
The Shopworn Angel, 1938
    (with James Stewart)
The Shop Around the Corner, 1940
    (with James Stewart)

The Mortal Storm, 1940
    (with James Stewart)
Appointment for Love, 1941
So Ends Our Night, 1941
Back Street, 1941
Cry 'Havoc,' 1943
No Sad Songs for Me, 1950

ELIZABETH TAYLOR

There's One Born Every Minute, 1942
Lassie Come Home, 1943
National Velvet, 1944
Courage of Lassie, 1946
Life with Father, 1947
Cynthia, 1947
A Date with Judy, 1948
Julia Misbehaves, 1948
Little Women, 1949
Conspirator, 1949
The Big Hangover, 1950
Father of the Bride, 1950
Father's Little Dividend, 1951
A Place in the Sun, 1951
Love Is Better Than Ever, 1952
Ivanhoe, 1952
The Girl Who Had Everything, 1953
Rhapsody, 1954
Elephant Walk, 1954
Beau Brummell, 1954
The Last Time I Saw Paris, 1954
Giant, 1956
Raintree County, 1957
Cat on a Hot Tin Roof, 1958
    (with Paul Newman)
Suddenly, Last Summer, 1959
Butterfield 8, 1960
Cleopatra, 1963 (with Richard Burton)
The V.I.P.s, 1963 (with Richard Burton)
The Sandpiper, 1965 (with Richard Burton)
Who's Afraid of Virginia Woolf?, 1966
    (with Richard Burton)
The Comedians, 1967 (with Richard Burton)
The Taming of the Shrew, 1967
    (with Richard Burton)
Doctor Faustus, 1967 (with Richard Burton)
Reflections in a Golden Eye, 1967
Boom!, 1968 (with Richard Burton)
Secret Ceremony, 1968
The Only Game in Town, 1970
Zee and Co., 1972
Under Milk Wood, 1972
    (with Richard Burton)
Hammersmith Is Out, 1972
    (with Richard Burton)
Night Watch, 1973
Ash Wednesday, 1973
Identikit/The Driver's Seat, 1974
The Blue Bird, 1976
A Little Night Music, 1977
The Mirror Crack'd, 1980
Il Giovane Toscanini/Young Toscanini, 1988
The Flintstones, 1994

ROBERT TAYLOR

Handy Andy, 1934
There's Always Tomorrow, 1934
A Wicked Woman, 1934
Society Doctor, 1935
Times Square Lady, 1935
West Point of the Air, 1935
Murder in the Fleet, 1935
Broadway Melody of 1936, 1935
Magnificent Obsession, 1935
Small Town Girl, 1936
Private Number, 1936
His Brother's Wife, 1936
The Gorgeous Hussy, 1936
Camille, 1936 (with Greta Garbo)
Personal Property, 1937
This is My Affair, 1937
Broadway Melody of 1938, 1937
A Yank at Oxford, 1938
Three Comrades, 1938
The Crowd Roars, 1938
Stand Up and Fight, 1939
Lucky Night, 1939
Lady of the Tropics, 1939
Remember?, 1939
Waterloo Bridge, 1940
Escape, 1940
Flight Command, 1940
Billy the Kid, 1941
When Ladies Meet, 1941
Johnny Eager, 1942
Her Cardboard Lover, 1942
Stand By for Action, 1942
Bataan, 1943
Song of Russia, 1944
Undercurrent, 1946
High Wall, 1947
Ambush, 1950
The Bribe, 1949
Conspirator, 1949
Devil's Doorway, 1950
Westward the Women, 1951
Quo Vadis, 1951
Ivanhoe, 1952
Above and Beyond, 1952
Knights of the Round Table, 1953
Ride, Vaquero!, 1953
All the Brothers Were Valiant, 1953
Valley of the Kings, 1954
Rogue Cop, 1954
Many Rivers to Cross, 1955
Quentin Durward, 1955
The Last Hunt, 1956
D-Day the Sixth of June, 1956
The Power and the Prize, 1956
Tip on a Dead Jockey, 1957
Saddle the Wind, 1958
The Law and Jake Wade, 1958
Party Girl, 1958
The Hangman, 1959
The House of the Seven Hawks, 1959
Killers of Kilimanjaro, 1960
Miracle of the White Stallions, 1963
Cattle King, 1963
A House Is Not a Home, 1964
The Night Walker, 1964
Johnny Tiger, 1966
Savage Pampas, 1966
La sfinge d'oro/The Golden Sphinx, 1967
Return of the Gunfighter, 1967
Le rouble à deux faces/
     The Day the Hot Line Got Hot, 1968
Where Angels Go, Trouble Follows, 1968

GENE TIERNEY

The Return of Frank James, 1940
Hudson's Bay, 1941
Tobacco Road, 1941
Belle Starr, 1941
Sundown, 1941
The Shanghai Gesture, 1941
Son of Fury, 1942 (with Tyrone Power)
Rings on Her Fingers, 1942
Thunder Birds, 1942
China Girl, 1942
Heaven Can Wait, 1943
Laura, 1944
A Bell for Adano, 1945
Leave Her to Heaven, 1945
Dragonwyck, 1946
The Razor's Edge, 1946
     (with Tyrone Power)
The Ghost and Mrs. Muir, 1947
The Iron Curtain, 1948
That Wonderful Urge, 1948
     (with Tyrone Power)
Whirlpool, 1949
Night and the City, 1950
Where the Sidewalk Ends, 1950
Close to My Heart, 1951
The Mating Season, 1951
On the Riviera, 1951
The Secret of Convict Lake, 1951
Way of a Gaucho, 1952
Plymouth Adventure, 1952
Never Let Me Go, 1952
Personal Affair, 1953
The Egyptian, 1954
Black Widow, 1954
The Left Hand of God, 1955
Advise & Consent, 1962
*Las cuatro noches de la luna llena/*Four
     Nights of the Full Moon, 1963
Toys in the Attic, 1963
The Pleasure Seekers, 1964

SPENCER TRACY

Up the River, 1930
Quick Millions, 1931
Six Cylinder Love, 1931
Goldie, 1931
She Wanted a Millionaire, 1932
Sky Devils, 1932
Disorderly Conduct, 1932
Young America, 1932
Society Girl, 1932
The Painted Woman, 1932
Me and My Gal, 1932
20,000 Years in Sing Sing, 1932
The Face in the Sky, 1933
Shanghai Madness, 1933
The Power and the Glory, 1933
Man's Castle, 1933
The Mad Game, 1933
The Show-Off, 1934
Looking for Trouble, 1934
Bottoms Up, 1934
Now I'll Tell, 1934
Marie Galante, 1934
It's a Small World, 1935
The Murder Man, 1935
Dante's Inferno, 1935
Whipsaw, 1935
Riffraff, 1936
Fury, 1936
San Francisco, 1936
Libeled Lady, 1936
They Gave Him a Gun, 1937
Captains Courageous, 1937
Big City, 1937
Mannequin, 1937
Test Pilot, 1938
Boys Town, 1938
Stanley and Livingstone, 1939
I Take This Woman, 1940
Northwest Passage, 1940
Edison, the Man, 1940
Boom Town, 1940
Men of Boys Town, 1941
Dr. Jekyll and Mr. Hyde, 1941
Woman of the Year, 1942
     (with Katharine Hepburn)
Tortilla Flat, 1942
Keeper of the Flame, 1942
     (with Katharine Hepburn)
A Guy Named Joe, 1943
The Seventh Cross, 1944
Thirty Seconds over Tokyo, 1944
Without Love, 1945
     (with Katharine Hepburn)
The Sea of Grass, 1947
     (with Katharine Hepburn)
Cass Timberlane, 1947
State of the Union, 1948
     (with Katharine Hepburn)
Edward, My Son, 1949
Adam's Rib, 1949 (with Katharine Hepburn)
Malaya, 1949
Father of the Bride, 1950
Father's Little Dividend, 1951
The People Against O'Hara, 1951
Pat and Mike, 1952
     (with Katharine Hepburn)
Plymouth Adventure, 1952
The Actress, 1953
Broken Lance, 1954
Bad Day at Black Rock, 1955
The Mountain, 1956

Desk Set, 1957 (with Katharine Hepburn)

The Old Man and the Sea, 1958
The Last Hurrah, 1958
Inherit the Wind, 1960
The Devil at 4 O'Clock, 1961
Judgment at Nuremberg, 1961
It's a Mad Mad Mad Mad World, 1963
**Guess Who's Coming to Dinner, 1967
(with Katharine Hepburn)**

LANA TURNER

They Won't Forget, 1937
The Great Garrick, 1937
The Adventures of Marco Polo, 1938
Love Finds Andy Hardy, 1938
Rich Man, Poor Girl, 1938
Dramatic School, 1938
Calling Dr. Kildare, 1939
These Glamour Girls, 1939
Dancing Co-Ed, 1939
Two Girls on Broadway, 1940
We Who Are Young, 1940
Ziegfeld Girl, 1941
Dr. Jekyll and Mr. Hyde, 1941
Honky Tonk, 1941
Johnny Eager, 1942
Somewhere I'll Find You, 1942
The Youngest Profession, 1943
Slightly Dangerous, 1943
Marriage Is a Private Affair, 1944
Keep Your Powder Dry, 1945
Week-End at the Waldorf, 1945
**The Postman Always Rings Twice, 1946
(with John Garfield)**
Green Dolphin Street, 1947
Cass Timberlane, 1947
Homecoming, 1948
The Three Musketeers, 1948
A Life of Her Own, 1950
Mr. Imperium, 1951
The Merry Widow, 1952
The Bad and the Beautiful, 1952
Latin Lovers, 1953
Flame and the Flesh, 1954
Betrayed, 1954
The Prodigal, 1955
The Sea Chase, 1955
The Rains of Ranchipur, 1955
Diane, 1956
Peyton Place, 1957
The Lady Takes a Flyer, 1958
Another Time, Another Place, 1958
Imitation of Life, 1959
Portrait in Black, 1960
By Love Possessed, 1961
Bachelor in Paradise, 1961
Who's Got the Action?, 1962
Love Has Many Faces, 1965
Madame X, 1966
The Big Cube, 1969
Persecution, 1974
Bittersweet Love, 1976
Witches' Brew, 1980
Thwarted, 1991

JOHN WAYNE

Bardelys the Magnificent, 1926
Words and Music, 1929
The Big Trail, 1930
Girls Demand Excitement, 1931
Three Girls Lost, 1931
Arizona, 1931
Range Feud, 1931
Maker of Men, 1931
The Shadow of the Eagle, 1932
Texas Cyclone, 1932
Two-Fisted Law, 1932
Lady and Gent, 1932
The Hurricane Express, 1932
Ride Him, Cowboy, 1932
The Big Stampede, 1932
Haunted Gold, 1932
The Telegraph Trail, 1933
The Three Musketeers, 1933
Somewhere in Sonora, 1933
His Private Secretary, 1933
The Life of Jimmy Dolan, 1933
Baby Face, 1933
The Man from Monterey, 1933
Riders of Destiny, 1933
Sagebrush Trail, 1933
The Lucky Texan, 1934
West of the Divide, 1934
Blue Steel, 1934
The Man from Utah, 1934
Randy Rides Alone, 1934
The Star Packer, 1934
The Trail Beyond, 1934
The Lawless Frontier, 1934
'Neath the Arizona Skies, 1934
Texas Terror, 1935
Rainbow Valley, 1935
The Desert Trail, 1935
The Dawn Rider, 1935
Paradise Canyon, 1935
Westward Ho, 1935
The New Frontier, 1935
Lawless Range, 1935
The Oregon Trail, 1936
The Lawless Nineties, 1936
King of the Pecos, 1936
The Lonely Trail, 1936
Winds of the Wasteland, 1936
Sea Spoilers, 1936
Conflict, 1936
California Straight Ahead!, 1937
I Cover the War, 1937
Idol of the Crowds, 1937
Adventure's End, 1937
Born to the West, 1937
Pals of the Saddle, 1938
Overland Stage Raiders, 1938
Santa Fe Stampede, 1938
Red River Range, 1938
Stagecoach, 1939
The Night Riders, 1939
Three Texas Steers, 1939
Wyoming Outlaw, 1939
New Frontier, 1939
Allegheny Uprising, 1939

Dark Command, 1940
Three Faces West, 1940
The Long Voyage Home, 1940
Seven Sinners, 1940
A Man Betrayed, 1941
Lady from Louisiana, 1941
The Shepherd of the Hills, 1941
Lady for a Night, 1942
Reap the Wild Wind, 1942
The Spoilers, 1942
In Old California, 1942
Flying Tigers, 1942
Pittsburgh, 1942
Reunion in France, 1942
A Lady Takes a Chance, 1943
In Old Oklahoma, 1943
The Fighting Seabees, 1944
Tall in the Saddle, 1944
Flame of Barbary Coast, 1945
Back to Bataan, 1945
They Were Expendable, 1945
Dakota, 1945
Without Reservations, 1946
Angel and the Badman, 1947
Tycoon, 1947
Fort Apache, 1948
Red River, 1948
3 Godfathers, 1948
Wake of the Red Witch, 1948
The Fighting Kentuckian, 1949
She Wore a Yellow Ribbon, 1949
Sands of Iwo Jima, 1949
Rio Grande, 1950 (with Maureen O'Hara)
Operation Pacific, 1951
Flying Leathernecks, 1951
The Quiet Man, 1952 (with Maureen O'Hara)
Big Jim McLain, 1952
Trouble Along the Way, 1953
Island in the Sky, 1953
Hondo, 1953
The High and the Mighty, 1954
The Sea Chase, 1955
Blood Alley, 1955
The Conqueror, 1956
The Searchers, 1956
**The Wings of Eagles, 1957
(with Maureen O'Hara)**
Jet Pilot, 1957
Legend of the Lost, 1957
The Barbarian and the Geisha, 1958
Rio Bravo, 1959
The Horse Soldiers, 1959
The Alamo, 1960
North to Alaska, 1960
The Comancheros, 1961
The Man Who Shot Liberty Valance, 1962
Hatari!, 1962
The Longest Day, 1962
How the West Was Won, 1962
McLintock!, 1963 (with Maureen O'Hara)
Donovan's Reef, 1963
Circus World, 1964

The Greatest Story Ever Told, 1965
In Harm's Way, 1965
The Sons of Katie Elder, 1965
Cast a Giant Shadow, 1966
El Dorado, 1966
The War Wagon, 1967
The Green Berets, 1968
Hellfighters, 1968
True Grit, 1969
The Undefeated, 1969
Chisum, 1970
Rio Lobo, 1970
Big Jake, 1971 (with Maureen O'Hara)
The Cowboys, 1972
The Train Robbers, 1973
Cahill U.S. Marshal, 1973
McQ, 1974
Brannigan, 1975
Rooster Cogburn, 1975
The Shootist, 1976

JOHNNY WEISSMULLER

Glorifying the American Girl, 1929
Tarzan the Ape Man, 1932
   (with Maureen O'Sullivan)
Tarzan and His Mate, 1934
   (with Maureen O'Sullivan)
Tarzan Escapes, 1936
   (with Maureen O'Sullivan)
Tarzan Finds a Son!, 1939
   (with Maureen O'Sullivan)
Tarzan's Secret Treasure, 1941
   (with Maureen O'Sullivan)
Tarzan's New York Adventure, 1942
   (with Maureen O'Sullivan)
Tarzan's Desert Mystery, 1943
Tarzan Triumphs, 1943
Tarzan and the Amazons, 1945
Swamp Fire, 1946
Tarzan and the Leopard Woman, 1946
Tarzan and the Huntress, 1947
Jungle Jim, 1948
Tarzan and the Mermaids, 1948
The Lost Tribe, 1949
Jungle Jim in Pygmy Island, 1950
Captive Girl, 1950
Mark of the Gorilla, 1950
Jungle Manhunt, 1951
Fury of the Congo, 1951
Voodoo Tiger, 1952
Jungle Jim in the Forbidden Land, 1952
Killer Ape, 1953
Valley of Head Hunters, 1953
Savage Mutiny, 1953
Cannibal Attack, 1954
Jungle Man-Eaters, 1954
Devil Goddess, 1955
Jungle Moon Men, 1955
The Phynx, 1970
   (with Maureen O'Sullivan)
Won Ton Ton, the Dog Who Saved Hollywood, 1976

ORSON WELLES

Too Much Johnson, 1938
Citizen Kane, 1941
Journey into Fear, 1943
Jane Eyre, 1944
Follow the Boys, 1944
The Stranger, 1946
Tomorrow Is Forever, 1946
The Lady from Shanghai, 1948
   (with Rita Hayworth)
Macbeth, 1948
The Third Man, 1949
Black Magic, 1949
Prince of Foxes, 1949
The Black Rose, 1950
Trent's Last Case, 1953
L'uomo, la bestia e la virtù, 1953
Trouble in the Glen, 1954
Napoléon, 1955
Mr. Arkadin, 1955
Three Cases of Murder, 1955
Othello, 1955
Moby Dick, 1956
Si Versailles m'était conté/
   Royal Affairs in Versailles, 1957
Man in the Shadow, 1957
Touch of Evil, 1958
The Long, Hot Summer, 1958
The Roots of Heaven, 1958
Austerlitz, 1959
Compulsion, 1959
Crack in the Mirror, 1960
Ferry to Hong Kong, 1961
David e Golia/David and Goliath, 1961
I Tartari/The Tartars, 1962
Ro.Go.Pa.G, 1962
The V.I.P.s, 1963
La Fayette, 1963
Le Procès/The Trial, 1963
A Man for All Seasons, 1966
La fabuleuse aventure de Marco Polo/
   Marco the Magnificent, 1966
*Paris brûle-t-il?/*Is Paris Burning?, *1966*
The Sailor from Gibraltar, 1967
Campanadas a medianoche/Falstaff, 1967
Casino Royale, 1967
Oedipus the King, 1968
I'll Never Forget What's 'is Name, 1968
Tepepa/Long Live the Revolution, 1968
Kampf um Rom I/The Last Roman, 1968
The Immortal Story, 1969
Kampf um Rom II—Der Verrat, 1969
The Southern Star, 1969
House of Cards, 1969
12 + 1, 1969
*Bitka na Neretvi/*The Battle of Neretva, 1969
The Kremlin Letter, 1970
Catch-22, 1970
Waterloo, 1971
*Malpertuis'/*The Legend of Doom House, 1972
A Safe Place, 1971

La décade prodigieuse/
   Ten Days Wonder, *1971*
Necromancy, 1972
Get to Know Your Rabbit, 1972
Treasure Island, 1972
F for Fake, 1973
Voyage of the Damned, 1976
The Muppet Movie, 1979
Tajna Nikole Tesle, 1980
Butterfly, 1981
In Our Hands, 1983
Where Is Parsifal?, 1984
Someone to Love, 1987
Hot Money, 1989

MAE WEST

Night After Night, 1932
She Done Him Wrong, 1933
I'm No Angel, 1933
Belle of the Nineties, 1934
Goin' to Town, 1935
Klondike Annie, 1936
Go West Young Man, 1936
Every Day's a Holiday, 1937
My Little Chickadee, 1940
   (with W.C. Fields)
The Heat's On, 1943
Myra Breckinridge, 1970
Sextette, 1978

FAY WRAY

Gasoline Love, 1923
Just a Good Guy, 1924
The Coast Patrol, 1925
Sure-Mike!, 1925
Isn't Life Terrible?, 1925
Thundering Landlords, 1925
Chasing the Chaser, 1925
Madame Sans Jane, 1925
No Father to Guide Him, 1925
Unfriendly Enemies, 1925
Your Own Back Yard, 1925
Moonlight and Noses, 1925
One Wild Time, 1926
Don Key, Son of Burro, 1926
The Man in the Saddle, 1926
Don't Shoot, 1926
The Wild Horse Stampede, 1926
The Saddle Tramp, 1926
The Show Cowpuncher, 1926
Lazy Lightning, 1926
Loco Luck, 1927
A One Man Game, 1927
Spurs and Saddles, 1927
The Honeymoon, 1928
The Legion of the Condemned, 1928
Street of Sin, 1928
The First Kiss, 1928
The Wedding March, 1928
Thunderbolt, 1929

The Four Feathers, 1929
Pointed Heels, 1929
Behind the Make-Up, 1930
Paramount on Parade, 1930
The Texan, 1930
The Border Legion, 1930
The Sea God, 1930
Captain Thunder, 1930
The Conquering Horde, 1931
Three Rogues, 1931
Dirigible, 1931
The Finger Points, 1931
The Lawyer's Secret, 1931
The Unholy Garden, 1931
Stowaway, 1932
Doctor X, 1932
The Most Dangerous Game, 1932
The Vampire Bat, 1933
Mystery of the Wax Museum, 1933
***King Kong*, 1933 (with King Kong)**
Below the Sea, 1933
Ann Carver's Profession, 1933
The Woman I Stole, 1933
Shanghai Madness, 1933
The Big Brain, 1933
One Sunday Afternoon, 1933
The Bowery, 1933
Master of Men, 1933
The Clairvoyant, 1934
Madame Spy, 1934
The Countess of Monte Cristo, 1934
Once to Every Woman, 1934
Viva Villa!, 1934
Black Moon, 1934
The Affairs of Cellini, 1934
The Richest Girl in the World, 1934
Cheating Cheaters, 1934
Woman in the Dark, 1934
Mills of the Gods, 1934
Come Out of the Pantry, 1935
Bulldog Jack, 1935
White Lies, 1935
When Knights Were Bold, 1936
Roaming Lady, 1936
They Met in a Taxi, 1936
It Happened in Hollywood, 1937
Murder in Greenwich Village, 1937
The Jury's Secret, 1938
Smashing the Spy Ring, 1939
Navy Secrets, 1939
Wildcat Bus, 1940
Melody for Three, 1941
Adam Had Four Sons, 1941
Not a Ladies' Man, 1942
Treasure of the Golden Condor, 1953
Small Town Girl, 1953
The Cobweb, 1955
Queen Bee, 1955
Hell on Frisco Bay, 1955
Rock, Pretty Baby, 1956
Crime of Passion, 1957
Tammy and the Bachelor, 1957
Summer Love, 1958
Dragstrip Riot, 1958

ABOUT THE AUTHORS

Text

Frank Miller is head of the theater program at Georgia State University, where he also lectures. He is the author of *Casablanca: As Time Goes By* and *Censored Hollywood: Sin, Sex & Violence on the Screen*. He also wrote the companion volumes to this book, *Leading Ladies: The 50 Most Unforgettable Actresses of the Studio Era* and *Leading Men: The 50 Most Unforgettable Actors of the Studio Era*.

Editor

Genevieve McGillicuddy is brand manager for Turner Classic Movies. She has a master's degree in film studies from Emory University.

Researcher

Alexa L. Foreman is the senior researcher/producer at Turner Classic Movies. She is the author of *Women in Motion*, coauthor of *In the Picture: Production Stills from the TCM Archives*, and a contributor to *The St. James Women Filmmaker's Encyclopedia* and *International Dictionary of Films and Filmmakers*.